Albatros D.Va reproduction wearing the paint scheme of Jasta 5's Vfw Josef Mai, who scored 11 of his total 30 victories on this type. This aircraft was built by The Vintage Aviator Ltd and is powered by an original Mercedes D.IIIa engine. It is seen at Hood Aerodrome, Masterton, on New Zealand's North Island on 14 November 2009. **Jarrod Cotter**

Contents

Dawn patrol! The Vintage Aviator Ltd's meticulously restored original Royal Aircraft Factory BE.2f is silhouetted by a dramatic skyscape at Hood Aerodrome, Masterton, New Zealand. **Jarrod Cotter**

Cover image: Two-ship formation of The Vintage Aviator Ltd's Royal Aircraft Factory SE.5a reproductions, with John Bargh flying B507 nearest the camera and Tim Sullivan in F5690. **Jarrod Cotter**

Editor: Jarrod Cotter
jcotter@mortons.co.uk
Production editor: Janet Richardson
Publisher: Dan Savage
Contributors: Nick Blacow, Kathryn (KT) Budde-Jones, Martyn Chorlton, Gavin Conroy, Norm DeWitt, Douglas C Dildy, Juanita Franzi, Alastair Goodrum, Rob Leigh, Alex Mitchell, Ryan K Noppen, François Prins, DG Ridley-Kitts, Desmond Seward.

Designers: Justin Blackamore, Charlotte Pearson
Production manager: Craig Lamb
clamb@mortons.co.uk

Divisional advertising manager: Tracey Glover-Brown
tglover-brown@mortons.co.uk

Advertising sales executive: Jamie Moulson
jmoulson@mortons.co.uk
01507 529465

Magazine sales manager: Paul Deacon
pdeacon@mortons.co.uk
Brand manager: Sarah Downing
sdowning@mortons.co.uk
01507 529549

Operations Director: Dan Savage
Commercial Director: Nigel Hole
Business Development Director: Terry Clark
Managing Director: Brian Hill

Editorial address: Aviation Classics
Mortons Media Group Ltd
PO Box 99
Horncastle
Lincs LN9 6JR
Website: www.aviationclassics.co.uk

Customer services, back issues
and subscriptions: 01507 529529 (24 hour answerphone)
help@classicmagazines.co.uk

Archive enquiries: Jane Skayman
jskayman@mortons.co.uk
01507 529423

Distribution: COMAG
Tavistock Road, West Drayton,
Middlesex UB7 7QE
01895 433800

Printed: William Gibbons and Son,
Wolverhampton

Having trouble finding a copy of this magazine? Why not just ask your local newsagent to reserve you a copy

Introduction

Called the 'Great War', it was a name which described the extensive destruction and impact it left on the world. Highlighting the mass carnage of World War One, when the Battle of the Somme began at 07:30 on 1 July 1916 – following a brief and eerie silence as tens of thousands of men considered their fate in the next few minutes – whistles blew and the first British and French infantrymen left their muddy trenches to meet a deadly hail of machine-gun fire. By the end of this first day the British alone had almost 20,000 men killed, over 35,000 wounded, more than 2000 missing and hundreds more taken prisoner – the total loss was almost 60,000 in just one day and the offensive was to go on until November.

Above the devastation of the trenches, a new form of warfare had been rapidly evolving in the air which was transforming military strategy. Planning for the Somme offensive was based on the aerial reconnaissance photographs provided by the Royal Flying Corps. 'Winged' warriors were now duelling in the sky, which was their very own field of honour where they often fought by a gentleman's code that would seldom be repeated in modern warfare. This chivalry in the air contrasted with the slaughter below, although war it still was and many young and inexperienced airmen were killed within days of their arrival on the front line. During the months of the Somme offensive almost 800 aircraft were lost,

taking with them the lives of hundreds of airmen. These early flyers certainly played their part in the eventual Allied victory.

Flying in fragile fabric-covered aircraft, being shot at from the air and ground and without parachutes, the risks were high. There are some incredible stories of courage from this period though, as is evident with those of Alan Arnett McCleod and Albert Ball who both feature in this issue of *Aviation Classics*.

As a boy I became fascinated with the aerial conflict of World War One after watching classic films such as *The Blue Max* and *Aces High*. I built models of an all-red Albatros and Sopwith Camel and remember spending hours on the stairway landing playing out dogfights between the two. Later I read much about the exploits of the daring early military airmen of the era and was often left in awe of their bravery

and achievements in the line of duty. It only further fuelled my desire to join the Royal Air Force, which had been established during this conflict on 1 April 1918.

Today's airshow audiences can see this aspect of the evolution of military aviation well represented the world over. For example, in the UK the Shuttleworth Collection has a wonderful fleet of 1914-1918 period machines. In the USA there are numerous airworthy World War One types at Old Rhinebeck. Over in New Zealand The Vintage Aviator Ltd has in the past few years made great progress with both the restoration of original aircraft and the multiple construction of perfect reproductions of types from the era.

I was invited out to witness the results and the reproduction Albatros D.Va that was about to fly particularly caught my eye. It has been built to exact specifications and is powered by an original engine, so is as close to seeing an original Albatros D.Va fly as can be. Add to that TVAL's superb Sopwith Camel and it all brings to life those model dogfights of my youth.

I'd very much like to thank the following at TVAL for all their assistance and kindness in many ways during my visit to gather material for this issue: Gene DeMarco, Tim Sullivan, Stuart Goldspink, Keith Skilling, John Bargh, Gary Yardley, David Cretchley and – last but certainly by no means least – camera ship pilot Kerry Conner. Without their passion to showcase these wonderful aircraft to a wide audience this issue would not have been possible. ■

Jarrod Cotter
Jarrod Cotter
Editor

Two Fokker Dr.I Triplanes making a ferry flight over the Cook Strait between New Zealand's North and South Islands.
Jerry Chisum

Medal inset: British Allied Victory Medal from World War One, which features a winged 'victory' figure on its obverse. An inscription on the reverse reads 'The Great War For Civilisation 1914-1919'. This example features an oak leaf cluster denoting Mentioned in Despatches on its 'double rainbow' ribbon.

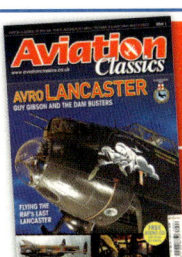
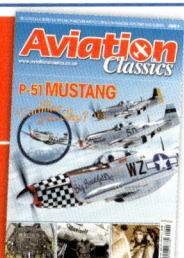
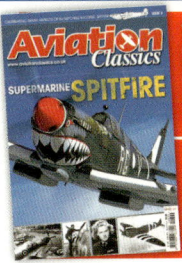

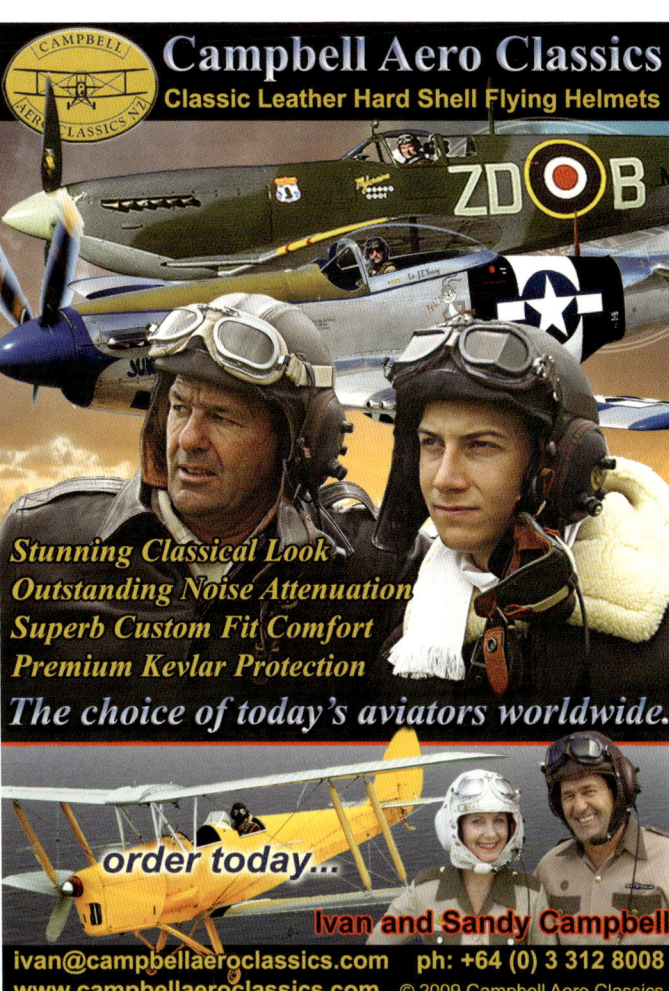

Founding the Royal Flying Corps

The name David Henderson has slipped from view, but François Prins tells the story of the real founder of military aviation in Britain.

Born in Scotland in 1862, David Henderson studied engineering at Glasgow University, and on qualifying joined the Army. He passed out at Sandhurst and was gazetted into the Argyll and Sutherland Highlanders, joining his regiment in Cape Town in August 1883. Although the main Zulu wars were over, there were several minor skirmishes and Henderson saw action during the following year.

He was a popular and much-liked officer who entered all aspects of regimental life, including coaching the Argylls at rowing, earning them the nickname 'the Marine Highlanders'. Henderson was gifted artistically and organised amateur theatrical performances for which he even painted the scenery himself.

Back in Britain in 1890, Henderson was promoted to Captain and attended a Staff College course at Camberley. In 1895, he married Henrietta Caroline, daughter of Henry Robert Dundas and grand-daughter of the First Baron Napier of Magdala (of Indian Mutiny fame).

Following graduation from Camberley, Henderson briefly served on the War Office staff in London before joining Lord Kitchener in the Sudan, as ADC to Brigadier-General Lyttelton. David Henderson was with the army as they advanced on Khartoum and was present at the Battle of Omderman in September 1898. Mentioned in Despatches, Henderson was posted back to the War Office as a Brevet Major.

In 1899, as Director of Military Intelligence under Lord Kitchener, Henderson was in Pretoria, South Africa, when the Boer War broke out. He fought at Reitfontein and Lombard's Kop where his unit gained much respect for their daring and courage. His group was among those trapped at Ladysmith and rather than wait for rescue he led several patrols against enemy gun positions. On one of these sorties, David Henderson was wounded in the thigh, but pressed home the attack. He recovered ➤

RFC BE.2a flying past HM King George V and the Imperial General Staff on the King's Birthday – Salisbury Plain, 3 June 1914. **All via author**

A fine portrait of
General Sir David
Henderson taken at the
War Office in 1917.

quickly from his injuries and was back in action within a month.

Following the relief of Ladysmith, Henderson was attached to Sir Redvers Buller's Headquarters and took part in several operations, including battles at Laing's Nek, Belfast and Lydenburg. He was Mentioned in Despatches four times; made a Brevet Lieutenant-Colonel, awarded the Distinguished Service Order (DSO) and the Queen's Medal with four clasps.

TAKING FLIGHT

Henderson read with interest the newspaper reports of 1908 on Wilbur Wright's demonstration flights in France. He had seen the value of observation balloons in the Sudan and the Boer War and his thoughts turned to aircraft in a military role. The army had a small flying facility at Larkhill, Wiltshire, but there was no governmental support. Further, the Committee of Imperial Defence suggested that army experiments with aeroplanes should be discontinued and aviation left to civilian pilots. However, this changed on 28 February 1911, with the creation of the Air Battalion of the Royal Engineers, which came into existence on 1 April.

That year, Henderson enrolled at the British & Colonial Aeroplane Company Flying School at Brooklands, Surrey, using the alias Henry Davidson. On 17 August 1911, at the age of 49, David Henderson gained his Royal Aeronautical Club certificate No.118. At the time he was the oldest pilot in Britain.

Meanwhile, the Committee of Imperial Defence expressed their concern that the few airships and aeroplanes of the Air Battalion were not enough to be an effective force in time of war. After discussions, the formation of a Flying Corps, with a Naval Wing, Military Wing and a Central Flying School, was recommended. David Henderson was co-opted onto a committee to work out the details. Their report was presented on 27 February 1912, and by Royal Warrant, the Royal Flying Corps – with its Military Wing and Naval Wing – was constituted on 13

The 'Concentration Camp' of the Royal Flying Corps at Netheravon on 29 June 1914. Aircraft include Blériots, Avro 500s, BE.2s, Henri and Maurice Farmans.

April. A month later, on 13 May, the Air Battalion and its reserve were absorbed into the Military Wing of the new Corps.

On 1 July 1912, David Henderson was appointed to the War Office as Director of Military Training which included the Military Wing of the Royal Flying Corps (RFC). From its formation, the RFC was divided into two wings, but later, on 1 April 1914, the Naval Wing became the Royal Naval Air Service (RNAS) and the title 'Military Wing' was dropped from the RFC.

David Henderson was appointed Director General of Military Aeronautics on 1 September 1913, and was determined that the RFC should have the best available aircraft of the day.

Less than a year later, war was declared on 4 August 1914, and British forces were mobilised. For the Channel crossing from Dover, pilots were instructed to carry the following items in their aircraft: a revolver, field-glasses, a spare pair of goggles, a roll of tools, a water-bottle containing boiled water, a small stove and, in a haversack, biscuits, cold meat, a piece of chocolate and a packet of soup-making material.

On 13 August, General Sir David Henderson (he had been created KCB in June 1914), as Commander in the Field, took his Air Service to France. At 06:25hrs, Lt HD Harvey-Kelly took-off from Dover in his BE.2a and set course for France; he was the first to land at 08:20 in a small field near Amiens. Altogether, 41 aircraft successfully made the crossing that day.

Soon after arriving in France, the RFC went into action; the first of regular reconnaissance flights was made on 19 August. One of the reports Henderson took personally to GHQ was the sighting by a pilot from 4 Squadron of the large German column that had been marching on Ninove, but had altered course for Mons. Had GHQ ignored the report, the outcome at Mons may have been different.

When the RFC mobilised in 1914, they did not have many vehicles, so assorted civilian vans were commandeered, including this from Maple's in London's Tottenham Court Road. Pencil sketch by Lt Col EW Powell MC of Henderson's HQ at Mehun in 1915.

'Henry Davidson' (an alias used by David Henderson) photographed on the Bristol Boxkite he learned to fly at Brooklands in 1911.

Commander of the British Expeditionary Forces, Sir John French, later reported: 'I wish particularly to bring to your Lordship's notice the admirable work done by the Royal Flying Corps under Sir David Henderson; their skill, energy and perseverance have been beyond all praise. They have furnished me with the most complete and accurate information, which has been of incalculable value in the conduct of operations. Fired at constantly by both friend and foe and not hesitating to fly in every kind of weather, they have remained undaunted throughout.'

INDEPENDENT AIR FORCE

As the war progressed, Henderson felt he would serve the Corps better in London as DGMA and handed over Field Command to Brigadier-General Hugh Trenchard. On 19 August 1915, Sir David was back in the War Office working to improve the RFC with the latest available developments in aircraft and armaments.

In 1917, Henderson was promoted Lieutenant-General and that same year the first of the daylight raids by German bombers on London took place, which once again focussed attention on the RFC/RNAS, and pressure was brought on the government to act.

General Jan Smuts, the famous Boer leader and now a member of the War Cabinet, was given the task of examining home defence arrangements by the two air services. Smuts relied heavily on Henderson, who made several recommendations that he had long wished to

see come into being. He reported that there should be one complete air service dealing with all air operations and administered by a single ministry with full powers.

General Smuts considered the facts before making his final report, which concluded: 'We can only defend this island effectively against air attack by offensive measures, by attacking the enemy in his air bases on the Continent and in that way destroying his power of attacking us across the Channel… air supremacy may in the long run become as important a factor in the defence of the Empire as sea supremacy.'

Between August and October 1917, a Bill was drafted for the new Ministry, and in November, the Air Force (Constitution) Act 1917 was placed before Parliament; it was passed unopposed and on 29 November received the Royal Assent. The Air Ministry and the Air Council came into being on 2 and 3 January 1918 respectively. Lord Rothermere was made President of the Air Council and Sir David appointed Vice-President with Trenchard as the first Chief of Air Staff. On 1 April 1918, the RFC and RNAS became the Royal Air Force.

Unfortunately, neither Henderson nor Trenchard agreed with Rothermere's policies and they resigned from the Air Council. Thus

ended Sir David's association with the aerial force he had helped to create.

As one of the most senior officers in Britain, he was appointed Area Commandant, British Armies in France, in August; and in October, he was made the Military Counsellor at the British Embassy in Paris.

Sir David Henderson was created KCVO in the 1919 New Year's Honours List; and as Military Counsellor, served at the Peace Negotiations in Paris. From Paris he left, in June 1919, for Switzerland to organise and direct the newly formed League of Red Cross Societies in Geneva. He relished his new task and looked like remaining Director for some time, but on 17 August 1921, just six days after his 59th birthday, he died in Geneva. His ashes are interred at Girvan in Ayrshire.

Tributes to this able man poured in: *The Times* of Friday 19 August 1921 called him 'The Maker of the RAF' and went on to state that 'Sir David was one of the most attractive and loveable of men, extremely quick in brain power but also with a good sense of humour.' They ended their obituary with: 'Sir David Henderson performed services for which this country should always be grateful to him.' What a pity, therefore, that Britain has all but forgotten this modest man who founded the Royal Air Force. ∎

> "…I wish particularly to bring to your Lordship's notice the admirable work done by the Royal Flying Corps under Sir David Henderson…"

Cheery bunch of 85 Squadron pilots and their numerous mascots celebrate receiving their excellent SE.5a fighters at Hounslow in May 1918.

'Day One' of the RAF

Martyn Chorlton lists the RAF's Order of Battle as at 1 April 1918, the day of its formation as the world's first independent air service.

On the Western Front the Germans had gained air superiority over the Somme during March 1918 and on the 21st opened a major offensive. By nightfall that day 17 Royal Flying Corps squadrons had been forced to evacuate their airfields before they were overrun by enemy forces. As the days went by the scale of the air fighting grew rapidly, with single dogfights amassing up to 70 aircraft. Meanwhile RFC and Royal Naval Air Service aircraft were hitting the advancing

forces on the ground to such effect that by month's end it had caused the offensive to slow in its advancement – the first time the use of large scale air power had given such a direct influence on such a strategically important battle.

So, when the RAF was officially formed on 1 April 1918, with such a high level of aerial operations still ongoing to stem the tide of the offensive there was little time for any pomp or ceremony to mark the occasion. While RFC squadrons retained their 'numberplates' as was, RNAS units had '200'

added to theirs – thus 1 Squadron RNAS became 201 Squadron RAF.

The RAF's performance over the Western Front was to be crucial, as it was considered that the war would be either won or lost in this theatre. It began its now more than 90 years of service by continuing to blunt the German offensive of spring 1918, and carried on right to the final counter-attacks of the Allied Armies which led to the surrender of the German forces in November 1918. The scale of air fighting remained undiminished from the formation of the RAF through to war's end.

RAF IN THE FIELD

1ST BRIGADE – CHATEAU 'TENBY'

1st (Corps) Wing – Hill 180, 1 mile NE of Baralle

2 Sqn	Hesdigneul	FK.8
4 Sqn	Chocques	RE.8
5 Sqn	Ascq (det Les Moëres)	RE.8
16 Sqn	Chamblain l'Abbé	RE.8
42 Sqn	Chocques	RE.8

10th (Army) Wing – Bruay

18 Sqn	Treizennes	DH.4
40 Sqn	Bruay	SE.5a
203 Sqn	Treizennes	Camel

2ND BRIGADE – OXELAERE (CASSEL)

2nd (Corps) Wing – Mont Rouge

7 Sqn	Proven	RE.8
9 Sqn	Proven	RE.8
10 Sqn	Droglandt	FK.8
21 Sqn	La Lovie	RE.8
53 Sqn	Boisdinghem	RE.8

11th (Army) Wing – Hondeghem

1 Sqn	St Marie Cappel	SE.5a
19 Sqn	Savy	Dolphin
20 Sqn	St Marie Cappel	F.2b
29 Sqn	La Lovie	Nieuport 27
57 Sqn	Le Quesnoy	DH.4

3RD BRIGADE – BEAUVAL

12th (Corps) Wing – Avesnes-Le-Comte

8 Sqn	Vert Galand	FK.8
12 Sqn	Soncamp	F.2b & RE.8
13 Sqn	Le Hameau	RE.8
15 Sqn	Fienvillers	RE.8
59 Sqn	Vert Galand	RE.8 & F.2b

13th (Army) Wing – Vert Galant

11 Sqn	Fienvillers	F.2b
22 Sqn	Vert Galand	F.2b
41 Sqn	Alquines	SE.5a
43 Sqn	Avesnes-le-Comte	Camel
46 Sqn	Filescamp Farm	Camel
49 Sqn	Petite Synthe	DH.4 & DH.9
56 Sqn	Valheureux	SE.5a
60 Sqn	Fienvillers	SE.5a
61 Sqn	Valheureux	SE.5a
70 Sqn	Fienvillers	Camel

5TH BRIGADE – VERS NR DURY

15th (Corps) Wing – Drucat

35 Sqn	Abbeville	F.2b
82 Sqn	Agenvillers	FK.8
205 Sqn	Bois-de-Roches	DH.4

22nd (Army) Wing – Tutencourt

23 Sqn	Bertangles	Dolphin
24 Sqn	Conteville	SE.5a
48 Sqn	Conteville	F.2b
54 Sqn	Bertangles	Camel
65 Sqn	Conteville	Camel
84 Sqn	Bertangles	SE.5a

7TH BRIGADE –
REFORMED WITH 64TH & 65TH WINGS AT SPYCKER

51st (Corps) Wing – en route for Candas (No.3 AP) & en route Novon

6 Sqn	Le Crotoy (and dets)	RE.8
74 Sqn	St Omer	SE.5a
98 Sqn	St Omer	DH.9
208 Sqn	La Gorgue	Camel

8TH BRIGADE –
CHATEAU DE FROVILLE, NR BAYON (HQ OPENED WITH 41ST WING)

41st Wing – Villesneux nr Reims

55 Sqn	Tantonville	DH.4
100 Sqn	Tantonville	FE.2c
216 Sqn	Villesneux (and dets)	HP O/400

9TH (GHQ) BRIGADE
(FORMED ON 3 APRIL 1918)

9th (GHQ) Wing – Wamin

25 Sqn	Ruisseauville	DH.4
27 Sqn	Ruisseauville	DH.4
32 Sqn	Beauvois	SE.5a
62 Sqn	Planques	F.2b
73 Sqn	Beauvois	Camel
79 Sqn	Beauvois	Dolphin
80 Sqn	Belleville Farm	Camel

54th (GHQ) Wing – Lambus

58 Sqn	Auchel	FE.2b
68 Sqn	Fouquerolles	SE.5a
83 Sqn	Auchel	FE.2b
101 Sqn	Haute Vissee	FE.2b
102 Sqn	Le Hameau	FE.2b ➤

RAF Communiqué No.1 recorded the following concerning this period: "57 enemy aircraft were brought down, 37 were driven out of control, 7 lost to anti-aircraft fire while RAF losses were 43; and 85 tons of bombs were dropped, 380,173 rounds fired at ground targets and 3302 photographs were taken."

While a historically significant day in the annals of our military aviation heritage, to those on the ground 1 April 1918 was a day like any other…

No.205 Squadron, originally 5 (N) Squadron, was one of many units which were renumbered on 1 April 1918 when the RNAS merged with the RFC to become the RAF. Operating from Bois-de-Roche, this is a rare air-to-air view of one of its DH.4s.

HOME DEFENCE

6TH BRIGADE: HQ –
HORSE GUARDS PARADE,
WHITEHALL, LONDON

46th Wing: HQ York - Burnholme, Henworth

36 Sqn HQ	Jesmond	Pup, F.2b
36 Sqn 'A' Flt	Hylton	Pup, F.2b
36 Sqn 'B' Flt	Ashington	Pup, F.2b
36 Sqn 'C' Flt	Seaton Carew	Pup, F.2b
76 Sqn HQ	Ripon	BE.12b
76 Sqn 'A' Flt	Copmanthorpe	BE.12b
76 Sqn 'B' Flt	Helpenby	BE.12b
76 Sqn 'C' Flt	Catterick	BE.12b
77 Sqn HQ	Edinburgh	
77 Sqn 'A' Flt	Whitburn	BE.12b
77 Sqn 'B' Flt	Penston	BE.12b

47th Wing: HQ - Leighton House, Trumpington, Cambridge

38 Sqn HQ	Melton Mowbray	
38 Sqn 'A' Flt	Stamford	FE.2b
38 Sqn 'B' Flt	Buckminster	FE.2b
38 Sqn 'C' Flt	Leadenham	FE.2b
51 Sqn 'A' Flt & HQ	Marham	BE.12b
51 Sqn 'A' Flt	Tydd St Mary	BE.12b
51 Sqn 'C' Flt	Mattishall	BE.12b
190 Sqn	Newmarket	BE.2c/e, DH.6, 504K
191 (N)TS	Marham	BE.2d/e, DH.6, FE.2b
192 (N)TS	Newmarket	FE.2d, BE.2d/e

48th Wing: HQ - The Lawns, Summerhill Rd, North Sandfields, Gainsborough

33 Sqn HQ	Gainsborough	
33 Sqn 'A' Flt	Brattleby	FE.2d
33 Sqn 'B' Flt	Kirton in Lindsey	FE.2d
33 Sqn 'C' Flt	Elsham	FE.2d

187 Sqn	East Retford	Various
188 Sqn	East Retford	504K
189 (N) TS	Suttons Farm	BE.12b, RE.8, SE.5a
199 Sqn	East Retford	BE.2e
200 TS	East Retford	FE.26, DH.6, 504J/K

49th Wing: HQ - Upminster Hall, Upminster

39 Sqn	North Weald Bassett	F.2b
44 Sqn	Hainault Farm	Camel
78 Sqn	Hornchurch	Camel
141 Sqn	Westerham	F.2b

50th Wing: HQ - The Vineyards, Great Baddow, Chelmsford

37 'A' & 'B' Flt	Woodham Mortimer	BE.12b
37 Sqn 'C' Flt	Goldhangar	BE.12b
61 Sqn	Rochford	SE.5a
75 Sqn HQ & 'B' Flt	Elmswell	BE.12b
75 Sqn 'A' Flt	Harling Road	BE.12b
75 Sqn 'C' Flt	Hadleigh	BE.12b
198 (N)TS	Rochford	504J/K, Pup, 1½ Strutter, BE.2d/e, BE.12a, Camel, FB.12c, RE.7

53rd Wing: HQ - Stede Court, Harrietsham, Maidstone

50 Sqn	Bekesbourne	BE.12b
112 Sqn	Throwley	Camel
143 Sqn	Detling	SE.5a
186 (N)TS	Throwley	DH.6, 504J/K

The perils of flying artillery spotting missions are clearly evident from the flak in this 21 Squadron RE.8 which was based at La Lovie in April 1918.

Typical battlefield over which the early RAF was fighting – this is the war-torn Somme. **Crown Copyright**

No.55 Squadron was the first RFC unit to equip with the DH.4 in January 1917 and it retained these through the formation of the RAF until it was disbanded at Shotwick in January 1920.

An 81 Squadron group photo taken post RAF formation differs little from the collections of uniforms and badges seen with the old corps.

OTHER THEATRES

MIDDLE EAST

TRAINING BRIGADE HQ – HELIOPOLIS

20th (Training) Wing: HQ - Aboukir

23 TS	**Aboukir**	504J, Pup, Scout, Elephant, BE.12, DH.6
193 Sqn	**Amriya**	Various
194 TS	**Amriya**	DH.6, BE.2e, FE.2b

32nd (Training) Wing: HQ - Ismailia

21 TS	**Ismailia**	DH.6
58 TS	**Suez**	BE.2e, 504K, SE.5a, S.1, Scout D, 1½ Strutter, FB.5, Pup
195 TS	**Abu Sueir**	504J, Pup, Nieuport, BE.2e, Camel

38th (Training) Wing: HQ - Heliopolis

AOS	**Heliopolis**	Various
SofAF	**Heliopolis**	504K, Pup, Nieuport, BE.2e, SE.5a, Scout D
SofAG	**Heliopolis**	DH.6

PALESTINE

5th (Corps) Wing - Ramleh

14 Sqn	**Junction Station**	RE.8 & Nieuport 17
113 Sqn	**Sarona**	RE.8, Nieuport 17, 23 & 24

40th (Army) Wing - Deir El Baleh

111 Sqn	**Ramleh**	SE.5a & Nieuport
142 Sqn	**Ramleh**	BE.12a & G.102

SALONIKA

16th (Corps) Wing - 110 Rue Reine Olga, Salonika

17 Sqn	**Lahana**	BE.2c, BE.12a & FK.8
47 Sqn	**Yanesh**	FK.3, FK.8 & M.1C
150 Sqn	**Kirec**	M.1C & SE.5a

MESOPOTAMIA

31st (GHQ) Wing - Baghdad

30 Sqn	**Baquba**	RE.8 & S.VII
63 Sqn	**Samarra**	BE.2c & DH.4
72 Sqn	**Baghdad**	DH.4, SE.5a, S.VII & M.1C

INDIA

52nd (Corps) Wing - Peshawar

31 Sqn	**Risalpur**	BE.2c & BE.2e
114 Sqn	**Quetta**	BE.2c & BE.2e

SOUTH AFRICA

26 Sqn	**Cape Town**	Henry Farman F.27

ITALY

14th (Army) Wing - Sarcedo

28 Sqn	**Grossa**	Camel
34 Sqn	**Villaverla**	RE.8 & F.2b
45 Sqn	**Grossa**	Camel
66 Sqn	**San-Pietro-in-Gu**	Camel ➤

One of 87 Squadron's Sopwith Dolphins pictured at Hounslow only weeks before the unit headed for France for the first time in late April 1918.

TRAINING DIVISION

HQ – 13 ALBEMARLE, PICCADILLY, LONDON

Northern Training Brigade: HQ – Fossgate, York

8th Wing: HQ – 26 Blossom Street, York

14 TS	Tadcaster	504A, S.1, BE.2c
49 TS	Doncaster	504J/K, RE.8, BE.2e, DH.4
72 TS	Beverley	504J/K, SE.5a, Camel

19th Wing: HQ – 10 Osborne Villas, Jesmond, Newcastle-upon-Tyne

52 Sqn	Catterick	RE.8 (Main unit operating from Abbeville)
75 TS	Cramlington	DH.6, DH.9, Elephant, BE.2e, RE.8
115 Sqn	Catterick	Formed for O/400 plus various types
118 Sqn	Catterick	Formed for O/400 plus various types
127 TS	Catterick	Formed for DH.9 plus various types
SDF	Cramlington	DH.6

23rd Wing: HQ – South Carlton, Lincoln

60 TS	Scampton	504J/K, SV.II, 1½ Strutter, Pup, Camel, Dolphin, SE.5a, BE.2e, BE.12, RE.8
61 TS	South Carlton	DH.5, DH.6, BE.2c/e, Elephant, Camel, Pup, RE.8, 504J, FK.8
81 Sqn	Scampton	Camel plus various types

24th Wing: HQ – Spittlegate

50 TS	Spittlegate	FK.8, DH.6, F.2b, 504J/K, JN.4, RE.7
64 TS	Harlaxton	Nieuport 17, RE.8, BE.2c/e, DH.6

27th Wing: HQ – Waddington

51 TS	Waddington	RE.8, BE.2c/e, DH.6, DH.9, Elephant, FE.2b, FK.8
117 Sqn	Hucknall	DH.4, RE.8
130 Sqn	Hucknall	DH.9
135 Sqn	Hucknall	Formed for DH.9 plus various types

30th Wing: HQ – 15 Panmore Place, Montrose

36 TS	Montrose	JN.4, BE.12, BE.2c/e, 1½ Strutter, Pup, Camel, 504J/K, RE.8

SOUTHERN TRAINING BRIGADE: HQ – SALISBURY

4th (Reserve) Wing: Netheravon

97 Sqn	Netheravon	HP O/400
116 TS	Netheravon	Various

17th WING: HQ – Beaulieu

73 TS	Beaulieu	Camel, Pup, 504J, 1½ Strutter

28th Wing: HQ – Yatesbury

66 TS	Yatesbury	BE.2c/e, BE.12, RE.8, Pup, DH.6

33rd Wing: HQ – 2A Winchester Street, Salisbury

99 Sqn	Old Sarum	DH.9
103 Sqn	Old Sarum	DH.9
107 Sqn	Lake Down	DH.9
108 Sqn	Lake Down	DH.9
109 Sqn	Lake Down	DH.9
136 Sqn	Lake Down	DH.9

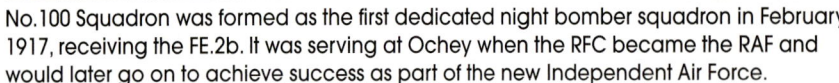

No.100 Squadron was formed as the first dedicated night bomber squadron in February 1917, receiving the FE.2b. It was serving at Ochey when the RFC became the RAF and would later go on to achieve success as part of the new Independent Air Force.

Above: The RAF BE.12 with marginally better performance over its older sibling served with many Home Defence squadrons. This BE.12a displays a 50 Squadron unofficial skull and cross bones with '50 HD' written within.

RAF'S FIRST HQ

On 30 March 2008, celebrations to mark the 90th anniversary of the formation of the RAF began with the unveiling of a green plaque at the site of its first headquarters in central London. This was in a requisitioned hotel in the Strand and the Westminster City Council green plaque was unveiled by the then Chief of the Air Staff, Air Chief Marshal Sir Glenn Torpy. The RAF's first HQ was in the Hotel Cecil at 80 Strand, once London's largest hotel but requisitioned for the war effort in 1917. In 1919 the RAF left for larger premises and the Hotel Cecil, with the exception of the northern block overlooking the Strand, was demolished and redeveloped by Shell as an art deco office block. It is within the façade of the remaining part of the original structure that the plaque now lies. ACM Sir Glenn Torpy commented: "I cannot think of a more fitting start to our 90th celebrations than by laying a plaque here on the building where our story began in the last year of the First World War." **Photo: Jarrod Cotter**

Right: No.25 Squadron had changed roles from fighter to day bomber unit when it re-equipped with the DH.4 in June 1917 and was scheduled to receive the DH.9 before the war ended, but this failed to materialise before the squadron was disbanded in January 1920.

34th Wing: HQ – Phiprus Cottage, Stockbridge

43 TS	Chattis Hill	Scout D, 1½ Strutter, Camel, 504J/K, Pup, Elephant, Nieuport 20

36th Wing: HQ – Upper Croft, Thruxton

104 Sqn	Andover	DH.9
105 Sqn	Andover	RE.8
106 Sqn	Andover	RE.8

EASTERN TRAINING BRIGADE:
HQ – ST JAMES, LONDON

6th Wing: HQ – Barming Place, Maidstone

40 TS	Croydon	Scout D, 1½ Strutter, DH.5, Pup, Camel, Scout C, 504J/K
42 TS	Wye	504J/K, RE.7, RE.8, BE.2d/e, BW.12, JN.4/4a, Pup, Camel, M.1c, DH.6, Elephant
65 TS	Dover	FK.8, Scout D, Camel, BE.2d/e, Elephant, RE.8, 504J, Pup
63 TS	Joyce Green	504J/K, DH.5, Pup, Camel

7th Wing: HQ – Belgrave, St. Johns Terrace, King's Lynn

9 TS	Sedgeford	504D, FE.2d, BE.2d/e, FB.5, S.1, RE.8, DH.9
69 TS	Narborough	DH.6, BE.2e, BE.12, RE.8
110 Sqn	Sedgeford	DH.4, DH.9
121 Sqn	Narborough	DH.9
122 Sqn	Sedgeford	DH.9

18th Wing: 23 Ryde Street, St James, London

3 TS	Shoreham	BE.12, FK.8, SE.5a, Pup, 504J, SE.5a, Camel
4 TS	Northolt	BE.2c, S.1, JN.3, FK.3, DH.6
19 TS	Curragh	BE.2c/e, FE.2b, FB.5, BE.12, 504J, RE.8, Elephant

27 Sqn	London Colney	BE.2
56 TS	London Colney	BE.2e, BE.12, 504J, SV.II, SE.5a, Pup, Scout D, Camel, DH.6
85 Sqn	Hounslow	SE.5a
86 Sqn	Northolt	Various
87 Sqn	Hounslow	Dolphin
91 Sqn	Tangmere	RE.8
92 Sqn	Tangmere	SE.5a
93 Sqn	Tangmere	SE.5a
148 Sqn	Ford Junction	FE.2b, FE.2d
149 Sqn	Ford Junction	FE.2b, FE.2d

26th Wing: St Mary's, Ely

5 TS	Wyton	BE.2e, DH.6, DH.9, S.1, RE.7/8, Camel
25 TS	Thetford	DH.6, BE.2e, RE.8, DH.9, 504J, DH.4, Camel, FE.2d, Pup
119 Sqn	Duxford	Various
123 Sqn	Duxford	DH.9
124 Sqn	Fowlmere	DH.4
125 Sqn	Fowlmere	DH.9
128 Sqn	Thetford	DH.9
129 Sqn	Duxford	DH.9

39th Wing: 79 London Road, Brandon

88 Sqn	Harling Road	F.2b
89 Sqn	Harling Road	Various
94 Sqn	Harling Road	Camel plus various types

WESTERN GROUP COMMAND:
HQ – EDGBASTON, BIRMINGHAM

21st Wing: Cirencester Castle

24 TS	Witney	F.2b, DH.6, FK.8, 504J, BE.2e
59 TS	Rendcomb	DH.6, FE.2d, BE.2e, BE.12a, F.2b, RE.8
71 TS	Port Meadow	BE.2e, BE.12, Camel, F.2b

35th Wing: Castle Bromwich

54 TS	Castle Bromwich	SV.II, SE.5a, Pup, DH.5/6, 1½ Strutter, 504J/K, Camel, Dolphin
55 TS	Lilbourne	Camel, SE.5a, 504J, BE.12, Pup
74 TS	Castle Bromwich	Pup, SE.5a, 504J & K, Camel

29th Wing: Shawbury

10 TS	Shawbury	Scout C/D, DH.5, FE.8, Pup, BE.2e, BE.12a, Elephant, JN.3/4, RE.8, Camel, 504J/K, SE.5a
131 Sqn	Shawbury	Formed for DH.9; used FE.2b plus various types
132 Sqn	Tern Hill	Formed for HP O/400; used DH.9 plus various types
133 Sqn	Tern Hill	FE.2b
134 Sqn	Tern Hill	HP O/400
137 Sqn	Shawbury	DH.9

37th Wing: The Oaks, Ledsham, Little Sutton

67 TS	North Shotwick	Camel, Pup, Nieuport 12, 1½ Strutter, 504J/K
90 Sqn	North Shotwick	FE.2b, 504K plus various types
95 Sqn	North Shotwick	Various
96 Sqn	North Shotwick	BE.2c plus various types

1ST TRAINING WING AFC:
HQ – TETBURY

HQ Training Division

CFS	Upavon	All RFC aircraft in service at the time
SofSF	Redcar	504J, DH.6, Scout D, Pup, Camel
SofAG	Redcar	Various
1S of AF	Ayr & Turnberry	Camel, S.7, 504J, SE.5a, M.1c, F.2b
2S of AF	Eastburn (Driffield)	M.1c, FK.8, DH.9, 504J, Dolphin, Camel
1(O)S ofAG 2(Aux)	Eastburn (Driffield)	Various
SofAG 4(Aux)	Turnberry	Camel, BE.2e, FE.2b, DH.9, SE.5a
SofAG	Marske	SE.5a, FK.8, Pup, M.1c, F.2b, DH.9/9a, Camel, 504J ■

Formed in Palestine in August 1917, 111 Squadron remained in this theatre to support the army offensive against Turkish forces in Palestine and Syria. It received the SE.5a in October 1917 and these aircraft are pictured at Ramleh a few weeks after the formation of the RAF.

For Valour

Jarrod Cotter highlights the heart-rending story behind the award of the Victoria Cross to 18-year-old Canadian pilot Lt Alan Arnett McLeod.

Lt Alan Arnett McLeod VC.

As a result of courage shown in the face of combat while at the same time being in the midst of the many dangers encountered while flying the fragile aircraft of the era, it is perhaps not surprising that during World War One the Victoria Cross was awarded for numerous acts of valour in the air. Of them, one which makes particularly emotive reading is that for 2nd Lt Alan Arnett McLeod. At just 18 years old he was severely injured in a dogfight with eight Fokker Dr.Is, but managed to get his badly damaged aircraft on the ground and then saved the life of his observer in a most incredible way, only to sadly die some months later from influenza.

By 21 March 1918 the final German offensive had resulted in a fierce advance that was pushing the Allies back. As part of the effort to stop the advance, Allied aircraft were detailed to attack German infantry and artillery batteries.

Early on the morning of 27 March – just days before the formation of the Royal Air Force – Lt McLeod and his observer Lt AW Hammond MC of 2 Squadron Royal Flying Corps took off in their Armstrong Whitworth FK.8 to bomb enemy positions at Bray-sur-Somme, near Albert. The weather that day was bad, and the crew lost their way in fog. They were forced to land at the airfield of 43 Squadron and slightly damaged the aircraft while doing so.

Just after noon the FK.8 had been repaired, and despite continuing poor weather Lts McLeod and Hammond took off with the intention of carrying out their planned task. On reaching the target area they found an artillery battery to attack, but as they were preparing for the bombing run a Fokker Dr.I Triplane appeared out of some cloud slightly below them. Even though the enemy scout was faster and more agile than the heavily bombed-up FK.8, the teenage pilot skilfully manoeuvred it so that his observer could get a clear shot at their attacker. With several accurate bursts from Lt Hammond's Lewis gun the Dr.I plunged to earth. However, another seven Triplanes appeared out of the cloud and immediately set upon the FK.8.

SWARMING TRIPLANES

The German machines literally swarmed around the RFC machine, taking turns firing at the lumbering bomber. With further skilful flying Lt McLeod again gave his observer a good line of fire at the attacking Triplanes, two of which he hit causing them to fall earthwards on fire.

The remaining Germans continued the frantic attacks, and bullets hit the FK.8 in the petrol tank which caught alight. The fire quickly spread and soon the pilot's basket seat was ablaze. Lt McLeod had been wounded five times, but despite his injuries he climbed out of the cockpit onto the lower left wing, then somehow with flames licking all around him still managed to maintain some directional control of the FK.8 in an attempt keep the flames away from Lt Hammond so that he could continue to fire at the enemy scouts to keep them at bay. The

Royal Flying Corps pilot's wings.

pilot evaded the Triplanes and brought the badly-hit bomber in low over the German lines, then, with his right hand on the control stick in the burning cockpit, flattened out its approach angle ready to crash-land in 'No Man's Land'.

The young Canadian got the burning aircraft down on the ground as best as he could, and having survived the ordeal he then proceeded to drag his severely wounded and badly burned observer free from the burning wreckage. With the FK.8's bomb load still in place, this had to be done immediately. Lt McLeod ignored his own injuries and pulled Lt Hammond – who had been hit six times – out of the flaming aircraft and towards a shell hole for protection from German machine-gun fire which was by then being aimed at them.

The aircraft exploded, and the blast from the bombs wounded the RFC pilot further. Despite this and with German bullets flying all around him, Lt McLeod managed to get himself and his observer into what protection the shell hole provided. They had to remain there until dusk, when it was safer for nearby Allied infantrymen to use the cover of darkness to rescue them.

The aircrew received treatment for their wounds and were then moved to a casualty clearing station; both had incredibly survived the ordeal. Alan McLeod was shipped back to 'Blighty' and was admitted to the Prince of Wales Hospital in London where he remained in a critical state for months. Lt Hammond had lost a leg as a result of his injuries.

FINEST FLOWER OF CHIVALRY

It was later announced that the Canadian pilot had been awarded the Victoria Cross for his actions on 27 March. Lt Hammond received a Bar to his Military Cross.

An extract from Lt McLeod's citation for the VC in the *London Gazette*, dated 1 May 1918, stated: 'Whilst flying with his observer (Lt AW Hammond, MC), attacking hostile formations by bombs and machine-gun fire, he was assailed at a height of 5,000 feet by eight enemy triplanes, which dived at him from all directions, firing from their front guns. By skilful manoeuvring he enabled his observer to fire bursts at each machine in turn, shooting three of them down out of control.

The Victoria Cross with its crimson red ribbon.

VICTORIA CROSS

The Victoria Cross is the premier military award for gallantry in the presence of the enemy which has been issued to members of the British armed forces and those of Commonwealth countries and previous British Empire territories. It can be awarded to all ranks of the services and may be awarded posthumously, plus civilians under military command can receive it. It is a bronze cross, and the obverse (face) of the medal bears a lion statant gardant on the Royal crown, with the simple but powerful inscription FOR VALOUR on a semi-circular scroll. The reverse has a circular panel inside which is engraved the date of the act for which the decoration was awarded. The cross is suspended by a ring from a seriffed 'V' to a bar ornamented with laurel leaves. The reverse of the suspender bar is engraved with the rank, name and ship, regiment or squadron of the recipient. The ribbon is of plain crimson, though prior to 1918 a dark blue ribbon had been issued for Royal Navy recipients. A bronze bar ornamented with laurels can be issued to VC holders performing a further act of such bravery which would have merited award of the medal. When the ribbon alone is worn, a replica of the cross in miniature is affixed to its centre.

The Victoria Cross was instituted by Queen Victoria, from whom it gets its name, to cover all actions since the outbreak of the Crimean War in 1854. It has been awarded 1356 times, with only three bars ever having been added. The medal is made from the bronze of Russian guns captured at Sebastopol and it is estimated that from the remaining metal no more than 85 further VCs can be cast.

"…2nd Lt McLeod, not withstanding his own wounds, dragged him away from the burning wreckage at great personal risk from heavy machine-gun fire from the enemy's lines."

By this time Lt McLeod had received five wounds, and whilst continuing the engagement a bullet penetrated his petrol tank and set the machine on fire. He then climbed out on to the left bottom plane, controlling his machine from the side of the fuselage, and by side-slipping steeply kept the flames to one side, thus enabling the observer to continue firing until the ground was reached. The observer had been wounded six times when the machine crashed in No Man's Land, and 2nd Lt McLeod, not withstanding his own wounds, dragged him away from the burning wreckage at great personal risk from heavy machine-gun fire from the enemy's lines. This very gallant pilot was again wounded by a bomb whilst engaged in this act of rescue, but he persevered until he had placed Lt Hammond in comparative safety, before falling himself from exhaustion and loss of blood.'

Shortly after the award Alan McLeod attended an investiture at Buckingham Palace with his father, who had sailed to England from Canada to be with his son. By the beginning of September Alan appeared to be sufficiently on the road to recovery that he and his father could return to Canada to continue his recuperation at home.

At the time a highly virulent strain of Spanish Influenza was widespread in Canada, and Alan unfortunately contracted the virus. Adding to this, in his weakened state he developed pneumonia and, after going through all that he had done during his courageous actions of 27 March, died from these complications in Winnipeg on 6 November – just five days before the Armistice.

A moving tribute to him written by Dr David Christie of Westminster Church, Winnipeg, appeared in the *Manitoba Free Press* the day after his death: "Alan McLeod was the finest flower of chivalry. The old days of knighthood are over, but for the very fairest blossoms of the spirit of knighthood the world has had to wait till the twentieth century. It is these dauntless boys who have saved civilization. The heroism of the Crusades pales before the incredible and quiet courage of such boys who gave us a new interpretation of Calvary. I saw Alan within a few hours of his death. He faced the last enemy with the same joyous confidence with which he started on what he called the very happiest part of his life. For our children's children names like Alan McLeod's will be written in letters of splendour in the annals of Canada." ∎

'King of the Air Fighters'

Jarrod Cotter gives an overview of the famous Sopwith Camel, in which pilots shot down more enemy aircraft than any other Allied type during World War One.

Although the Sopwith Triplane and Pup were very capable aeroplanes for their time; as the Germans developed their machines, there became an urgent need for a faster and better armed fighter for the Royal Naval Air Service and Royal Flying Corps. Such was the Pup's success that the new aircraft was largely based around its design, but was to be fitted with a more powerful engine and – as gun synchronisation had become more reliable by late 1916 – be armed with twin Vickers machine guns. It was Britain's first production fighter to feature synchronised twin guns.

Designated as the F.1, for ease of manufacture, designer Herbert Smith settled on a flat top wing; and to compensate for that, the dihedral of the lower wing was doubled.

Powered by a 110hp Clerget rotary engine, the first prototype took to the skies on 22 December 1916. During flight tests, the aircraft's superb manoeuvrability became

Standard Sopwith
F.1 Camel, c1917.
Via François Prins

TVAL's Sopwith Camel reproduction 'B3889' being flown by Gene DeMarco. **Alex Mitchell**

"The Camel was held in such high regard by those who flew it during World War One that it has often been likened to having the iconic status gained by the Spitfire in World War Two."

evident, although it was noted that this was at the price of causing some very tricky handling characteristics. The combination of the torque from the rotary engine with the concentration of masses (engine, guns, fuel and pilot) in a compact area of the fuselage led to the type dropping its nose in a starboard turn and rising in a turn to port. Without large inputs of rudder to counteract this, the aircraft could violently enter a spin. However, once pilots were experienced with its idiosyncrasies, the Camel's manoeuvrability was unmatched by previous British designs and most of its German contemporaries, with only the Fokker Dr.I able to rival it in this aspect of flight.

Firstly a nickname, the aircraft became called the 'Camel' as a result of the humped fairing over the gun breeches being likened to the hump of the desert animal of the same name.

Production machines began to arrive on the front line in early May 1917; firstly arriving on the strength of 4 (Naval) Squadron, soon followed by more RNAS units. In July, 70 Squadron became the first RFC unit to receive Camels and the following month, Home Defence squadrons were issued with the type which was later modified for night-fighter operations. This most notably

saw its twin nose-mounted Vickers machine guns – the flash from which had been causing pilots to lose their night vision – replaced by two Lewis guns mounted above the top wing.

There was also a naval version of the Camel, the 2F.1. This had a joint in its fuselage so that it could be taken apart for stowage on board a ship, featured a reduced wingspan and narrower track undercarriage, plus had a revised armament configuration.

MOST FAMOUS DOGFIGHT

On 21 April 1918, Canadian Captain AR Brown DSC* was flying Camel B7270 when he entered into combat with an all-over red Dr.I Triplane flown by Baron Manfred von Richthofen – perhaps becoming the single most famous aerial dogfight of World War One due to the notoriety of his opponent, who had claimed 80 Allied aircraft. Brown attacked the Dr.I as he'd noticed that it was about to fire on one of his comrades, and after firing a sustained burst the Triplane went down. The Canadian pilot was credited with the victory, although recent research has attributed the death of the 'Red Baron' to a bullet fired from the ground during the by then low-level combat.

Brown's combat report included: 'Went back again and dived on pure red triplane which was firing on Lieut May. I got a long burst into him and he went down vertical and was observed to crash…'

For the actions of that day, Brown was awarded a Bar to his DSC, and the citation in the *London Gazette* of 21 June 1918 read: 'For conspicuous gallantry and devotion to duty. On 21 April 1918, while leading a patrol of six scouts he attacked a formation of twenty hostile scouts. He personally engaged two Fokker triplanes, which he drove off; then, seeing that one of our machines was being attacked and apparently hard ➤

Twin Vickers gun arrangement of a standard F.1 Camel.

SOPWITH F.1 CAMEL SPECIFICATION

Dimensions: Wingspan 28ft 0in; Length 18ft 9in; Height 8ft 6in
All-up weight: 1453lb
Powerplant: One nine-cylinder rotary of either 130hp Clerget, 150hp BR 1, 110hp or 180hp Le Rhone, 100hp or 150hp Gnome Monosoupape
Performance: Maximum speed 117mph at sea level, 113mph at 10,000ft; Climb to 10,000ft 10 minutes 35 seconds; Service ceiling 19,000ft (figures for 130hp Clerget)
Armament: Two 0.303in synchronised Vickers 0.303in machine guns on top of forward fuselage with Sopwith-Kauper mechanical or Constantinesco hydraulic interrupter gear. Many also carried up to four 25lb bombs under the fuselage. Home defence fighters fitted with twin 0.303in Lewis guns fitted on Foster mounts above the top wing centre section

pressed, he dived on the hostile scout, firing all the while. This scout, a Fokker triplane, nose dived and crashed to the ground. Since the award of the Distinguished Service Cross, he has destroyed several other enemy aircraft and has shown great dash and enterprise in attacking enemy troops from low altitudes despite heavy anti-aircraft fire.'

At the time of the Armistice, Camels were in service with many front line RAF squadrons in France. As well as with UK Home Defence squadrons, they also served in Italy, Greece and Russia. The type also equipped some United States Air Service squadrons in France. Around 1300 enemy aircraft were downed by pilots flying Camels. Its continued use in the post-war RAF was limited by the arrival of the Sopwith Snipe, though it did continue to fly with the air arms of other countries well into the 1920s.

EXACT REPRODUCTION

Of the more than 5500 built, few original Sopwith Camels survive today. The Vintage Aviator Ltd's flying reproduction 'B3889', as illustrated within these pages, may not be an original airframe but is as close as can be to seeing the real thing fly – especially

as it is powered by an original Gnome rotary engine.

This wonderful aeroplane wears the colours of New Zealander Captain Clive Collett, who was the first pilot to score a victory with the Sopwith Camel. He eventually scored 12 confirmed 'kills', but died in a crash while test flying a captured Albatros during 1917.

This aircraft made its debut at the 2001 Classic Fighters airshow held at Omaka, Blenheim, Marlborough, on New Zealand's South Island. This was particularly appropriate, as Clive Collett originated from Marlborough. It has gone on to appear at many further airshows including subsequent biennial Classic Fighters and at its home at Hood Aerodrome, Masterton, on New Zealand's North Island. As well as its engine, the Camel features some other original components too, adding to its authenticity.

The Camel was held in such high regard by those who flew it during World War One, that it has often been likened to having the iconic status gained by the Spitfire in World War Two. With its impressive combat record, it later gained a more glamorous nickname than its first – 'King of the Air Fighters'. ■

TVAL's Camel is powered by an original Gnome rotary, which is lubricated with castor oil. With rotary engines, the crankshaft remains fixed, while the cylinders and propeller rotate around it. This results in a great amount of torque giving a significant 'pull' to the right, which in the hands of an experienced pilot could be exploited to give great manoeuvrability in a dogfight.

'B3889' awaits its next sortie at Hood Aerodrome, Masterton, in November 2009.
All Jarrod Cotter unless noted

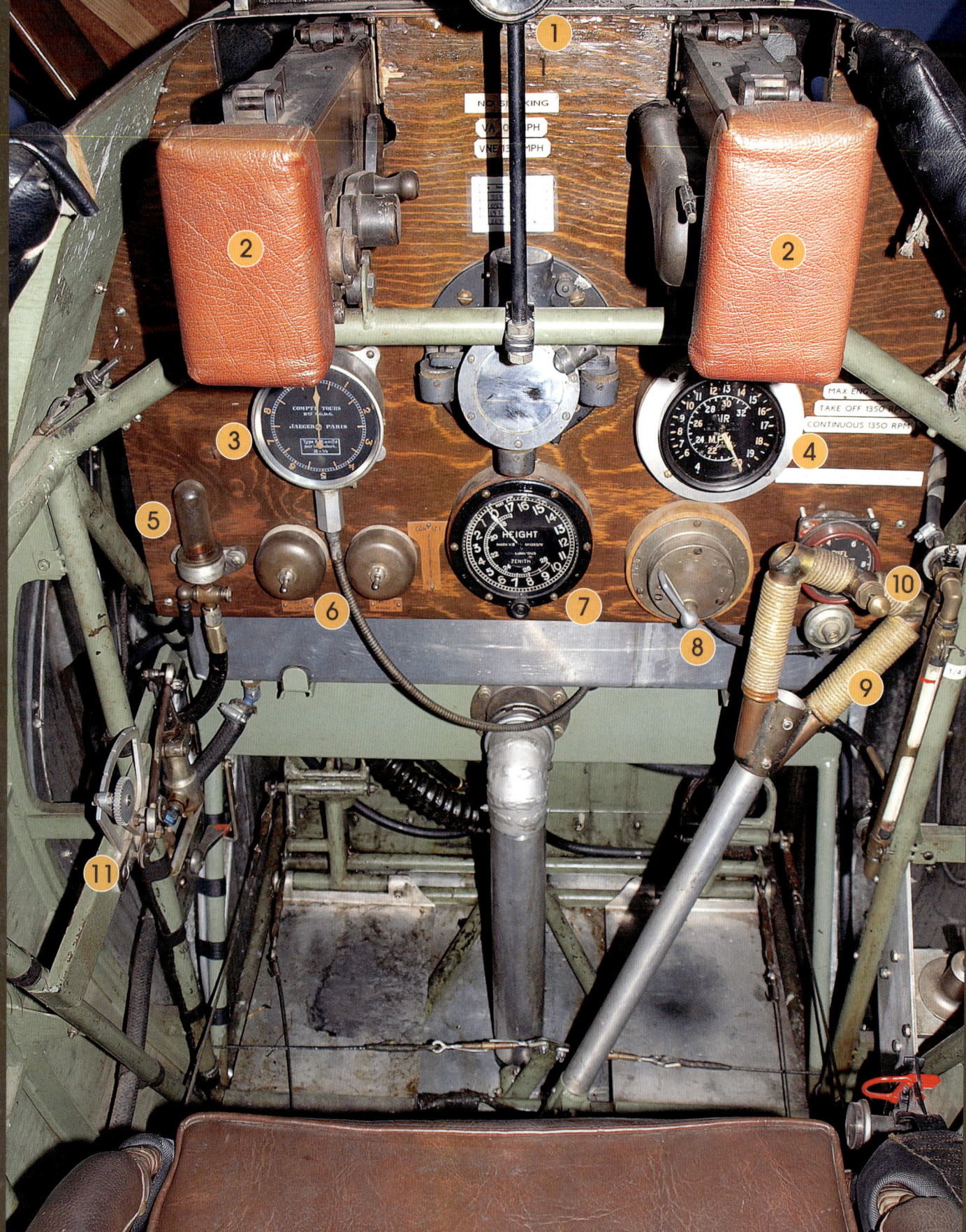

SOPWITH CAMEL COCKPIT

The number of instruments and their placement was not uniform with the Sopwith Camel. Those fitted with a Gnome engine did not have a throttle and were at full power while the ignition was on. They could be 'throttled' with a selector switch which cut the ignition to some of the cylinders to reduce power for landing. There was also a control column-mounted 'blip' switch which turned the ignition off and on and could be used intermittently to reduce power during manoeuvres.

1	Aldis gunsight	7	Altimeter
2	Machine gun padding	8	Variable cylinder selector control
3	Tachometer	9	Control column with spade grip
4	Airspeed indicator	10	'Blip' switch
5	Pulsator	11	Petrol regulating control
6	Magneto switches		

Above: The Sopwith Snipe was designed to replace the company's superb Camel. This photograph showing the production of Snipes was taken at the Sopwith works at Ham on 12 September 1918. A ferocious German offensive that opened in the spring of that year stretched the newly formed RAF to its limits trying to keep the front-line fighter squadrons up to strength, so it wasn't an ideal time to introduce a new type into widespread service. The first unit to receive the Snipe was 43 Squadron in August, followed by 201 Squadron in October. The only other unit to enter combat with the Snipe during World War One was 4 Squadron Australian Flying Corps. Major WG Barker VC DSO* MC*, flying a Snipe, single-handedly engaged large formations Fokker D.VIIs on 27 October 1918 for which he was awarded his Victoria Cross. The citation in the *London Gazette* of 30 November 1918 tells the story: 'On the morning of the 27 October 1918, this officer observed an enemy two-seater over the Foret de Mormal. He attacked this machine and after a short burst it broke up in the air. At the same time a Fokker biplane attacked him, and he was wounded in the right thigh, but managed, despite this, to shoot down the enemy aeroplane in flames. He then found himself in the middle of a large formation of Fokkers who attacked him from all directions, and was again severely wounded in the left thigh, but succeeded in driving down two of the enemy in a spin. He lost consciousness after that, and his machine fell out of control. On recovery, he found himself being again attacked heavily by a large formation, and singling out one machine he deliberately charged and drove it down in flames. During this fight his left elbow was shattered and he again fainted, and on regaining consciousness he found himself still being attacked, but notwithstanding that he was now severely wounded in both legs and his left arm shattered, he dived on the nearest machine and shot it down in flames. Being greatly exhausted, he dived out of the fight to regain our lines, but was met by another formation, which attacked and endeavoured to cut him off, but after a hard fight he succeeded in breaking up this formation and reached our lines, where he crashed on landing. This combat, in which Major Barker destroyed four enemy machines (three of them in flames), brought his total successes to fifty enemy machines destroyed, and is a notable example of the exceptional bravery and disregard of danger which this very gallant officer has always displayed throughout his distinguished career.'

Sopwith works

Two images from the collection of François Prins showing Sopwith Snipes under production towards the end of World War One.

Late production Snipes at the Ham factory in December 1918. Soon after the Armistice large numbers of newly built Snipes were scrapped, but three years later it was realised this decision had been made in haste and in 1921 the scrapping was stopped. A programme of salvage and rebuilding then took place and more than 200 Snipes were returned to service. Powered by a Bentley BR 2 engine, the Snipe was capable of more than 120mph and remained in RAF service until 1926.

The Camels that came over water

Ryan K Noppen details the world's first aircraft carrier strike.

In the afternoon haze of 17 July 1918, a force of Royal Navy cruisers and destroyers quietly steamed under the Forth Bridge, heading through the Firth of Forth out to the North Sea. In the middle of the force was a large, dazzle-painted warship of a type that had not been seen before; with seven Sopwith 2F.1 Camels on its forward flight deck, HMS *Furious* set out to take the naval war to inland Germany. The mission of *Furious'* air group was to approach the dens of the German giants that had brought modern aerial warfare to the civilian population of Great Britain, the Zeppelin hangars at the German Naval Airship Service base at Tondern in Schleswig-Holstein. The British pilots were to perform the first strike from an aircraft carrier in history.

"Nach England" was the popular call for the Zeppelins among the German population. Zeppelin raids on cities diminished the prestige of the Royal Navy, the highly vaunted guarantor of the nation's defence, in the eyes of the British public. This caused the Royal Navy to turn to aircraft to hunt down the giant "Baby Killers".
All author's collection unless noted

When World War One began, the concept of strategic aerial bombardment was in its infancy and the only aircraft at the time that had the range to drop bombs on targets far behind the enemy's front lines were Germany's Zeppelins. The first attacks against the heart of the British Empire began in 1915, with the worst raid to hit London occurring on the evening of 8-9 September 1915. Zeppelin L13, with nearly 4000 pounds of bombs aboard, under the command of Kapitänleutnant Heinrich Mathy released a rain of fire and destruction from the air the likes of which had never been experienced by a civilian population. Thirty-two people were killed and a large fire broke out among an area of textile warehouses. In an interview with the New York World, Kapitänleutnant Mathy showed no qualms about the attack: "London is a vast military centre and a military defended city in every sense. The laws of war, written or unwritten, as applicable to aerial warfare, therefore properly point to aerial attack, so far as concerns everything usable for military purposes, such as the big railway stations, banks, docks, shipyards, industrial establishments, etc.

"If anyone believes that London is not 'defended', and pretty well defended at that, he should have stood by my side in the front gondola of my Zeppelin in my last attack on London, a few nights ago, and seen the red, angry flashes of scores of cannon belching shrapnel at my craft."

Mathy's comments surely stoked the anger of the Admiralty and the British population. Seemingly overnight, the Germans had put into use a new weapons platform that negated the protection that had been offered to Britain by the Royal Navy for centuries; the Zeppelins cruising high over the ships of the Grand Fleet signified to the British that their island nation was no longer safe from attack. Demands went out for the Royal Navy to counter the new 'Zeppelin Menace'.

As seaborne bombardments of German naval bases were out of the question due to the difficult geography and the extensive German minefields, the British Admiralty pursued a novel tactic to strike the German Navy in its home ports. Before a German Zeppelin dropped the first bomb on English soil, the British executed the world's first attack on a ground target from naval aircraft. On Christmas Day, 1914, the seaplane tenders HMS *Empress, Engadine,* and *Riviera* sailed into the German Bight; their mission was to launch several Short Folder floatplanes to bomb the German Navy's Zeppelin sheds at Cuxhaven. Of the nine aircraft lowered into the water, seven made it into the air but only one managed to fly over Cuxhaven. No substantial damage was done but the mission served as good propaganda material for the Royal Navy and also planted the seeds of future naval aircraft operations in the minds of air-minded naval officers.

The raids mounted by Royal Naval Air Service floatplanes based from seaplane tenders were a nuisance to the German naval airship stations, but their material effects were negligible. The range and payload of the floatplanes was limited by the low weight they had to maintain in order to take off from the water. They were also extremely vulnerable to land-based fighters stationed at the airship bases. The British needed land-based aircraft that had the necessary range,

payload, and defensive capacity to carry out successful strikes. The Admiralty eventually conceived the idea of creating a ship with a flying-off platform that could launch land-based aircraft. A ship suited for such a conversion appeared in 1917.

HMS *Furious* began her operational life as a one-of-a-kind warship; she was the third of the three Courageous class shallow-draft battlecruisers, purpose-designed for First Sea Lord Admiral John 'Jackie' Fisher's Baltic Project, a pre-war plan calling for an amphibious invasion of Germany from the Baltic. Unlike her sister ships that mounted four 15-inch guns in two turrets, *Furious* mounted two 18-inch guns in two turrets, earning her the nickname 'Outrageous' among the sailors in the Grand Fleet. As the Baltic Plan was never put into action, the Admiralty decided to convert this awkward ship into a large seaplane carrier since her fast speed would enable her to cruise with the Grand Fleet (the other seaplane tenders in the Royal Navy being too slow). A take-off deck was constructed on the forward part of the ship and a landing deck was later added behind the funnel, although landing on the short deck proved to be too dangerous. After her conversions, *Furious* was finally ready for sea on 15 March 1918. ➤

A Sopwith Pup is being prepared for take-off during one of the many flight trials aboard HMS *Furious*. The bridge structure behind the Pup clearly shows the ship's battlecruiser origins. **IWM Q80452**

Above: *Furious'* air group of seven Sopwith 2F.1 Camels during the journey into the German Bight prior to the launch of the attack. **IWM Q20627**

Below: An aerial photo taken over Scapa Flow of HMS *Furious* showing her configuration at the time of the Tondern raid. **IWM Q19557**

LAUNCH FROM *FURIOUS*

The aircraft that made up *Furious'* air group were Sopwith 2F.1 Camels, a naval version of the land-based fighter. Bearing the range of this fighter in mind, an appropriate target was selected for the first strike at an inland target made by carrier-borne aircraft: the Zeppelins based at the German naval airship station at Tondern in Schlewig-Holstein.

On 17 July 1918, Operation F.7 commenced as HMS *Furious* set sail and was escorted into the German Bight by Force B, made up of the Revenge Class dreadnoughts of the First Battle Squadron and accompanying cruisers and destroyers. In the early hours of 19 July, *Furious* arrived in the German Bight off the Schleswig coast and prepared to launch her aircraft. The weather was poor but the British decided to press on with the attack. The pilots, Captains WD Jackson, WF Dickson, BA Smart and TK Thyne, and Lieutenants S Dawson, NE Williams and WA Yeulett, climbed into their aircraft. Shortly after 03:00, seven Sopwith 2F.1 Camels, each armed with two 50lb bombs, started their engines and flew off the flight deck. Captain Thyne developed engine trouble shortly after take-off and was forced to head back.

At 04:32 the still of the early morning on the ground at Tondern was disturbed by the drone of aircraft engines in the distance, but not the characteristic low drone made by the base's Zeppelins. A sentry on duty phoned the base headquarters, warning of the approach of aircraft. They were definitely enemy aircraft as there were no German ones based nearby or expected at this hour. Unfortunately for the Germans, the five Albatros D.IIIs which had been assigned to the base for defence had been relocated to a different airfield in March. There were a handful of anti-aircraft batteries, but these were spread around the base; at the sheds all that was available to the base personnel for defence were pistols and rifles. Three minutes after the incoming aircraft had been reported, the German ground crews heard the roar of rotary engines diving down from above. To

their surprise, they were not floatplanes but land-based pursuit aircraft; with no bases in range, where could they have come from?

The three attacking Camels belonged to Dickson, Jackson, and Williams. The target they selected was the large 'Toska' double shed. Approaching it, they put their Camels into a dive and released their bombs at 100ft just before pulling out of the dive at around 50ft. Captain Dickson recalled the following: "I saw Captain Jackson at about 3000ft above me and a good distance to the east of the town, coming down in a dive, with Lieutenant Williams about half a mile astern of him…

"… Captain Jackson dived right onto the northernmost shed and dropped two bombs, one a direct hit in the middle and the other slightly to the side of the shed. I then dropped my one remaining bomb and Williams two more. Hits were observed. The shed then burst into flames and enormous conflagration took place rising to at least 1000ft and the whole of the shed being completely engulfed."

Three of the bombs crashed through the roof of the 'Toska' shed and exploded as they hit the Zeppelins inside or the shed floor. Inside the shed, the gas cells of the L54 and

L60 caught fire, sending an eruption of flame gradually along the lengths of the airships. Smoke poured out of the shed's doors and the holes in the roof, but fortunately for the ground crews, the airships did not explode. As the gas cells disintegrated in the flames, the airships crashed to the hangar floor, crumpling into a tangled mess of smouldering duralumin girders.

SECOND WAVE

Ten minutes after the bombs of the first attack wave were dropped, the Camels of the second wave arrived overhead. These pilots targeted the small 'Tobias' shed, which at the time housed a captive balloon. Two bombs plummeted through the shed's roof, exploding and destroying the balloon inside. That was to be all the damage that the British inflicted. The other four bombs dropped by the Camels fell near a wagon loaded with hydrogen cylinders, but all four bombs failed to explode. While the airships were destroyed, the base was spared due to these duds. As the Camels flew off, the Germans tallied up their losses: four men wounded but no fatalities; two airships and a balloon destroyed, but the 'Toska' shed was still intact.

The Sopwith 2F.1 Camel ship-borne fighter, armed with one synchronized Vickers machine gun mounted above the fuselage and one Lewis gun mounted on the centre wing section plus two 50lb bombs. This particular aircraft was flown on the Tondern raid by Captain Smart.

The Marine Luftschiff Abteilung base at Tondern in Schleswig-Holstein. The 'Toska' double shed is in the background while the small 'Tobias' shed is in the foreground. At the time of the attack, Zeppelins L54 and L60 were berthed in the 'Toska' shed.

Camel lifting off from the flight deck of the *Furious*.

Out in the North Sea, the crew of the *Furious* pensively kept a look out, hoping that the Camels would return. There was a collective sigh of relief when the first Camel approached; Dickson ditched his near the *Furious* and was picked up by the destroyer *Violent*. The sense of relief aboard the *Furious* turned to joy when Dickson reported that the mission had been a success. Smart arrived over the task force at 06:30, ditched, and was also picked up. The *Furious* and her escorts stayed in the vicinity for another hour (this was judged to be the maximum endurance time for the Camels based upon the amount of fuel they took off with), at which point the ships turned north and proceeded back to Britain. After leaving the Tondern area, Dawson, Jackson, and Williams all believed that they did not have enough fuel to reach the task force at sea. They opted to land in neutral Denmark, whose border lay just to the north of Tondern. The fate of Yeulett remains a mystery; presumably he had to make a forced landing on the water and was lost at sea.

The aerial strike from the *Furious* achieved more than just a tactical objective: it forced the German Naval Airship Division to go on the defensive for the rest of the war. No further airships were based at Tondern for the rest of the war, its location being then deemed too exposed to the front. The Marine Luftschiff Abteilung took measures to heavily defend its other bases, greatly fearing another attack made by a 'land-based aircraft mother ship'. The High Seas Fleet even went so far as to push for the conversion of the uncompleted passenger ship *Ausonia* into a flush-deck aircraft carrier in the late summer of 1918. Despite all of these German defensive precautions, *Furious* never attacked another German target for the rest of the war. Its flight deck configuration at the time made it an awkward ship for aircraft to operate from, particularly in light of the fact that the Royal Navy's first flush-deck carrier, HMS *Argus*, was preparing to enter service. Nevertheless, *Furious* and her pilots had demonstrated the effectiveness of a weapons platform that since has dominated naval planning to the present day. ∎

"The mission of *Furious'* air group was to approach the dens of the German giants that had brought modern aerial warfare to the civilian population of Great Britain..."

BIBLIOGRAPHY

Bruce, JM Sopwith 2F1 Camel. Wind Sock Datafiles, No.6 (2004).
Friedman, Norman. British Carrier Aviation: The Evolution of the Ships and their Aircraft. Annapolis: Naval Institute Press, 1988.
Gardiner, Ian. The Flatpack Bombers: The Royal Navy and the 'Zeppelin Menace'. Barnsley: Pen & Sword Military, 2009.
Gröner, Erich. German Warships, 1815-1945. London: Conway Maritime Press Limited, 1990.
Heiss, Friedrich. Das Zeppelinbuch. Berlin: Volk und Reich, 1936.
Jackson, Robert. Strike from the Sea: A Survey of British Naval Air Operations, 1909-69. London: Arthur Barker Limited, 1970.
Layman, RD. Furious and the Tondern Raid. Warship International, 10 No.4 (1973) : 374-385.
Robinson, Douglas H. The Zeppelin in Combat: A History of the German Naval Airship Division, 1912-1918. Atglen: Schiffer Military/Aviation History, 1994.
Thetford, Owen. British Naval Aircraft Since 1912. Annapolis: Naval Institute Press, 1991.

Smoke billowing out of the large 'Toska' shed at Tondern following the raid. The shed was only lightly damaged but it would never house another Zeppelin.

The charred and crumpled remains of Zeppelin L54 on the floor of the 'Toska' shed. The Germans were fortunate that the Zeppelins simply burned rather than exploded, which could have resulted in significant casualties.

London's first 'Blitz'

German Gotha III airborne; together with Gotha IVs these aircraft carried out bombing raids on London in 1917 which eventually led to the question of home defence and the integration of the two air services as the RAF in 1918.
All via author

Although Zeppelins bombed Britain early in World War One, it was the later raids by aircraft that caused the most damage, as François Prins details.

As aviation technology progressed, the idea of using an aeroplane to carry bombs to a target was an obvious military progression. By 1912, the Naval Wing experimented by dropping heavy objects – not bombs – on a target and the idea of a dedicated bomber did not seem too far off.

Several light bombers were produced for use by the RFC/RNAS, but it was not until December 1914 that Commander Murray Sueter ordered the development of a "bloody paralyser" of an aeroplane to bomb Germany. He asked that it could carry at least six 112lb bombs. The result was the Handley Page O/100, which went into service with the Royal Naval Air Service in 1916 and was used for daylight sea patrols near Flanders; it made its first operational bombing mission on

the night of 16/17 March against the railway yards at Metz. The O/100 could carry up to 16 112lb bombs and served effectively until the end of the war.

However, it was the Germans who developed one of the most famous bombers of World War One. Their Zeppelins may have had a psychological effect on the civilian population, but they were limited in speed and bomb load. More potent were the Gotha bombers which had two Mercedes engines, a wingspan of over 77ft and could carry more than 1000lb of bombs.

On 23 May 1917, a fleet of 21 Gothas appeared over the south coast and bombed Folkestone, leaving 95 dead and 195 injured. Questions were asked in the Houses of Parliament as to why the defence forces had not intercepted the bombers. Then, at noon on 13 June, 14 Gothas bombed London, destroying buildings and leaving 162 dead and many injured. Although the bombers were met by 90 fighters, not one was shot down. The Germans were elated by the success and carried out almost daily raids on London and elsewhere, still meeting little by way of opposition.

Morale dropped and the public demanded that the military protect them and stop the bombers. There was little opposition from aircraft based in and around London and the role of the RFC and RNAS was called into question.

UK-based RFC and RNAS fighters kept intercepting the Gothas, but not always with success: on 7 July 1917 over 100 defensive sorties were flown against a 22 aircraft raid. On this occasion, one Gotha was shot down and three were damaged, at the cost of two fighters shot down by the Gotha's gunners.

The dissatisfaction with the two air services regarding the defence of the capital came to a head. The German bombers had been getting through with little or no aerial opposition and pressure was brought on the government to act. General Jan Smuts, the famous Boer leader and now a member of the War Cabinet, was given the task of examining the home defence arrangements by the two air services against air raids. He relied heavily for advice and information from the Director General of Military Aeronautics, Sir David Henderson, who reported directly to Smuts.

In a now famous memorandum, written in July 1917, Sir David dealt with the problems facing the two air arms and made several recommendations that he had long wished to see come into being. He reported that there should be one complete air service dealing with all operations in the air and administered by a single ministry with full powers. Smuts also dealt with the defence of London and the unification of the two air services. On receiving this report, Prime Minister Lloyd George set up a committee, under the chairmanship of General Smuts, to establish an Air Ministry. Henderson

Workmen set about clearing a London street following a night raid by Gotha bombers in 1917.

relinquished his post as DGMA to work with Smuts on the Air Organisation Committee.

Between August and October 1917 – while London was being bombed – they drafted a Bill for the new Ministry; and in November, the Air Force (Constitution) Act 1917 was placed before Parliament; it was passed unopposed and on 29 November received the Royal Assent. The Air Ministry and the Air Council came into being on 2 and 3 January 1918 respectively. On 1 April 1918, the two air arms became the Royal Air Force.

FIGHTING BACK

By now, the defence of the capital had been co-ordinated and with an increase of anti-aircraft guns and fighters, the enemy found it hard to attain success. Home defence was greatly improved when 44 Squadron, based at Hainault Farm, re-equipped with the Sopwith Camel in August 1917 and began to seriously impede the enemy. Consequently, that same month, the Germans ceased the daylight raids and switched to night bombing, which continued until May 1918, when they were discontinued due to heavy losses of aircraft and crews.

Pilots of 44 Squadron had trained hard at flying the tricky Camel at night and their work led to a dedicated night-fighter version of the Camel being built. It was found that the muzzle-flash of the two Vickers guns on the cowling destroyed the pilots' night vision. Sopwith replaced the Vickers guns with twin Lewis guns on Foster mounts on the upper

wing section. To enable the pilot to aim and reload the guns, the cockpit was repositioned about 12 inches aft; the fuel tank was moved from behind the pilot to the front fuselage to compensate for the cockpit move.

It is worth noting that on 16 February, four Gothas raided London and one dropped a 2200lb bomb – the largest used by anyone in the war – and blew up a wing of the Chelsea hospital. A direct hit on St Pancras railway station was scored the following night, despite the ring of barrage balloons and heavy anti-aircraft fire. By now the Gothas were joined by the massive Zeppelin-Staaken Riesenflugzeug Giant with a wingspan of 138ft on raids against Britain. The last raid of the war was carried out on the night of 19/20 October 1918. This was a combined Gotha/Giant raid, and of the 38 Gothas taking part, three were shot down by fighters and a further three were brought down by anti-aircraft fire. A total of 61 Gotha aircraft were lost over Britain between September 1917 and May 1918, but no Zeppelin-Staaken Giants were brought down, although some were damaged in combat.

Germany had mounted 27 Gotha bombing raids and it was reported that there had been 835 killed and 1990 wounded. Damage from

German Gotha III bomber of the type that attacked London in 1917 and forced a reorganisation of the RFC and RNAS.

the raids was estimated at some £3,000,000, but the loss of war production due to workers having to seek shelter in the middle of the day, or suffering exhaustion from having to leave their beds to seek shelter at night, had a far greater impact.

While the Zeppelin and Gotha raids were insignificant when compared with the Blitz of 1940, it was the fact that the enemy brought the battle to Britain, an invasion of sorts and something that had not happened since the Norman conquest of 1066. The effect was to spread fear and that was what the enemy had counted on – what they did not count on was the concentrated defence by the ground and air services. These raids and those carried out by the Allies showed just how easy it was to bomb targets miles behind the front lines; it also laid down a blueprint for the future of the strategic bomber. ■

The destruction at Folkstone after a raid by the German bombers in 1917.

Still on the
front line

Jarrod Cotter describes how 3 Squadron RFC was the first unit to be equipped with 'heavier-than-air' machines, and almost 100 years later is now flying the RAF's state-of-the-art fighter, the Typhoon.

No.3 Squadron was formed as one of the founder units of the Royal Flying Corps, at Larkhill, Wiltshire, on 13 May 1912, when No.2 (Aeroplane) Company was given a new name – 3 Squadron Royal Flying Corps (Military Wing). It was the first RFC unit to fly 'heavier-than-air' machines and during its formative years flew a variety of early types including the Blériot XI, Deperdussin, Farman, BE.2a and Bristol Boxkite.

In the 1912 manoeuvres, 3 Squadron was involved in the first serious use of aircraft in co-operation with the Army. Major Brooke-Popham returned from a recce flight with sketch maps showing 'enemy' positions, which he gave to General Grierson who used the intelligence to outflank General Haig's forces with such efficiency that the exercise finished long before it was due to.

Following the outbreak of war in August 1914, on the 12th 3 Squadron deployed to France as part of the British Expeditionary Force flying seven Blériots, four Henry Farmans and one BE.8 to Amiens and was one of the first squadrons to arrive in France. The RFC's first reconnaissance duties were carried out on 19 August by a Blériot from No.3 and a BE from 4 Squadron. The unit was also ordered to be ready to attack Zeppelins – its aircrew were armed with three bombs and a revolver. The bombs were to be dropped on the Zeppelin and the revolvers used for air fighting.

While on an artillery spotting sortie, a 3 Squadron pilot in a Henry Farman reported an incident where he entered aerial combat with a German Etrich Taube. The British observer was firing at the Taube with a rifle, while the enemy aircraft was trying to position itself to be able to drop a bomb on its pursuer. Shots were then fired from the German aircraft also before it made off for the German lines, initially chased by the British crew until they came in range of anti-aircraft fire and returned to continue with their observations.

It wasn't until early 1916 that the unit standardised on one type; the Morane Parasol which continued to be used on artillery spotting duties.

One of the squadron's aircraft was involved in a remarkable incident on 26 July 1916, when 2nd Lt LG Wood and his observer were directing artillery fire on a German strongpoint. The crew then called for the bombardment to cease, and flew in low along the enemy trenches strafing the infantrymen with machine-gun fire. After this attack the crew saw the German troops waving their hands and white handkerchiefs in surrender. A message was dropped from the aircraft to the British lines reporting this, and around 370 German soldiers were taken prisoner.

With the advent of specialised fighter squadrons No.3 changed to such duties until war's end, equipped with Sopwith Camels from September 1917. It still continues in this role in its contemporary form.

Over the course of its history 3(F) Squadron has had a number of 'firsts', and so it was apt that it was the first to go operational

The highly capable Typhoon is powered by two Eurojet EJ200 turbojets, each producing 20,000lb of thrust – making the jet capable of getting to high altitude very quickly and travelling at Mach 2 at 65,000ft. **Jarrod Cotter**

Left: On 31 March 2006, No.3 moved to Coningsby to become the third RAF, and first front line squadron, equipped with the Typhoon. The fourth is 11 Squadron, which led the RAF's Typhoon in the ground attack role, to become fully operational in both air-to-air and air-to-ground operations giving the type its multi-role combat status. Initially single-seat Typhoons were designated F2, but as the type was to be multi-role capable it took on the FGR4 designation as modified aircraft came on strength. Its payload includes a maximum of eight air-to-air and up to six air-to-surface weapons. The avionics inside it include the advanced Captor ECR90 radar, which can track multiple targets at long range, and the pilot can even carry out many functions by voice command. And in the time it takes to read this sentence a Typhoon could have travelled more than two kilometres – all in stark contrast to the Morane Parasols pictured below! **Jarrod Cotter**

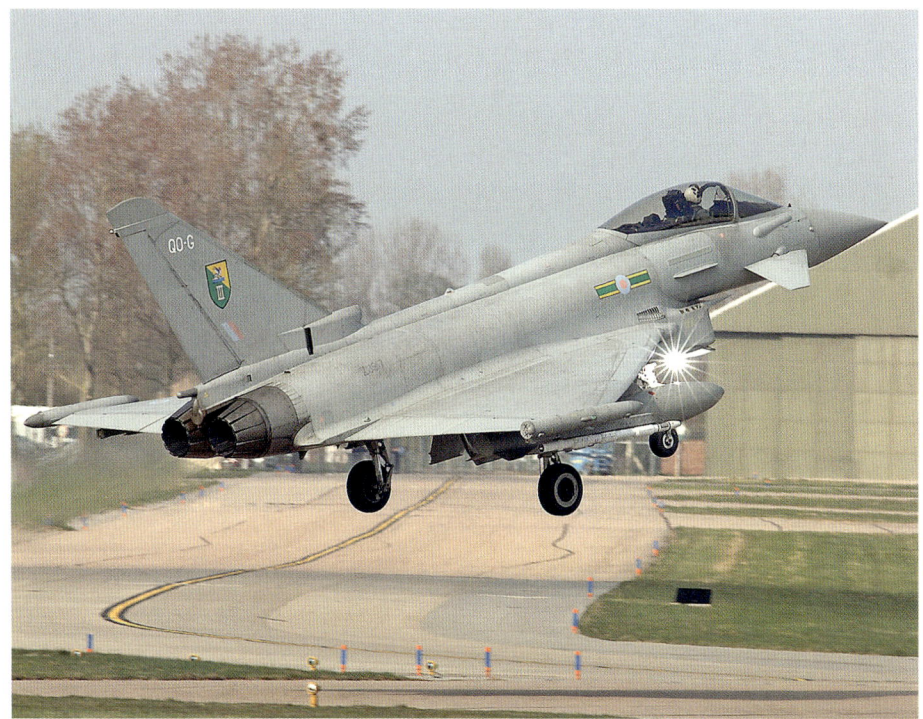

with the Eurofighter Typhoon F2 which arrived on strength in March 2006. The unit then became the lead squadron for developing RAF Typhoon air defence operations.

The squadron's Typhoons carry 'QO-' tail codes, which were reintroduced to commemorate its operations flying the Hawker Typhoon during World War Two. They are based on the codes worn by aircraft which participated on the first operational raids using 'Bombphoons' in 1943. The Commanding Officer led the first raid in QO-C, hence the aircraft now flown by the current CO wears QO-C on its tail.

No.3 Squadron's badge features on a monolith, a cockatrice. It was approved by King George VI in September 1937, and the cockatrice was chosen because in mythology it was the first creature to fly. The unit's motto is 'Tertius primus erit', which translates as 'The third shall be the first' referring to 3 Squadron being the first unit of the RFC to be equipped with 'heavier than air' machines. A modern take on the badge is applied to the tails of 3 Squadron's Typhoons, giving the squadron a strong sense of identity based on its proud heritage. ■

Below: Morane Parasols of 3 Squadron RFC seen at La Houssoye, France, in September 1916 outside makeshift canvas hangars erected to offer the aircraft some protection. **Via François Prins**

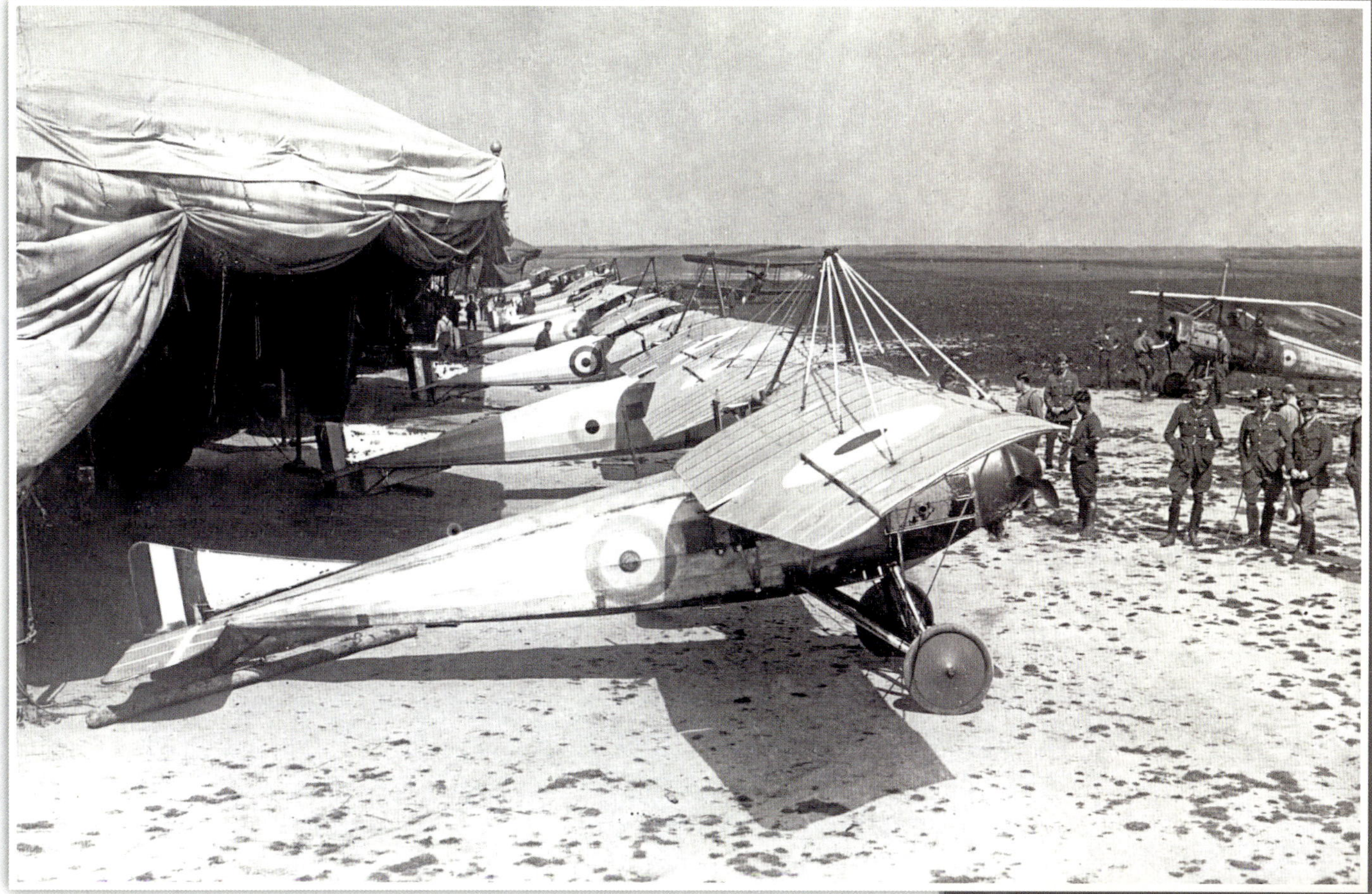

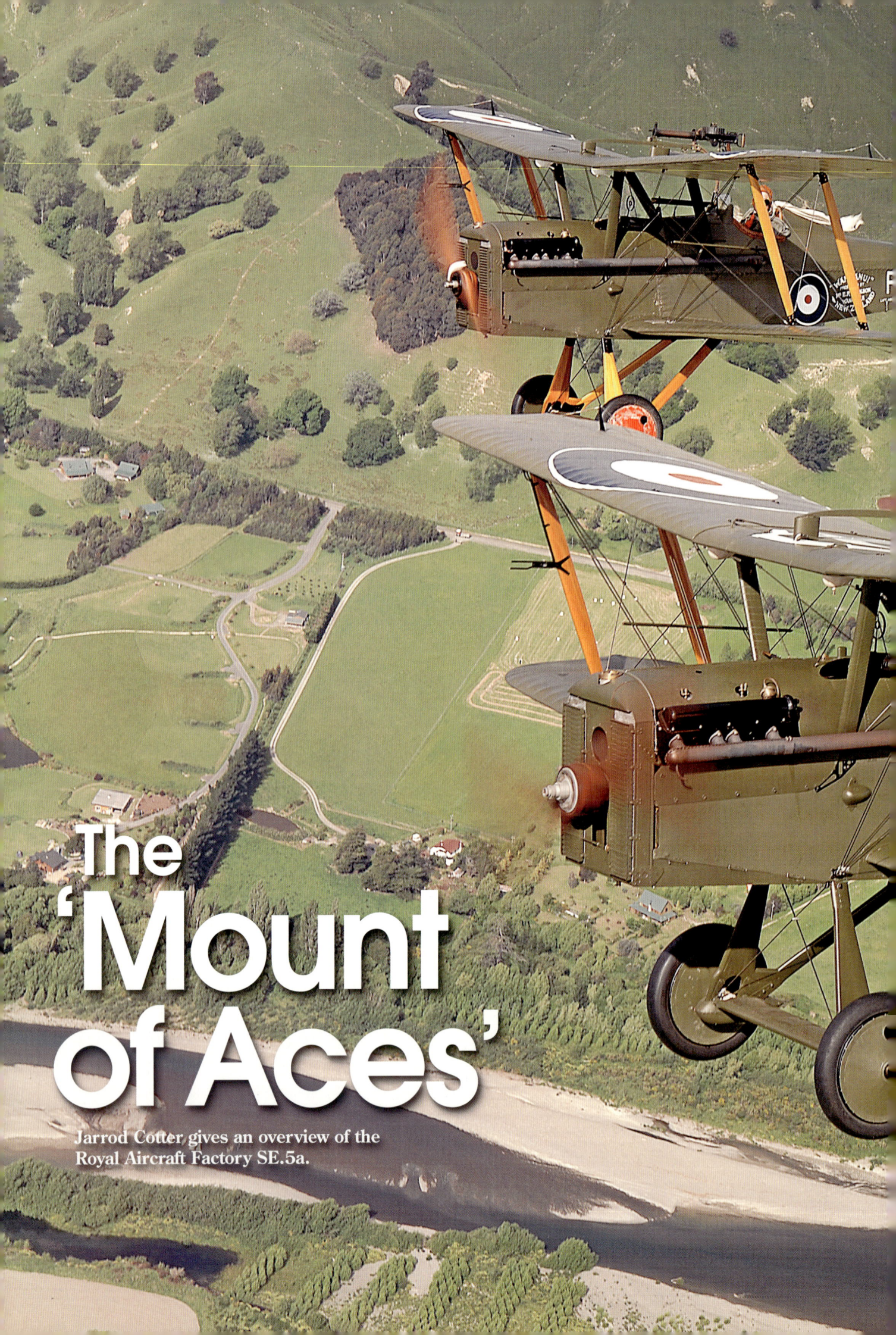

The 'Mount of Aces'

Jarrod Cotter gives an overview of the
Royal Aircraft Factory SE.5a.

Two-ship TVAL SE.5a formation, with John Bargh flying B507 nearest the camera and Tim Sullivan in F5690.

The three airworthy TVAL SE.5as taxi in after a sortie out of Masterton in November 2009.

It was strong, featured high performance and was a steady gun platform. Major James McCudden VC DSO* MC* MM said in his book *Flying Fury – Five Years in the RFC* that the SE.5a was: "a most efficient fighting machine, far and away superior to the enemy machines of that period." It is no wonder then that many regarded the SE.5a as the 'Mount of Aces'.

The SE.5a could be described as a 'next generation' fighter of its time. By late 1916/early 1917, rotary engines were reaching their limit, because the increased horsepower was making the centrifugal forces on the engine and the gyroscopic effect on the airframe too great. Very advanced for its time, one engine which could produce the high horsepower required without the difficult handling characteristics of the rotary was the inline Hispano-Suiza. The SE.5 (Scout Experimental) was designed to use this powerplant.

The first Hispano-Suiza arrived in August 1916 and three prototype SE.5s were built. The first, A4561, took to the air on 22 November. The second flew on 4 December and was sent to France for evaluation by 60 Squadron.

On 28 January 1917, the prototype crashed as a result of its wings collapsing in flight, killing chief pilot Major Frank Goodden.

Wing modifications were then introduced, which included strengthened rear spars, shorter wings with a reduced rake and stronger joints for both the struts and spars. This work solved the problem and gave the type its characteristic strength.

The first production SE.5s were delivered to 56 Squadron in March 1917, while it was working up for France at London Colney in Hertfordshire. The unit embarked overseas with the new fighter in April and initially there were several teething troubles, especially with the engines.

Meanwhile, a more powerful version of the Hispano-Suiza had been developed which increased output from 150hp to 200hp. Aircraft also began to be fitted with a Wolseley Viper direct drive V-8 engine. ➤

Nose detail showing the radiator shutters open.

TVAL's first airworthy SE.5a reproduction represents presentation aircraft F5690. It is seen being flown by TVAL pilot Tim Sullivan. **All Jarrod Cotter unless noted**

TVAL's SE.5as feature replica Lewis guns fitted on accurate Foster mounts.

Close-up of the presentation inscription on F5690.

Close-up of the 0.303in Vickers machine-gun.

Cockpit of F5690. Stowage for additional Lewis gun ammunition drums can be seen top centre and on the floor in front of the control column.

Mass 85 Squadron SE.5a line-up, c1918. **Crown Copyright**

Those fitted with the newer type of engines differed in their looks, as they had a slightly deeper forward fuselage. Combined with a fairing behind the pilot's head, the fitting of radiator shutters and the shorter wings, further production machines were re-designated as the SE.5a.

The improved design arrived on unit strength with 56 Squadron from June 1917. Due to production delays, by year's end only seven squadrons were equipped with the SE.5a. Teething troubles had also continued, but by the spring of 1918 the type was considered the best fighter of its era.

The SE.5's first combat victory occurred on 23 April 1917, when Captain Albert Ball shot down an Albatros D.III. Many of the top-scoring Allied aces of World War One claimed a large proportion of their scores in this type, including Major Edward 'Mick' Mannock VC DSO** MC* who achieved 54 of his 73 'kills' in SE.5as.

The fighter went on to equip numerous units in France, plus some Home Defence squadrons – although it wasn't ideally suited to this task as its engine took too long to warm up when needed to intercept a sighted target. It also served in Greece and Palestine.

Along with the Sopwith Camel, the SE.5a is regarded as being largely responsible for regaining air superiority over the Western Front. The two worked well together, as the more manoeuvrable Camel was generally used for low-level operations while the SE.5a's superior performance at higher altitude was used to good advantage in that environment. ➤

One of TVAL's three airworthy reproductions accurately represents D3540.

TVAL'S 'LATE MODEL' SE.5As

The Vintage Aviator Ltd (TVAL) has produced no less than three airworthy reproductions built to original specification, and each powered by an original Hispano-Suiza direct drive engine. Components were built using the same materials and processes that were used in 1917/1918. These include Ash and Spruce timbers and Irish linen. TVAL has a skilled team of craftsmen working on its aircraft production, and they have become adept at combining bygone techniques with modern technology in order to comply with current New Zealand CAA regulations for airworthy aircraft.

The 90-plus-year-old engines were sourced from around the world and all restored to 'as new' condition. Another good example of the many great lengths gone to in order to ensure accuracy were the propellers. TVAL scanned the three-dimensions of an original example into a computer, and then exact copies were machined using laminated mahogany.

After all the effort, the results emerged as just the most incredible reproductions

imaginable. TVAL craftsmen like to think of them as being 'late model' SE.5as.

The first example 'off the production line' took to the skies on 26 March 2007 from Hood Aerodrome, Masterton, on New Zealand's North Island. It then made its airshow debut at Classic Fighters, Blenheim, on the South Island over the Easter weekend of 6-8 April.

TVAL chief pilot, Gene DeMarco, commented: "It is the finest example of a World War One fighter I have ever flown! It is comfortable, manoeuvrable yet stable, fast and easy to fly. The cockpit is warm, not too windy and the visibility is very good even for a biplane.

"Best of all, the engine inspires confidence. It develops a tremendous amount of power, responds well and is extremely smooth and so far, very reliable. If I had any doubts about the reliability of the Hispano-Suiza engine, I would not have flown the SE.5a across the Cook Strait to attend the Classic Fighters Airshow." ∎

RFC pilot Gwilym Lewis flew many types, but is seen in his favourite, the fast and stable SE.5a. He is pictured in D3540, in which he scored at least four victories beginning with a Fokker Dr.I on 11 April 1918. **Via François Prins**

SE.5A SPECIFICATION

Dimensions:	Wingspan 26ft 7½in; Length 20ft 11in; Height 9ft 6in
All-up Weight:	1953lb
Powerplant:	One Hispano-Suiza engine producing 200hp, 220hp or 250hp; or one Wolseley Viper producing 200hp
Performance:	Maximum speed 135mph at sea level; Climb to 10,000ft 10 minutes 20 seconds; Service ceiling 22,000ft
Armament:	One fixed synchronised 0.303in Vickers machine-gun mounted faired into port cowling with Constantinesco CC interrupter gear and one 0.303in Lewis gun fitted to top wing on a Foster mount

"Along with the Sopwith Camel, the SE.5a is regarded as being largely responsible for regaining air superiority over the Western Front."

This view highlights the armament of an SE.5a, with a sychronised Vickers gun offset to port and the Lewis gun fitted to the top wing. Note also the optical Aldis sight visible in front of the pilot's windscreen.

The 'Red Baron'

A pictorial presentation of Rittmeister Baron Manfred von Richthofen, the most feared German pilot above the trenches of World War One.

Manfred von Richthofen (left) and aircraft designer Anthony Fokker sit on the wreckage of Sopwith Pup B1795, the Baron's 61st victory shot down on 3 September 1917. Fokker is wearing the flying helmet and jacket of the Pup's pilot, who survived the crash and became a prisoner of war. **Via François Prins**

Well-known portrait of Rittmeister (Cavalry Captain) Baron Manfred von Richthofen, who scored 80 aerial victories – the most of any pilot during World War One. He is seen wearing the Pour le Mérite, or Blue Max. The much-celebrated pilot was killed on 21 April 1918 during a low-level combat at around 11:00am in the vicinity of Vaux sur Somme, aged 25. Claims at the time said that Captain Roy Brown shot down the 'Red Baron' in a Sopwith Camel; however, later research suggests that it was actually ground fire that struck the fatal blow.

The 'Red Baron' takes-off in his Albatros D.III, another all-over red machine flown before he received the Triplane. As his reputation grew, 'The Red Knight of Germany' was painted on the fuselage of von Richthofen's all-red D.III.

FAMOUS VICTORY

Manfred von Richthofen's 11th victory was highly prized by the Germans, and a damaging blow to public morale for the British. His victim was Major Lanoe Hawker VC DSO, who when shot down by the 'Red Baron' on 23 November 1916 was a national hero. Hawker was credited with seven aerial victories, and his Victoria Cross was awarded after he single-handedly attacked and conquered three German aircraft. Lanoe Hawker became the first British flying ace, and a figure of considerable fame within the ranks of the RFC and the public too. As such, this victory elevated von Richthofen's standing as an air ace considerably. The British pilot was buried by German infantrymen near the crash site at Luisenhof Farm, though the site was later lost to the deluge of war and he now has no known grave. He is listed on the Arras Flying Services Memorial in France, which commemorates nearly 1000 airmen of the Royal Naval Air Service, the Royal Flying Corps and the Royal Air Force, either by attachment from other arms of the forces of the Commonwealth or by original enlistment, who were killed on the Western Front and have no known grave.
Photo: Via François Prins

The 'Red Baron's' trademark all-over red Fokker Dr.I Triplane, 425/17. While it is the Triplane that most people associate him with, von Richthofen predominantly flew Albatros D.IIs and D.IIIs.
Juanita Franzi / Aero Illustrations © 2010

Von Richthofen's trophy room in the family home at Schweidnitz, Silesia, decorated with items taken from his prey including serial numbers cut from the fabric of British aircraft and a chandelier made from a rotary engine.

Hauptman Oswald Boelcke was Germany's first leading fighter pilot. He showed the way to many younger pilots including von Richthofen. He was killed while flying an Albatros D.II as a result of a mid-air collision with one of his own side during an aerial combat with DH.2s of 24 Squadron on 28 October 1916.

Leutnant Max Immelman pioneered many aerial combat manoeuvres that were admired and have been copied by pilots over the years, especially the 'Immelman turn'. He was killed while flying a Fokker E.III during an aerial combat with FE.2bs of 25 Squadron on 18 June 1916. **Both via François Prins**

Manfred von Richthofen (right) with his younger brother Lothar pictured in front of a Fokker Triplane.

Sanke portrait of Manfred von Richthofen that was widely used as a postcard of the period.

Pilots of JG1, the 'Flying Circus', with von Richthofen at centre. His dog Moritz is also in the picture.

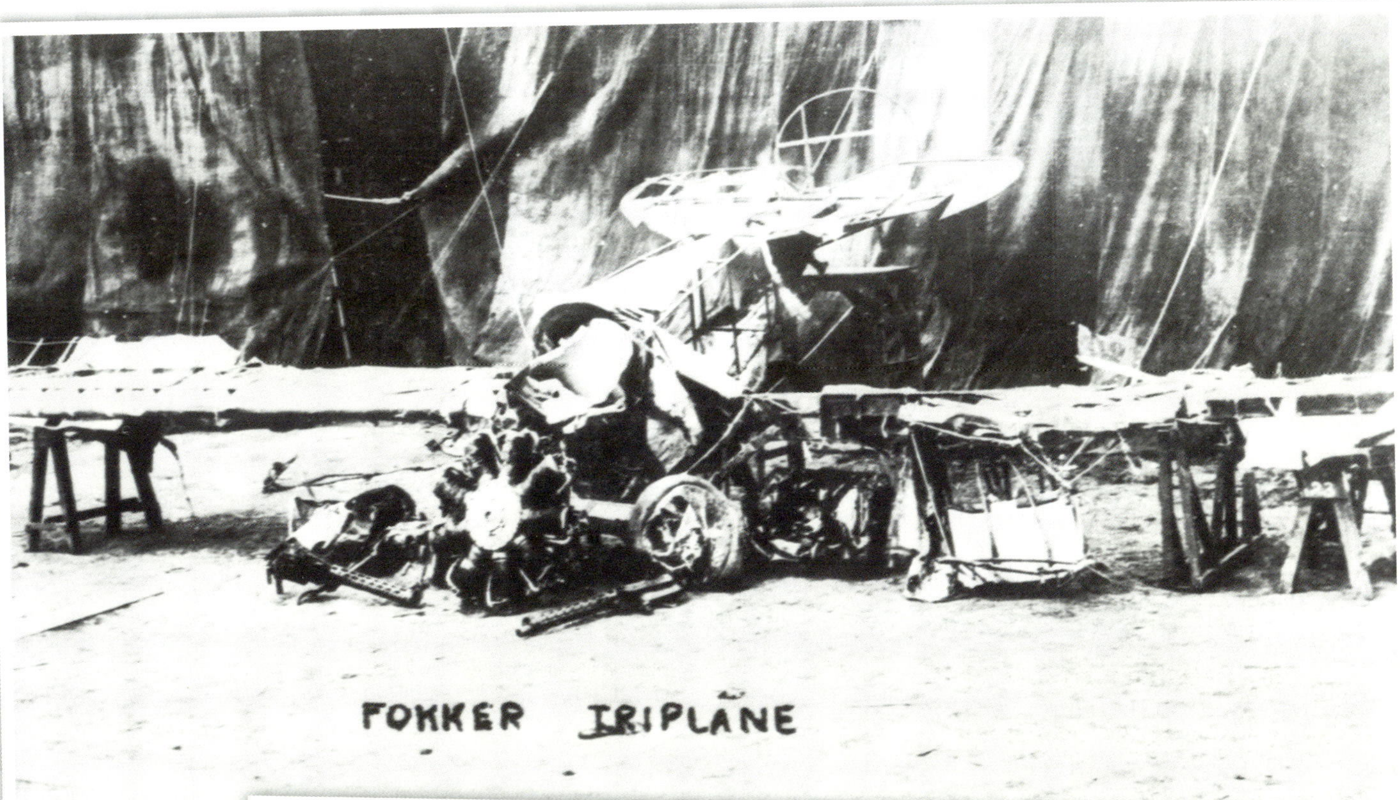

Wreckage of von Richthofen's Triplane after being shot down on 21 April 1918. After being shot in the air, the pilot is reported to have lived long enough to make a forced landing and the Triplane reportedly suffered little damage. However, such was its pilot's fame that the Dr.I was pulled apart by Allied infantry 'souvenir hunters' when on the ground.

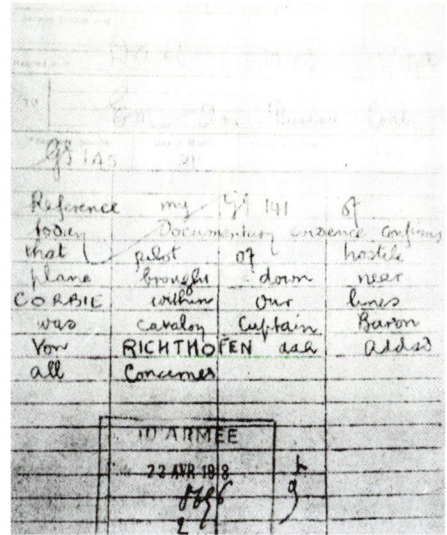

Letter confirming the shoot down of von Richthofen.

Fokker Dr.I Triplane of Manfred von Richthofen on display in the Zueghaus museum, Berlin. It was destroyed by Allied bombing during World War Two. **All via Time Line Images unless noted**

THE RED BARON FILM

Now available on DVD in Europe and the USA is *The Red Baron*, a modern film based on the story of the famous World War One pilot.

Set in the Europe of 1916, Baron Manfred von Richthofen (Matthias Schweighöfer) is, at the age of just 24, the crack pilot of the German aerial forces – a legend in his own time, a hero at home and a man both feared and respected by the enemy, including Allied forces' Canadian pilot, Captain Roy Brown (Joseph Fiennes).

Von Richthofen and his fellow officers see their duels in the sky as tactical, almost sportsmanlike challenges, that at least at first obscure their view of the horrors of the battlefields below. The provocative red paintwork of his aircraft earns him the nickname the 'Red Baron' and makes him famous the world over.

For millions of his countrymen, he becomes an idol, a symbol of hope and pride. But the German High Command increasingly misuses him for propaganda purposes – until the young pilot falls in love with Käte (Lena Headly), a beautiful and resolute nurse who opens his eyes to the fact that there is more to war than dogfights won and adversaries downed. Manfred von Richthofen finally becomes aware of his role in the propaganda machine of a senseless and barbarous war.

On another, more personal front, his ambitious and patriotic brother Lothar (Volker Bruch) questions his chivalrous code of honour. But despite the heavy losses in his squadron and torn between his disgust for the war and his responsibility to his fighter wing, von Richthofen cannot stop flying. But even for this living legend, each new combat mission could be his last… **Synopsis and film still courtesy Monterey Media Inc**

THE RED BARON

MATTHIAS SCHWEIGHÖFER AS MANFRED VON RICHTHOFEN

'Richthofen's Flying Circus' flies again! The seven Dr.I replicas in formation led by the all-red example representing Baron Manfred von Richthofen's machine fly in the Blenheim area on 7 April 2007. **Gavin Conroy**

'Flying Circus' Triplanes

One of the best known aircraft of World War One was Germany's Fokker Dr.I Dreidecker, which was made especially famous by flying in coats of many colours with JG1's Jasta 11 under the command of Manfred von Richthofen.

There are few aircraft of World War One that can be considered as distinctive as the Fokker Dr.I Dreidecker, or 'Triplane'. The fame of this agile fighter, which came into effective service from September 1917, was in the main made by the successes of the 'Red Baron' and his colourful Richthofen's 'Flying Circus'.

As the aerial war and the aircraft designs used advanced, there was a continual swing of air supremacy as both sides introduced new types that only gained an advantage for a matter of months before the other did likewise. At the turn of the year 1917, Royal Naval Air Service squadrons on the Western Front began to receive the first Sopwith Triplanes. This type offered excellent performance with its ingenious and radical wing design. All six wing sections had ailerons offering sharp handling, and a reduced wing chord gave the pilot good visibility.

Obviously the success of this type led to its design catching the eye of its opponents and Germany was keen to pursue it. Anthony Fokker's answer took to the air during June of the same year and was soon in production.

It was little surprise that Germany's leading fighter ace was given one of the first examples to test in combat. At the time it was designated Fokker F.I, and 102/17 was delivered to JG1 on 21 August. The machine wasn't red, but just finished in the standard factory applied dope-streaked finish.

FIRST PATROL, FIRST 'KILL'

Manfred von Richthofen took it on its first operational sortie during the early morning of 1 September 1917. During the patrol von Richthofen encountered RE.8 B782 of 6 Squadron RFC. It is widely thought that the British aircraft understandably believed the aircraft was an RNAS Sopwith Triplane and hence did not open fire.

In his combat report, Richthofen wrote: "Flying my Triplane for the first time, I attacked, together with four of my gentlemen, a very boldly flown artillery-reconnaissance aircraft. I approached and fired twenty shots from a distance of 50 metres, whereupon the adversary fell out of control and crashed this side, near Zonnebeke. Apparently the opponent had taken me for an English Triplane, because the observer in the machine stood upright without making a move for his machine gun."

His second victory in a Triplane came two days later when a Sopwith Pup was downed. Despite tough opposition, the German pilot confidently included in this report: "The Fokker Triplane F.I No.102/17 was absolutely superior to the British Sopwith." In fact, such were the flying capabilities of the Dr.I that von Richthofen commented that it "Climbed like a monkey and manoeuvred like the devil." ➤

View from a Fokker Dr.I looking out over the Cook Strait as two Triplanes make their way to Blenheim on New Zealand's South Island from Hood Aerodrome, Masterton, on the North Island. **Tim Sullivan**

Dr.I wings having their fabric stitched in the factory during 1917.

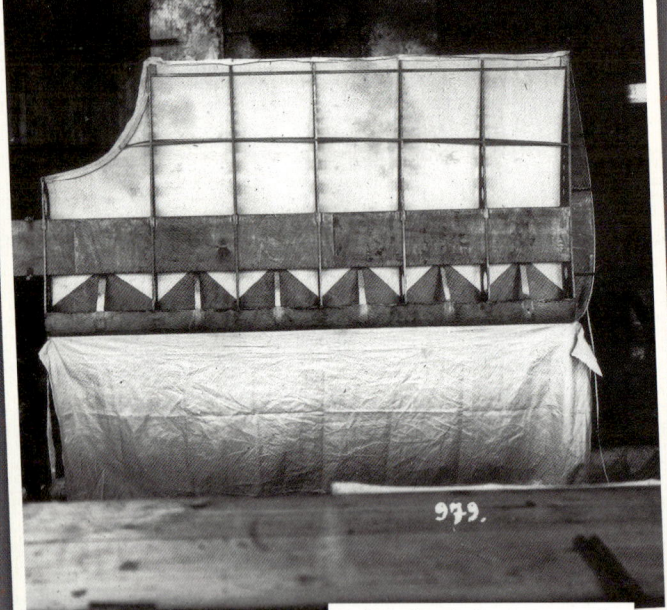

A Dr.I wing in the process of having its fabric fitted, c1917.

Painting of wings in progress, c1917.

Completed Dr.I 212/17 after being loaded onto a railway truck ready to be taken to the front. Its wings have yet to be placed on the truck alongside the fuselage. **All via Time Line Images**

"Apparently the opponent had taken me for an English Triplane, because the observer in the machine stood upright without making a move for his machine gun."

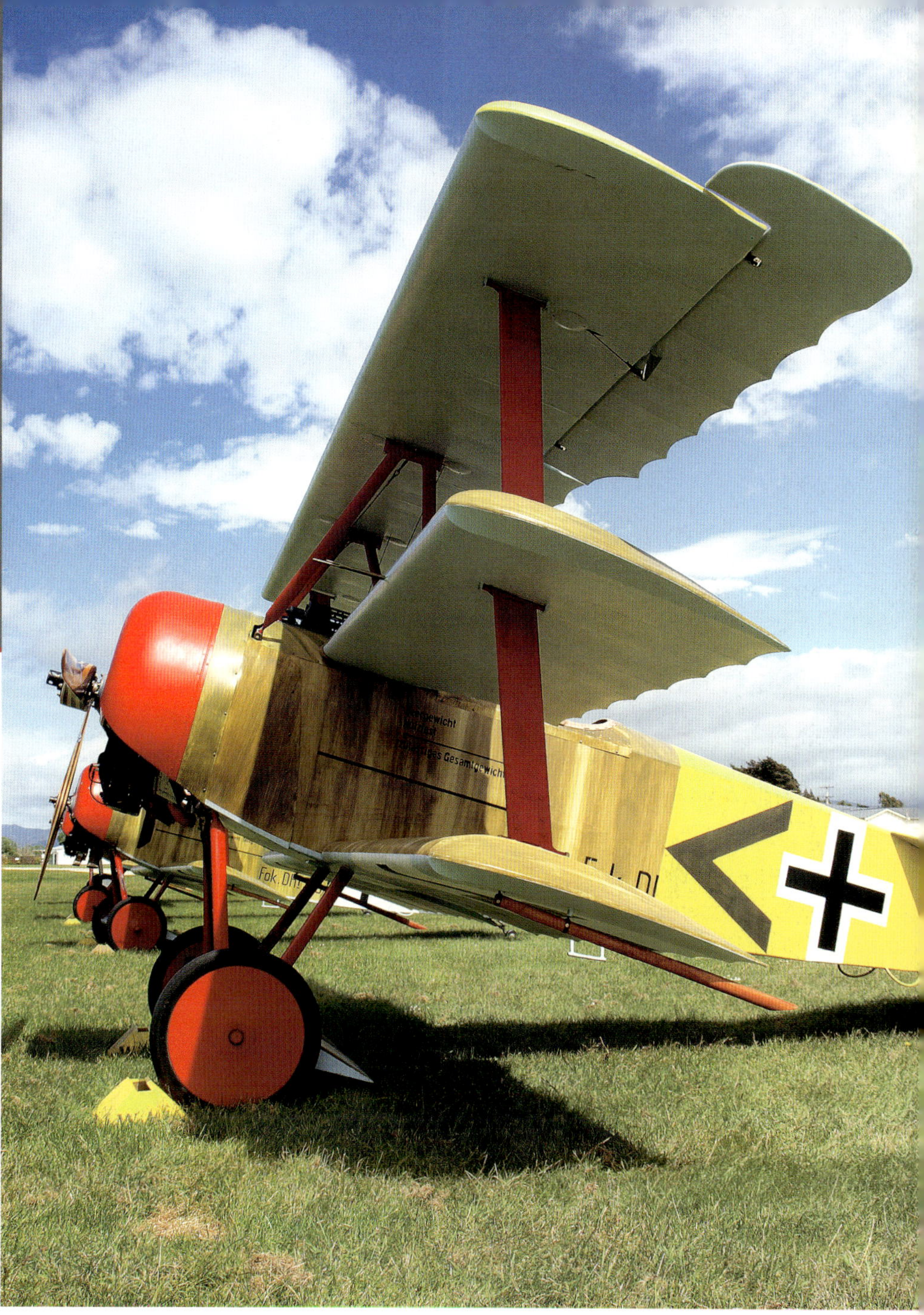

Right: Three Triplanes wearing the common red markings of Jasta 11 on their cowlings, wing struts and undercarriage at Hood on 12 November 2009. **Jarrod Cotter**

Bottom: Low angle view of one of the Dr.I replicas at Hood Aerodrome, Masterton, during the build-up to The Vintage Aviator Ltd's Remembrance Day Air Show in November 2009. **Jarrod Cotter**

However, the Fokker Triplane differed from its Sopwith counterpart in that only the top wing had ailerons. It also lacked the bracing wires that were so characteristic of other aircraft of its era. The Dr.I began to have recurring fatal crashes due to the upper-wing structure collapsing and this led to its premature withdrawal from service. By the time the fault was diagnosed, the superior Fokker D.VII was coming on stream and the number of Dr.Is built reached just 320, quite low in comparison to some of the superior fighters of its time.

'FLYING CIRCUS' FLIES AGAIN

Nowadays no original Dr.Is remain, the last surviving example – one flown by Richthofen – having been destroyed when the Zeughaus museum building in Berlin was bombed by the Allies during World War Two. However, there are numerous flying replicas, including seven in New Zealand which all wear the carefully researched accurate paint schemes of pilots who flew with Jagdstaffel 11 (11 Fighter Squadron) of JG1 around March 1918. At that time Manfred von Richthofen was the Jasta's leader and was flying his 'trademark' all-over red Triplane.

Jasta 11 was formed on 28 September 1916 when Germany decided to establish specialist fighter squadrons. Its first commanding officer was Oberleutnant Rudolf Lang who remained in post until January 1917, whereupon Rittmeister Manfred von Richthofen took over. At that point von Richthofen already had numerous aerial victories and had just received the Pour le Mérite, more commonly known as the Blue Max.

The aircraft of Jasta 11 had common red cowlings, wing struts and undercarriage, and then had an individual pilot's chosen paintwork applied over the predominantly dope-streaked olive camouflage.

One of the world's leading airshows is the biennial Classic Fighters held at Omaka, Blenheim, on New Zealand's South Island. At the 2007 event, all seven Fokker Triplanes flew together creating a sight not seen since 1918 as Richthofen's 'Flying Circus' took to the skies once more. ■

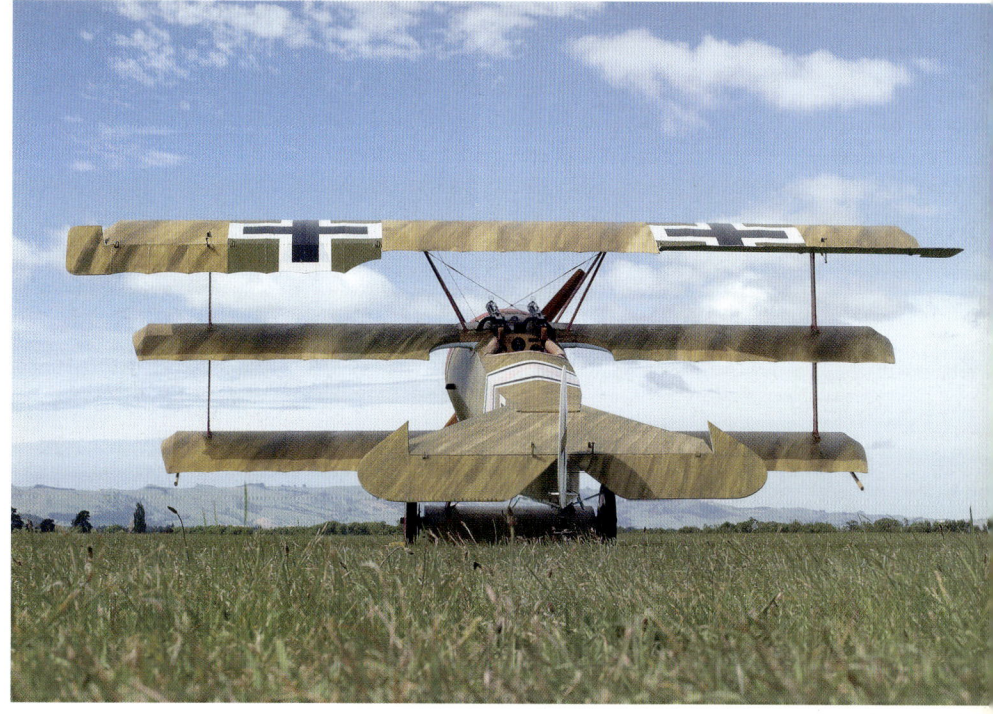

Absolute authenticity

A profile of the incredible craftsmanship of The Vintage Aviator Ltd, which is unique within the historic aviation community as it solely restores and manufactures aircraft from the 1914-1918 era.

An original Avro 504K powered by an original 100hp Gnome rotary engine is also part of the fleet at Hood; following restoration this aircraft returned to the skies in April 2009. **Jarrod Cotter**

ON THE WINGS OF HISTORY

A brand new largely pictorial book entitled *On The Wings Of History* by Allan Udy and Alex Mitchell features the results of the first 10 years' work of TVAL. Within the 116 pages of this softbound A5 format full colour publication are more than 260 photographs featuring 47 different paint schemes of 25 World War One aircraft types, including those on display at the Omaka Aviation Heritage Centre. More than 50 pages of the book are taken up by full-page colour photos, many of which are air-to-air. The book costs £17 including postage to the UK; for more details see the advertisement on the inside back cover. www.aviationfilm.com

With facilities in Wellington and at Hood Aerodrome, Masterton, on New Zealand's North Island, The Vintage Aviator Ltd (TVAL) has become highly regarded for building World War One era aircraft, engines and propellers to the same specifications that they were originally built to. TVAL's skilled craftsmen always set themselves the task of maintaining absolute authenticity to the original design – and as you can see from the numerous aircraft featured within this issue, the results are astounding. Both airworthy and static display aircraft for museums are constructed.

TVAL has worked closely with the New Zealand CAA to ensure it fully met its obligations as a certified aircraft manufacturer, gaining CAA approval and being issued with its Part 148 Manufacturing Organisation Certificate in 2007. Its pilots and engineers also maintain and operate the large collection of World War One aircraft owned by the 1914-18 Aviation Heritage Trust. Chairman of the Trust is film director Peter Jackson, best known for his incredible *Lord of the Rings* trilogy. Peter has a great interest in the aviation of the period.

While the company uses traditional techniques in the construction of the aircraft, it also uses modern technology such as CAD to ensure that its reproductions are the most accurate representation to the very last and minute detail. TVAL is capable of every aspect of aircraft and engine construction from this bygone era, with specialist woodworkers, machinists and craftsmen highly skilled in the art of fabric covering of aircraft.

The trio of airworthy Royal Aircraft Factory SE.5a reproductions (plus a fourth for museum display) aptly highlight that these aircraft can even be produced in what could be described as a 'factory output'. That's because once original drawings and components have been used to establish the build specification of a type, several can be constructed to the exact same standard. TVAL continues to source technical data and original parts for duplication so that other types may be constructed in a similar way in the years to come. The recent FE.2b 'pusher' is a perfect example of how this dedicated craftsmanship is bringing the world flying examples of aircraft that could have otherwise been 'lost in the skies of history'. ∎

TVAL manufactures perfect reproductions of World War One aircraft as well as restoring originals to accurate airworthy condition. BE.2f A1325 is an example of an original restoration, and in this picture highlights how the fruits of TVAL's labour of love is re-creating the 1914-1918 aviation era for a modern audience.
Photo Jarrod Cotter, sepia and graphic artwork by Simon Duncan

TVAL's incredible Albatros D.Va is silhouetted by the fading evening light at Hood Aerodrome. **Jarrod Cotter**

'KNIGHTS OF THE SKY'

The Omaka Aviation Heritage Centre is located at Omaka Aerodrome, near Blenheim on New Zealand's South Island – home to the biennial Classic Fighters Marlborough airshow.

Omaka's first exhibition, 'Knights of the Sky', comprises one of the world's largest collections of World War One aircraft and artefacts, including some very realistic and dramatically staged permanent dioramas. The collection is managed by the 1914-18 Aviation Heritage Trust, and gives a fascinating insight into the aviation of the era through the theatrical dioramas.

These realistically come to life via the 'film set' treatment given to them, depicting the aircraft in action in the skies over the trenches as well as some specific incidents. One of these depicts New Zealand's highest scoring ace 'Grid' Caldwell's amazing incident when he managed to regain control of his SE.5a after it was severely damaged in a mid-air collision, then managed to stabilise the aircraft by placing himself half in and half out of his cockpit for just long enough to make it back to friendly lines and jump clear moments before it crashed. Of the rare artefacts on display, highlights include the flying suit belonging to America's highest scoring ace 'Eddie' Rickenbacker, complete with his name and the 'Hat-in-the-Ring' insignia of the 94th Aero Squadron, and Ernst Udet's Blue Max.

The Etrich Taube (Dove) diorama is one of the most dramatic exhibits at Omaka, suspended in front of a huge photographic background and coming under fire from a BE.2c. It highlights an aspect of the very early war in the air with the observer turned around to fire a rifle at the British aircraft. **Norm DeWitt**

One exhibit which attracts a huge amount of attention is this representation of the scene after Manfred von Richthofen had been shot down and crashed on 21 April 1918. The bright red Fokker Dr.I Triplane has the 'Red Baron' lying beside it as Australian ground troops tear the aircraft apart for souvenirs, just as it really happened, and soldiers are even pulling the pilot's flying boots off. Near the exhibit is a remarkable display of original items relating to von Richthofen, including one of the fabric crosses cut from the Triplane. **Norm DeWitt**

GENE DeMARCO

Many of the picture captions in this issue state that the pilot is Gene DeMarco, who is TVAL's production manager and chief pilot. Gene has 25 years of experience on early aircraft types, having previously worked for the Old Rhinebeck Aerodrome Museum amongst others in the USA. He is also an FAA licensed mechanic with an inspection authorisation and nearly 13,000 hours flying predominately early types, so has a vast knowledge of these aircraft. Gene has flown many World War One aircraft and has a great deal of experience with rotary engines; hence when he takes to the skies in the Sopwith Camel in a mock dogfight, airshow visitors see the type flown just as it would have been in combat.

Another TVAL aircraft flown out of Hood is Sopwith Triplane replica 'N533' *Black Maria*, as flown by Canadian ace Lt Raymond Collishaw while with 10 (Naval) Squadron RNAS. **Jarrod Cotter**

'Hun chivalry'. Fliegerabteilung 300 with Lt Floyer and 2nd Lt Palmer (3 and 4) of 14 Squadron, whom they have just shot down and entertained to 'a damn good lunch' at Beersheba on 5 March 1917. Oberleutnant Gerhardt Felmy is marked '1' and Leutnant Richard Falke '2'. Picture from *The Gnome*, May 1917. **All author's collection**

'Hun chivalry'

Desmond Seward presents a story about airmen from 14 Squadron flying over the Sinai Desert in 1917 which shows a different side to war.

At sunrise on 5 March 1917 all the aircraft of 14 Squadron still in working order took off from an aerodrome at Ujret el Zol near El Arish in the Sinai Desert – known to the RFC as 'Kilo 143'. Comprising half of Colonel AE Borton's 5th Wing, they formed a motley collection, which included six two-seater BE.2cs and a lone two-seater 'pusher', a De Havilland DH.1, together with three single-seater Martinsyde 'Elephants' and two single-seat Bristol Scouts. Among the Martinsyde pilots was a 25-year-old, red-headed Franco-Irishman with a broken nose, Eric Seward, who had joined the squadron during the previous summer.

This was an unusually big reconnaissance patrol, its mission to investigate the Turkish lines around Gaza. The information was urgently needed for Major-General Sir Archibald Murray's imminent offensive to end Turkey's threat to the Suez Canal. The BE.2cs' job was to photograph the enemy artillery. The single-seaters and the

'pusher' were there to defend them from attack by Fliegerabteilung 300 of the Luftstreitkräfte (the name given to the German Army's recently re-organised air force), which was operating from aerodromes at Beersheba and Ramleh.

The airmen had risen from their camp-beds before dawn, some already woken by the cold, but the sun rose so swiftly that by the time they climbed into their aircraft it was oppressively hot, and when they set off from Kilo 143 they were grateful for the cooler world of the clouds. It soon became too cold again, however, in their open cockpits, since they flew without protective clothing. Yet despite the cold – and the deafening noise from their engines and the wind – they had more to think about than the temperature.

Everyone knew that the BE.2cs were dangerously vulnerable – on the Western Front they were nicknamed 'Fokker Fodder'. The Jumbo Martinsydes (or 'Tin-sides') were a bit faster, but their top speed was only 87mph. Like the tiny little Bristol Scouts,

each was armed with a Lewis gun mounted on the centre section of the upper wing, firing outside the radius of the propeller.

An attempt to intercept the flight by a handful of German scouts was driven off, even though the Huns had started to supplement their Aviatiks and Fokker monoplanes with 'bull-nosed' Albatross D.IIIs and Halberstadts that were technically six months in advance of the local RFC machines. Not only faster, the German aircraft were armed with Spandau machine-guns that had 'interrupter' gear enabling them to fire through the propeller. Luckily for the British, they amounted to no more than a squadron, less than the normal 'Jasta' on the Western Front, and today only a few were in evidence. Nor does 'Archie' fire from the enemy's anti-aircraft guns seem to have been particularly effective on this occasion. When the mission was completed, which was fairly soon since their aircraft had a very limited range, 14 Squadron turned back for home and breakfast.

MISSING IN ACTION

After landing, they were horrified to learn that one of the BE.2cs, piloted by Lt Floyer with 2nd Lt Palmer as observer, had failed to return. If shot down, they might have burned to cinders (since the RFC flew without parachutes); if they had made a forced landing, they would die from thirst or perhaps be tortured to death by Bedouin. Everyone knew they themselves might go the same way. TE Lawrence, who saw a lot of them, realised that airmen were bundles of nerves – like his Arabs, they 'lived for the day and died for it'. An aircraft set off to search for Floyer and Palmer, but found nothing. The colonel suggested that everybody have 'a damn good lunch', which was code for drown their sorrows in drink.

Three days later, on the morning of 8 March, while the only six machines of 14 Squadron now serviceable were out bombing Junction Station, north of Arak el Menshiye, a two-seater Rumpler dived down from 4000ft over the landing ground at Kilo 143 and dropped a 'smoke ball', followed by a message bag. Then it flew off. Mistaking this for a bombing attack, two Australian aircraft from 1 Squadron, which was also based at El Arish, took off to attack the Rumpler, but it was too fast for them.

The message was a letter from the Germans, saying they regretted having to inform their British opponents that they had shot down one of their machines. Luckily, however, pilot and observer had survived to enjoy an excellent lunch in their Mess. The bag also contained requests from Floyer and Palmer for pyjamas and shaving tackle, with a note from their captors promising that these might be delivered in safety. That afternoon, a British aircraft dropped the items at Beersheba, with a message of thanks and also an apology from the Australians for trying to intercept the Rumpler. German fliers, some in white tropical uniform, stood outside their Mess waving up at the pilot.

On 18 March another enemy aeroplane visited Kilo 143. Again, the pilot signalled with a smoke bomb, shut off his engine, came down to 1000ft and then dropped a satchel. This contained a photograph of Floyer and Palmer surrounded by German officers, including Gerhardt Felmy and Richard Falke, the two fliers who had delivered the first message. With them were two Austro-Hungarian pilots.

In addition, there was a letter from the German commander, Hauptmann Hellmuth Felmy (Gerhard's brother), to say that 14 Squadron's machines were always welcome to deliver messages and prisoners' kit: he gave his word that the German artillery would be ordered not to fire on British aeroplanes so long as they followed an agreed course at 1000m and signalled with a smoke ball over a specified point. He also invited everybody at Kilo 143 to stay with him at his house in the country in Pomerellen, 'as soon as this boring war is over'.

POLITE DECLINE

A British pilot dropped a reply on the enemy aerodrome, politely declining the offer. This chilly response can be explained by the British Army's fear that any form of fraternisation might weaken morale and the determination to destroy the enemy at all costs – no doubt a legacy of the famous 'Christmas Truce' of 1914 in Flanders. Yet the incident made a lasting impression on RFC pilots in Palestine, who began to see German fliers as human beings. Despite the prohibition, contact was discreetly maintained while, in the rare event of any enemies surviving after being shot down, they were invited to lunch and plied with champagne. On one occasion, the welcome was misunderstood by a Turkish observer (the Ottoman Air Force on the Sinai Front consisted of no more than a dozen pilots and observers in a single 'squadron' – in reality a flight – that in 1917 was based at El Kutrani), who looked noticeably glum throughout the meal, refusing to cheer up – only later did his hosts learn that he had expected to be tortured as soon as they finished eating.

I used to wonder if my father's memories of 'Hun chivalry' were exaggerated or wishful thinking. But, quite recently, I found among his papers a copy of the May 1917 issue of *The Gnome* (a magazine for the RFC on the Sinai Front edited by Capt JE Dixon while on active service with 14 Squadron). It contains a full account of the incident, together with a photograph of Floyer and Palmer surrounded by their captors at Beersheba.

The opening scenes of Jean Renoir's film of 1937, *La Grande Illusion*, re-create a similar incident on the Western Front, when captured French aircrew are invited to lunch at a German Mess by the officer who has shot them down. No.14 Squadron's experience shows that this sort of thing really took place. For the 'Great War' was another world, as my father never tired of telling me. In his own words, in his own, preferred language, 'autre temps, autre moeurs' – different times, different behaviour. ∎

Top: The DH.1 'pusher' (with the propeller at the back) was so under-powered that none were sent to the Western Front and only a few to the Sinai. The last surviving example in Palestine, this one was shot down in March 1917.

Above: A BE.2c of 14 Squadron ready to set off on a reconnaissance flight over the Sinai Desert. Because of its stability in the air, this type of machine (nicknamed 'Stability Jane') made an ideal camera platform for photographing enemy troop positions and fortifications – but was dangerously vulnerable to attack by enemy aircraft.

WINGS OVER THE DESERT

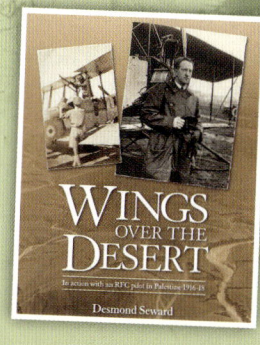

This article is extracted from the recently published book *Wings over the Desert – In action with an RFC pilot in Palestine 1916-1918* (ISBN 978 1 84425 672 3) by Desmond Seward and is used by kind permission of the author and Haynes Publishing. This fascinating book is based around the experiences of the author's father, WEL Seward MC, who was a pilot with 14 Squadron RFC. It is illustrated with remarkable photographs that have only recently come to light and provides a unique historical record. See pages 102-107 for another fascinating extract from this book. Priced at £25, it can be ordered from Haynes by calling 01963 442030 or online at www.haynes.co.uk

The Vintage Aviator Ltd's superb Albatros D.Va reproduction wearing the paint scheme of Jasta 5's Vfw Josef Mai. It is seen at Hood Aerodrome, Masterton, in New Zealand's Wairarapa region on 14 November 2009 – but it could easily pass as having been taken in late 1917! **Photo by Jarrod Cotter, sepia and graphic artwork by Simon Duncan**

Edward Vernon 'Eddie' Rickenbacker was the American 'Ace of Aces' in World War One. Born in Columbus, Ohio, in 1890, he gained fame as a race car driver before joining the service.
All photos US Air Force

America's 'Ace of Aces'

Kathryn (KT) Budde-Jones tells the story of Eddie Rickenbacker, the top-scoring US ace of World War One.

During World War One, Eddie Rickenbacker became the American 'Ace of Aces', but first made history as a race car driver, racing three times in the Indianapolis 500, setting speed records and making a fortune 'flying' around a racetrack before flying in the war.

When World War One broke out, Rickenbacker proposed a squadron of race car drivers to take their skill at speed and manoeuvring to the air over Europe.

Instead of flying for the army though, he was initially tasked to drive the leaders, becoming a driver for General 'Black Jack' Pershing and fixing Col Billy Mitchell's car. The encounter with Billy Mitchell changed his assignment to engineering officer at the Issoudun aerodrome setting him on course, at age 27, for a new career in aviation.

SPAD XIII at the National Museum of the United States Air Force, Dayton, Ohio, wearing the colours of S4523 as flown by Eddie Rickenbacker.

By March 1918, he was assigned to the newly formed 94th Aero Squadron flying cast-off Nieuports. The squadron eventually flew out of the aerodrome at Toul, France, where they selected the famous 'Hat-in-the-Ring' insignia for their ragtag, often ill-equipped squadron. After coaching by ace Raoul Lufbery, Rickenbacker's 26 aerial victories came in combat flying between the months of April to October. This was a spectacular achievement, especially considering the mistakes he made while traversing the steep learning curve of combat.

He readily admitted getting lost, mistaking friends for foes and falling into German aerial ambushes etc. He later reflected that these early lessons helped him accumulate his large tally. His fighting technique was to fire his guns as close to the enemy as he dared and good luck saw him through near escapes when his guns jammed. Rickenbacker lost several aircraft and he sometimes

Capt Eddie Rickenbacker was a recipient of the Congressional Medal of Honor for his aerial accomplishments in World War One, but not until 12 years after the conflict.

returned to base with a fuselage full of bullet holes – and once even with a mark on his flying helmet from a passing enemy bullet.

FIRST VICTORY

With a combination of skill and good luck, Lt Rickenbacker brought down his first enemy airplane on 29 April 1918 without taking a single shot. Working in concert with Lt Hall, they teamed up like sheep dogs culling a single sheep from the herd and setting their sights on him.

Rickenbacker scored his second aerial victory on 7 May and his third, and almost last of the war, on 17 May. On that day, Lts Rickenbacker and Chambers flew toward the German front to look for trouble. Over the aerodrome at Thiaucourt, he noticed three Albatros D.V scouts taking off. Rickenbacker dove, shooting at the aircraft at maximum speed, pulling up at the last moment, ripping off the upper wing covering of his Nieuport. He spun out of control but landed safely.

Lt Rickenbacker shot down another Albatros D.V on 22 May and became an ace on the 28th after claiming his fifth German aircraft. His success is remarkable considering the fragility of the Nieuports and their propensity for losing wing covering and gun jamming. The squadron was eager to step up to the beefier SPADs. By July, Lt Rickenbacker 'liberated' a SPAD from a US supply depot while on leave and flew it back to the 94th. ➤

Eddie Rickenbacker, who started in the US Army as a chauffeur to Gen John J Pershing, seen in a Nieuport 28.

"The experienced fighting pilot does not take unnecessary risks. His business is to shoot down enemy planes, not to get shot down. His trained hand and eye and judgment are as much a part of his armament as his machine gun, and a 50-50 chance is the worst he will take – or should take – except where the show is of the kind that… justifies the sacrifice of plane or pilot." Capt Edward V 'Eddie' Rickenbacker.

Rickenbacker did not add to his total victories throughout the summer of 1918 due to bad weather, bad health and bad luck. In September, his luck changed, adding six more victories, with his month's tally including four of the new and highly capable Fokker D.VIIs. He also assumed command of the 94th Aero Squadron around this time, helping his unit in recapturing the lead in number of total aerial victories by the end of the month, taking on flights of Fokkers and LVGs.

The 'Hat-in-the-Ring' 94th worked in concert with ground forces on 26 September 1918 to aid a huge offensive American effort across the Meuse River into the formidable Argonne Forest. The 94th's best pilots went after and brought down German observation balloons while Rickenbacker brought down one of the pursuing Fokker D.VIIs.

Rickenbacker teamed up with Chambers again on 2 October to share a Hannover CL reconnaissance aircraft victory. As the squadron made its way home, several SPADs encountered a flight of Fokkers, confirming another victory for Rickenbacker.

BELATED AWARD
Billy Mitchell was impressed with not only Rickenbacker's aerial successes, but his leadership qualities as well. These 'field-tested' skills would serve him well as he left the battlefield of Europe for the world of business. However, it took 12 years after the war's end for him to be acknowledged for his aerial accomplishments with the Medal of Honor.

Capt Edward V Rickenbacker receiving two Oak Leaf Clusters to his Distinguished Service Cross from Lt Gen Hunter Liggett, commander of the 1st US Army in France, in November 1918.

After the war, he applied his name and talents towards developing a new and innovative car design. The 1920s were not ready for his new four-wheel brake designs and his company went bankrupt. He then turned his attentions back to his first love, auto racing, buying a majority share in the Indianapolis Speedway (serving as the president until after World War Two).

In 1926, Rickenbacker joined the emerging commercial aviation industry. He founded Florida Airways, which he soon sold to Pan

Capt Eddie Rickenbacker and Lt Harold Goettler exhibits at the National Museum of the United States Air Force, including photographs, medals, insignia and documents.

The National Museum of the US Air Force's SPAD XIII while briefly taken outside for photos at Dayton.

Eddie Rickenbacker posing beside SPAD XIII S4523, in which he scored 20 aerial victories. These included 13 of the capable Fokker D.VIIs.

American Airlines, before becoming vice-president with General Aviation Corporation (formerly Fokker). In 1933, he joined North American Aviation as a vice-president and general manager of the subsidiary Eastern Air Transport, eventually reorganised as Eastern Air Lines. Rickenbacker became General Manager of Eastern Air Lines, securing a highly sought-after government airmail contract that kept the company well in the black for his 20-year tenure.

Rickenbacker joined the fight again during World War Two. Even though much older than his aviation counterparts, his vast combat and real-life experiences made him an important addition to the war effort, carrying out special assignments for Henry Stimson, the Secretary of War.

On one such mission, in October of 1942, the Boeing B-17 Flying Fortress in which Rickenbacker was flying went down in the vast Pacific Ocean. Surviving the crash, Rickenbacker and seven other crew members survived on a raft for 24 days before they were rescued.

His life experiences and self-reliance led to him becoming a spokesman and advocate for conservative causes, convinced that government 'socialist' programmes were ruining the country. Rickenbacker always believed that he knew the right answer for any problem. It is no wonder that Billy Mitchell thought well of him, for they seem to be made of the same cloth; a fabric that is woven into every aspect of our aviation history. ∎

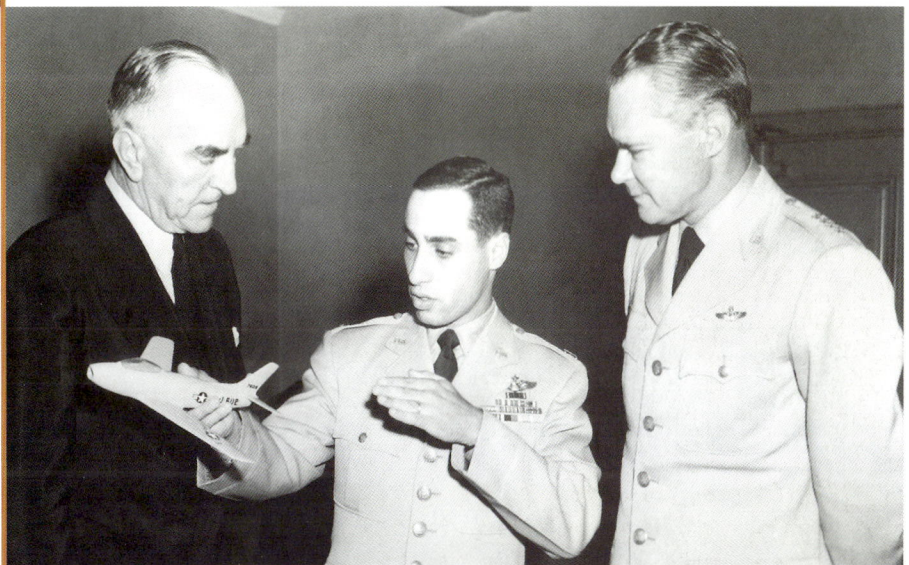

From left, retired Capt Eddie Rickenbacker, the first American fighter ace of World War One, meets Capt James Jabara, the first American jet ace in history. The two men met in the office of Gen Hoyt S Vandenberg, then Air Force Chief of Staff, on 31 May 1951.

Seen from a KC-135 Stratotanker from the 121st Refueling Wing of the Ohio Air National Guard based at Rickenbacker International Airport, Columbus, Ohio, a B-2 Spirit Stealth Bomber takes on fuel over the Pacific Ocean. As Eddie Rickenbacker was from the city, the airport was named after him in 1974. He died on 27 July 1973 and is buried in Columbus' Green Lawn Cemetery. **US Air Force/Senior Airman Brian Kimball**

Close up showing the radiator louvres closed. Not the curved cut-out on the top one, which gave clearance for the synchronized 0.303in Vickers gun aperture.

The cockpit of 'D8084'.

Detail shot of the compass mounted on the top wing and the Aldis optical gunsight.

'Biff'

Jarrod Cotter highlights the Bristol F.2b Fighter.

Along with such machines as the Royal Aircraft Factory SE.5a, Sopwith Pup, Triplane and Camel, the Bristol F.2b Fighter was one of the truly great British fighters of World War One. It differed significantly from the others listed though, in that it was a two-seat aircraft with a pilot at the front armed with a fixed forward-firing Vickers machine-gun and an observer/gunner directly behind, facing rearwards, with a rotating Lewis gun mounted on a Scarff ring.

The aircraft was designed as a much-needed replacement for the RAF BE.2, which due to its lack of manoeuvrability was suffering high losses in combat. Bristol's initial design was designated the R.2A and prototype A3303 carried out its maiden flight on 9 September 1916. The first of the 50 production Rolls-Royce Falcon I powered F.2as were delivered on unit strength to 48 Squadron in February 1917, with the new type moving to France the following month.

Its combat debut came on 5 April and ended in disaster, when six F.2as encountered five Albatros D.IIIs led by Rittmeister Manfred von Richthofen. Four of the British fighters were shot down. Over the next few days, more were lost, until it became apparent that the aircraft weren't being flown in the correct manner during combat, as the pilots were relying too heavily on the rear gun. Instead, they began to be flown as though it was a single-seat fighter using the pilot's gun as the primary offensive weapon and the observer's gun as defensive armament. This completely changed the fighter's results in dogfights.

Design refinements were made to the fighter, and the better F.2b was soon arriving on squadron strength. Although aircraft in the first batch were still fitted with the Falcon I engine (190hp), examples from the second batch had the more powerful Falcon II (220hp) and from the next order the definitive Falcon III (275hp) became the standard powerplant.

Its first combat occurred on 20 June 1917 when 11 Squadron pilot Lt AE McKeever was attacked head-on by an Albatros D.III. The Canadian fired a burst from his gun and shot down the Albatros, highlighting how the new two-seat aircraft and revised tactics were a good combination. Due to its continuing success, the F.2b was chosen as the standard aircraft for fighter and Corps-reconnaissance squadrons of the RFC from July 1917.

It was said that as the F.2b's reputation grew, German pilots began to avoid combat with the type if they could, unless they outnumbered the British machines. But even then, the aircraft wasn't necessarily doomed, as was proven on 30 November 1917.

Again, it was Lt McKeever at the controls with his observer Sgt LF Powell who encountered a brace of German reconnaissance aircraft escorted by seven Albatros scouts. The RFC crew accounted for both the two-seaters and two of their escorts during the combat before disengaging and heading for home.

The 'Biff', as it had affectionately become known, had a great impact over the Western Front and also equipped Home Defence squadrons; and some operated in Italy and Palestine. Post-war, the type continued to equip several squadrons, both at home and

'D8084' awaits its next sortie at Masterton in November 2009. **All Jarrod Cotter unless noted**

The Vintage Aviator Ltd's 'Biff' in the skies over Masterton, New Zealand. Note that features of the F.2b's wing sets were that they were mounted above and below the fuselage and it was a 'two-bay' biplane. In this view, the aircraft is fitted with the twin Lewis gun configuration rather than a single weapon. **Alex Mitchell**

overseas, including service in the Middle East and India. Later being referred to as the 'Brisfit', it remained in RAF service until March 1932, by which time 20 Squadron had totally re-equipped with the Westland Wapiti on the North West Frontier of India.

FROM FLOOR TO FLYER

One of the few airworthy original F.2bs remaining is operated by The Vintage Aviator Ltd out of Masterton, New Zealand. It was one of several airframes found in the floor of a barn in Oxfordshire during the 1960s. Following research, it was discovered that the aircraft was originally F4516, which served with 13 Squadron RFC.

The aircraft was restored for The Fighter Collection based at Duxford, Cambridgeshire,

with much of the work being carried out by Skysport Engineering. At TFC's Flying Legends airshow in July 2006, it was one of a trio of 'Brisfits' that made up a three-ship formation (with Shuttleworth's D8096 and Historic Aircraft Collection's then newly flown D7889); the first time this had been seen since the 1930s, and after another similar appearance at Old Warden, this was a sight which will perhaps not be repeated. 'D8084' made its way to New Zealand later that year, while D7889 left for Canada.

TVAL's F.2b currently wears the paint scheme of 139 Squadron's D8084 while based at Villaverla on the Italian Front, circa late 1918. It makes regular appearances at the various airshows held at Masterton's Hood Aerodrome. ■

Close up of the observer's Lewis gun fitted to the Scarff ring.

SPECIFICATION

Dimensions:	Wingspan 39ft 3in; Length 25ft 10in; Height 9ft 9in
All-up Weight:	2779lb
Powerplant:	One Rolls-Royce Falcon III 12-cylinder liquid-cooled inline engine producing 275hp
Performance:	Maximum speed 126mph at sea level, 105mph at 15,000ft; Climb to 10,000ft 11 minutes 15 seconds; Service ceiling 20,000ft
Armament:	One fixed synchronised 0.303in Vickers machine-gun mounted centrally beneath the top engine cowling with Constantinesco CC interrupter gear and one or two moveable 0.303in Lewis guns mounted on a Scarff ring; later aircraft could be fitted with up to 12 20lb Cooper bombs

'D8084' crewed up and ready to fly in the capable hands of pilot Stuart Goldspink. This view shows the pronounced taper of the type's rear fuselage, which increased the observer's lower field of fire. **Photo Jarrod Cotter, sepia and graphic artwork by Simon Duncan**

Flying with Daedalus

Alastair Goodrum looks at early flying and aerial gunnery training that took place at RNAS Cranwell and Freiston.

In classical mythology, Daedalus escaped captivity by constructing wings for himself and his son and flying to freedom. The ethos behind a father teaching a son to fly is enshrined in the history of RAF Cranwell in Lincolnshire, which opened in 1916 as a Royal Naval Air Service training establishment appropriately named HMS *Daedalus*.

Cranwell's primary task was to train service personnel in all types of airmanship, including piloting land- and seaplanes together with flying and handling balloons and airships for the RNAS. During the second half of 1916, Cranwell became home to examples of the main lighter-than-air type used by the Admiralty in World War One. These were Submarine Scout (SS) non-rigid airships. Compared to the mighty Zeppelins, examples of which reached over 650ft in length and contained up to two million cubic feet of hydrogen gas, these SS types were 'tiddlers' at 145ft and 70,000 cubic feet. One of the first of six SS models to serve at Cranwell was SS39

and it is this particular airship that managed to gain considerable notoriety for itself.

The erection of a portable hangar, in November 1916, to house such airships was the signal for SS39 to make the journey north from Wormwood Scrubs, London, heading for Cranwell. Nearing Thurlby in the Lincolnshire Fens on 15 November 1916 it flew slowly towards the village, getting ever lower until it only just cleared trees and telegraph poles. This alarming situation was caused by a pronounced loss of gas escaping through a broken valve. With its crew unable to check this descent, the sagging airship became uncontrollable, circling roof and chimney tops in the main street until it finally staggered to a halt, firmly locked against a chimney pot near the village school. Bricks, dislodged by the collision, fell into the control gondola, with one actually hitting a crewman on the head. These unfortunates were, however, able to clamber from their precarious perch to terra firma whereupon a local doctor tended the injured airman.

Thurlby's main street remained blocked for several hours, during which a strong smell of gas and petrol fumes pervaded the air. The next problem was to fully deflate and recover the craft, a task requiring drastic action in the form of slitting the fabric with knives. Petrol from fuel tanks was allowed to run away down the nearest drain – no environmental issues in those days!

SS39 must have been fated to be a maverick. Having been rebuilt after the Thurlby accident, it came to grief once more when its rigging fouled a tree and caused it to make a forced landing in May 1917. But on 20 July 1917, SS39 finally turned on its Naval masters with dire consequences.

Following an instructional flight, the airship was being 'walked' back into its shed at Cranwell, when a violent up-current of wind pulled SS39 from the grip of her handling party. Nearly all of these men let go. All, that is, except the Officer Commanding, Lieutenant Colonel Clive Waterlow of the Royal Engineers, attached to the RNAS as Wing Commander;

Avro 504B, N5253, after a crash. Flt Sub Lt Costain flew this aircraft at Freiston in June 1917.

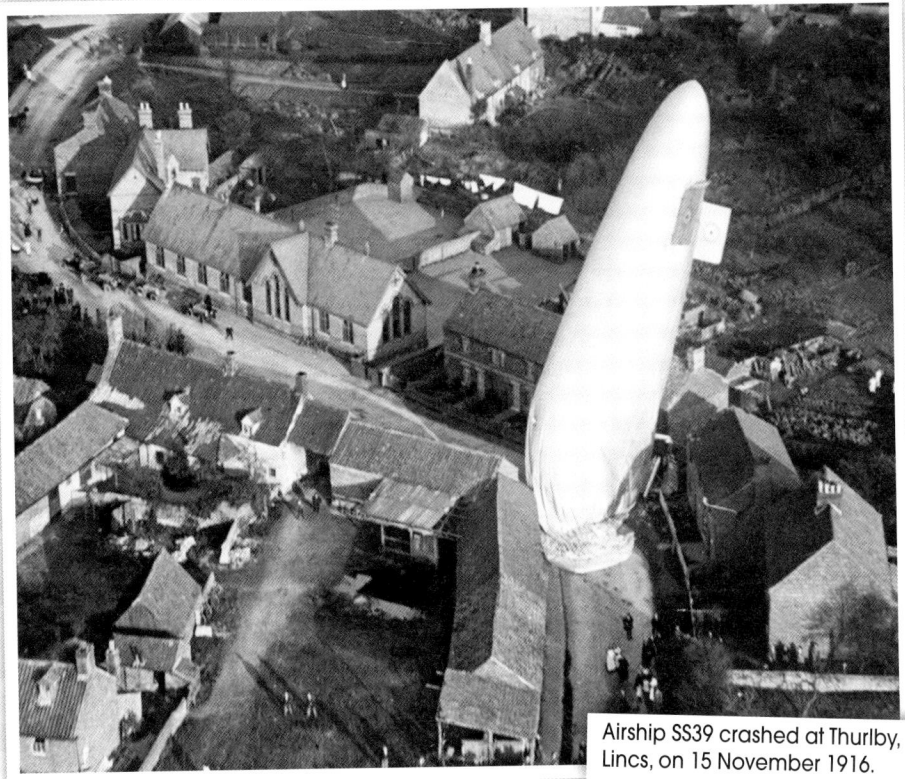

Sopwith Camel at Freiston in 1918 with OC 4 SAF&G, Sqn Cdr Harold Kerby DSC seen left.

RNAS Sopwith Pup pictured at Cranwell.

Airship SS39 crashed at Thurlby, Lincs, on 15 November 1916.

Petty Officer Mechanic Maurice Collins and Airman 2nd Class Simon Lightstone. These three clung to a rope and were swiftly carried aloft to a great height until their arms could no longer stand the strain and they fell to their deaths. SS39 floated back to earth a mile and a half away. Yet still the Admiralty persisted with this wayward craft. SS39 was rebuilt once more as SS39a but from then on seems to have led a trouble-free existence until 1919 when it was finally scrapped.

Sopwith Snipe, E6274, seen at Freiston during 1918.

GUNNERY SCHOOL

As outlined above, Royal Naval Air Station Cranwell's purpose was to train Navy officers to fly and operate not only airships and balloons but also aircraft. Officer aircrew destined for aeroplanes were generally posted in from preliminary RNAS flying training schools at Chingford, Redcar, Eastbourne and Eastchurch. The final two weeks of Cranwell's advanced aeroplane course was taken at its satellite airfield at Freiston before aircrew were posted to operational squadrons or for other specialist duties.

Soon after HMS *Daedalus* had opened it was decided that it would need a live gunnery and bombing facility for training purposes. An aerial survey of the Lincolnshire coast was carried out and from this it was decided that the desolate mud flats of The Wash to the south of the village of Freiston, near Boston, would provide just such a place and so began an association between air gunnery and the area that has lasted to the present day. As the war progressed there was a need for a growing number of aircrew to be trained in the art of fighting in the air and it was therefore decided to purchase grass fields on the landward side of the bombing range so that a fully functioning aerodrome could be established, thus saving the 40 minutes it took to fly to and from Cranwell to the range.

Initially 90 acres (40 hectares) were requisitioned adjacent to the sea bank near Freiston Shore, but this was later extended twice to allow for hangars and accommodation to be built. In some respects Freiston, near the mouth of the river Witham, can be seen as the World War One forerunner of 6 Operational Training Unit (OTU) located, 25 years later, only a stone's throw away across The Wash, at RAF Sutton Bridge. Bombing targets were laid out on the sand and mud flats together with a few dilapidated surplus aircraft dotted around to be used as targets for air-to-ground gunnery practice.

Initially known as the RNAS Gunnery School, it operated as a sub-station to RNAS Cranwell but in September 1917 the airfield began functioning as a joint facility for the RNAS and RFC (later RAF) until its closure in 1920. On the formation of the RAF on 1 April 1918 the resident unit became the School of Aerial Fighting & Bomb Dropping, only to be re-designated on 6 May as 4 School of Aerial Fighting & Gunnery and again on 29 May to 4 Fighting School. As we shall see later, aircrew officer cadets undertook their final 14 days flying training at Freiston after which, if considered proficient, they could find themselves pitched into combat.

As at 31 December 1917 the officer commanding Freiston was Squadron Commander JI Harrison, ably assisted by Flight Commander Noel Keeble DSC DFC (a fighter ace credited with six air victories) and Lts CK Jupp RNVR and EAB Tooth RNVR. Thirty-seven Flight Sub-Lieutenants were listed as receiving instruction at the airfield on that date. Records also show that during the eight months from January to August 1917 of the 485 officers that graduated from Cranwell/Freiston, 227 went on to fly seaplanes and 258 to fly land-based aeroplanes. Perhaps the most notable among Freiston's Officers Commanding was the Canadian, Harold Kerby DSC AFC. Kerby joined the RNAS in 1915 and learned to fly at the Grahame-White School in Hendon. While flying on the Western Front with 'Naval 9' then 'Naval 3' he was credited with shooting down, or sharing in the destruction of, seven enemy aircraft between 24 March and 27 May 1917. Posted back to England, he became CO of a Home Defence squadron based at Walmer in Kent and while there he destroyed two German Gotha bombers during daylight air raids in August. He was awarded a DSC and in 1918 took command of 4 SAF&G at Freiston with the rank of Major, where he was awarded an AFC in the New Year Honours list of 1919. ➤

Over the course of the war, in addition to a mixed bag of aeroplanes for training purposes, such as Avro 504, BE.2, Bristol F.2b Fighter, Sopwith 1½ Strutter, Pup, Triplane, Camel, Snipe and Dolphin, in the early days Freiston also maintained a flight of Bristol Scouts for anti-Zeppelin patrols as well as normal training.

GRADUATES

Sadly many trainee pilots from Freiston were ill-prepared to be pitched into operational flying as the following selections show.

In November 1916, Flight Sub-Lt A Kay noted in his logbook that he had accumulated 28 flying hours when he was posted to Freiston. He was sent off in the morning of the 15th for a 78-minute solo cross-country flight in BE.2c 8404 to Bourne, Spalding, Sutton Bridge and back to Freiston. That afternoon he was sent off again, this time in 8303, to find his way to Grantham, Newark and back for another 75 minutes in the air, then up again for a two-hour cross country in 8303, taking in Peterborough, Wisbech, Sutton Bridge, Boston and back to Freiston. Then they let him loose in a Sopwith 1½ Strutter and after a few circuits in 9893 he wrote rather proudly:

"Flew the Sopwith, very good machine. A little bumpy but good flying."

Flight Sub-Lt Mosley Woodhouse was posted to Cranwell from Redcar (Yorks) initial training station on 31 March 1917 with 20 hours in his logbook. Between 23 May and 8 June, his total flying for the fortnight he was 'finishing' at Freiston amounted to just four and a quarter hours, during which he wrote: "Ascended for firing in air. [in Avro 504B, N6156] Gun wouldn't fire owing to [ammunition] pan not being properly put on." He landed and had the fault rectified then took off again, noting: "Fired in the air. Started firing too soon."

These 25 minutes were his sole gunnery practice. The rest of the time was spent on bomb dropping practice in various BE.2cs.

At the tender age of 18 years, Sub-Lt Woodhouse was posted to France as a fighter pilot with 9 (Naval) Squadron on 4 August where he had his first flight in a Sopwith Camel. Two days later, on his first operational patrol he managed to lose contact with the formation and two days later on his second patrol the same thing happened again. Next day he was shot down in flames while flying as part of an escort to RE.8s of 52 Squadron RFC.

RNAS Sopwith 1½ Strutter at Cranwell.

RNAS Sopwith Triplane, N5370, at Cranwell.

RNAS BE.2e, B3707, at Freiston cFebruary 1918.

Flt Sub-Lt HH Costain arrived in June 1917 after six weeks at Eastbourne initial training school. He noted in his logbook that two hours and 45 minutes was flown on bomb dropping sorties using BE.2e aircraft A8694 and A8698 at Freiston, first using a mirror device then with dummy and live bombs. He, too, had just 25 minutes on three gunnery practice flights in Avro 504s N5253 and N5250, during which he fired the magnificent total of 173 rounds. On 14 August he was classed by Lt Jupp as 'a second-class bomb dropper' and posted to the RNAS Handley Page bomber training squadron at Manston and seems to have gone on to survive the war.

Flight Sub-Lt Geoffrey Bowman had a similar training profile, arriving at Cranwell from Chingford training station on 13 February 1917. By the time he reached Freiston he had 32 flying hours to his name and less than a month later he was considered ready for active service with a grand total of 12 minutes air gunnery firing and one hour and 40 minutes bomb dropping practice, all in BE.2cs, to his name. Sub-Lt Bowman was posted to 'Naval 10', a front line fighter squadron equipped with the Sopwith Triplane. Bowman was allowed over the lines on 1 April in a Nieuport 12 and noted in his logbook that he was "hit four times over Dixmude." He got his first flight in a Triplane on the 4th and managed to survive a month before being posted away to 'Naval 1' on 1 May. Sub-Lt Bowman was shot down in

flames while on patrol in Triplane N5461 on 19 May 1917, believed to have been one of Hauptmann Adolf Count von Tutschek's 27 air victories. Bowman was 19 years old.

It is interesting to note that some of the above pilots only came into contact with the aircraft they were to fly operationally, when they reached their squadrons. There were just not enough of the latest front-line fighter types to spare for the training units but officialdom eventually realised the foolishness of this situation so, as aircraft production gradually increased, Freiston records show the arrival of Sopwith Pups, Camels and a small number of Triplanes and Dolphins from mid-1917 onwards.

CANADIAN TRAGEDIES

In a quiet, tree-shaded corner of Freiston village churchyard lie three CWGC headstones marking the last resting place of a trio of Canadian pilots. Like thousands of their countrymen, these young men turned their backs on promising careers at home, to volunteer for a war raging far from their native land, only to lose their lives in most tragic circumstances.

The first of these young Canadians was 21-year-old Second Lieutenant John William Dowling from Vancouver. Records indicate that he was posted to Cranwell on 27 April 1918 and by the time he reached the gunnery school at Freiston he had accumulated 40 hours' flying experience. He lost his life when the aircraft in

which he was flying, Sopwith Camel C25, was seen to spin into the ground while making a turn at low altitude on 26 June 1918.

Second Lieutenant John Meek from Southwold, Ontario, was the next of the trio to die, not long after Dowling. In April 1916 he joined the Canadian Expeditionary Force when it went to France where he served with the 24th Battalion on the Ypres-St Eloi sector of the Western Front. He was severely wounded in one arm on 28 September and repatriated to Canada at the end of that year. While recuperating, Meek returned to his studies for a time but it appears he became restless for a return to the action in France. He applied to the Canadian Forces to allow him return to France, but was turned down due to the permanent injury to his arm. This did not deter John and he volunteered for service with the Royal Flying Corps, was accepted and underwent flying training in Canada. On completion of this training he returned to France in May 1918 for flying duties as a pilot. After a month in France he was posted back to England for a gunnery course at 4 School of Aerial Gunnery and Fighting at Freiston, after which he was scheduled to leave for service on the Italian front.

Meek's final flight came on 14 August 1918, when he took off in Sopwith Camel B7263 to carry out gunnery practice over The Wash firing range. What happened during that fateful flight was recalled by

Captain JST Fall at the subsequent inquest. He said that Meek had been at the air station for about three weeks and he was considered to be a very capable pilot. This was to be his last qualifying flight in his course of instruction, during which he had accumulated more than 100 hours' flying experience.

Captain Fall said he saw Lieutenant Meek fly over the range and watched him fire at a ground target in a dive from about 1000ft. Meek pulled out of the dive to climb away seaward. A few minutes later Captain Fall saw the Camel diving vertically and it disappeared from his view behind the sea bank. Captain Fall ran out to the water's edge and then swam out to the wreckage of the aeroplane, which he found to be upside down in about four feet of water. He was able to turn the tail of the aeroplane over and found Lieutenant Meek strapped into his seat but dead.

Second Lieutenant Edward Bach from Toronto is the final member of this unfortunate Canadian trio. He was just 20 years old when he died flying Sopwith Camel E1429 on 30 August 1918. At the time of his death Edward Bach had accumulated 80 flying hours and was coming to the end of his course at 4 Fighting School when he was killed in a spinning accident near the airfield, one of 58 pilots who – after falling from the sky like Daedalus' son Icarus – died in flying accidents at the two stations between September 1916 and November 1918. ■

First to France

Jarrod Cotter looks at a brace of aircraft that highlight the evolution of the BE.2, one of the RFC's earliest types to go to war.

Cockpit of the BE.2f.

Powered by a replica RAF 1a engine, note the BE.2f's high vertical exhaust stacks attached to the top wing.

Development roots of the BE.2 (Blériot Experimental) series can be traced back to the BE.1, which is of significant historical interest as it was the first aircraft to be purpose-designed for military use. Early variants of the Royal Aircraft Factory BE.2, the BE.2a and 'b, were by their very nature reconnaissance aircraft without any fixed armament. When the Royal Flying Corps deployed to France after World War One was declared, it is believed that a BE.2a flown by Lt HD Harvey-Kelly of 2 Squadron was the first to cross the Channel for military operations. It was BE.2bs which soon arrived in greater numbers though.

Next in line was the BE.2c, which became the best known of its breed and was built in the greatest numbers. Its staggered wings featured ailerons rather than relying on the wing warping of its predecessors and it had a fixed fin forward of the rudder. In April 1915, 8 Squadron became the first unit to be completely equipped with the BE.2c in France.

As the war grew in ferocity, the BE.2's role diversified and aircraft began to carry bombs. On 26 April 1915, 2nd Lt WB Rhodes-Moorhouse of 2 Squadron became the first British airman to be awarded the Victoria Cross as a result of his actions while flying a BE.2c. He successfully dropped a 100lb bomb on his objective, a railway junction at Courtrai, before coming under heavy ground fire. Fatally wounded by the gunfire, he flew for some 40 minutes to make it back to base whereupon he insisted on filing his report before being taken to hospital. He died from his injuries the following day and was awarded the medal posthumously.

That summer, the vulnerability of the BE.2c, which had little comparative speed or agility, became evident as the German Fokker monoplane scouts arrived on the front. With a synchronised machine-gun and high manoeuvrability, aircraft such as the E.I were having such success that the period became known as the 'Fokker Scourge'.

High angle view of BE.2c replica '347'. Note its wooden undercarriage skids.

Original BE.2f A1325 slowly patrols over the New Zealand countryside around Masterton on a glorious evening in November 2009, flown by John Bargh. An observer occupies the front seat. **All Jarrod Cotter unless noted**

The BE.2c has an original Renault engine fitted.

Aircrew attempted to remedy the situation by fitting Lewis guns on 'Strange Mounts', designed by Captain LA Strange, but this had the adverse effect of hampering the BE.2's already low performance. By September the 'Scourge' was really taking its toll and RFC losses were heavy. The type did have notable success in the UK though, because with it being such a steady gun platform Zeppelins were being brought down by Home Defence squadrons equipped with the BE.2c.

The most common engines fitted to the BE.2 became the 90hp RAF 1a, an improvement over the 70hp Renault units. In a bid to improve the type further, slight modifications resulted in the BE.2d which was followed by the BE.2e. This latter model featured a single bay wing structure and upper wing overhang. In October 1916 it was stated that only BE.2e models should be sent to France. To keep apace with demand, BE.2cs and 'ds were modified with the new wing structure. Modified BE.2cs gained the designation BE.2f, while the 'd models so converted became the BE.2g.

RAF BE.2C SPECIFICATION

Dimensions:	Wingspan 37ft 0in; Length 27ft 3in; Height 11ft 1½in
All-up Weight:	2142lb
Powerplant:	One 90hp RAF 1a air-cooled V-8 (various others also used)
Performance:	Maximum Speed 77mph at sea level; Climb to 10,000ft 45 minutes 15 seconds; Service ceiling 10,000ft (RAF 1a engine)
Armament:	One to four 0.303in Lewis guns; two 112lb bombs (bombing duties flown solo); maximum of 10 Le Prieur rockets on interplane struts for Home Defence

'An aircraft that while lacking in performance, became one of the longest serving and multi-role types of World War One.'

A comparative study of the two aircraft tin flight, with BE.2c '347' being flown by Gene DeMarco in the foreground and BE.2f A1325 with John Bargh at the controls behind it. **Alex Mitchell**

REPRODUCTION AND ORIGINAL

The Vintage Aviator Ltd has two BE.2s based at Hood Aerodrome, Masterton, on New Zealand's North Island, which highlight ideally the evolution of the type as well as having quite different provenance. One is a reproduction with an original engine, while the other is an original airframe with a reproduction engine.

BE.2c '347' is a fine reproduction of an early war machine, built using original drawings. It features bare wood and metal panels and its fabric is only covered with clear dope, not painted green. It also features Union Jacks rather than roundels, as it would have been when the real aircraft is thought to have arrived in France, circa October 1914, before national insignia roundels were introduced. It is also fitted with undercarriage skids, which later examples of its type did not have. Of great note, '347' is powered by an original Renault engine.

BE.2f A1325 is a World War One original, comprising a BE.2c fuselage with BE.2e specification wings. It was part of a batch of 15 aircraft sold to the Norwegian Army Air Service in 1917. Retired in 1925, after a period of storage it was sold into private hands.

Many years later it was donated to what is now the de Havilland Aircraft Heritage Centre in the UK, owing to the fact that the BE.2 was a very early de Havilland design. Later A1325 found its way back into private ownership and was put up for sale.

New Zealand-based 1914-1918 Aviation Heritage Trust purchased the BE.2f around 10 years ago. The fuselage was in very good condition, retaining a good deal of original

timber which could be preserved to airworthy standard. It also included an original RAF 1a engine, though this was in very poor condition.

The engine could have caused the project serious problems with its return to the air. However, The Vintage Aviator Ltd was at the same time in the process of creating reproduction BE.2s and, unable to locate an original in good enough condition to be restored or willing to settle for a modern replacement, set about the creation of a reproduction engine built to original specifications. After three years' work, a reproduction RAF 1a engine was ready for A1325 to ensure its authenticity, and importantly to return it to the air.

This wonderful historic machine took to the skies in April 2009 and made its public debut at Classic Fighters, Omaka, on New Zealand's South Island over the Easter weekend of 12-14 April. It is now complemented perfectly by TVAL's BE.2c to highlight the evolution of an aircraft that while lacking in performance, became one of the longest serving and multi-role types of World War One. ■

Inside the BE.2c's very basic pilot's cockpit.

Detail shot of the BE.2c's bracing wire joints.

Norm DeWitt looks at the fight for air supremacy and the steps that led to the design of the formidable Fokker D.VII.

Innovation
on the Western Front

By 1918, the fourth year of the 'Great War', the combat pilots of Germany were no longer enjoying the advantages they had the previous year. The re-designed Albatros D.III, first arriving in numbers by January 1917, was to become the most effective fighter, or 'scout', on the Western Front. Ernst Udet (62 kills) who was the sole surviving pilot from his days at Jasta 15, and Manfred von Richthofen (80 kills) both flew the D.III extensively during 1917. Once early wing failures were resolved, the aircraft were delivered in large quantity and April 1917 came to be known to the Allies as "Bloody April"… a time of German air supremacy.

However, their advantage was fleeting and with a ceiling of 20,500ft along with a superior rate of climb, the nimble Sopwith Triplane provided inspiration for the German aviation industry. Fokker's Reinhold Platz was to create a cantilever winged prototype design, known as the V.4.

Later in the year, his Fokker Dr.I Triplane appeared on the scene. This iconic image of German air power was soon to become the tool of choice for Manfred von Richthofen and his 20-year-old squadron leader at Jasta

10, Werner Voss (48 kills). The courageous Voss had only had the Triplane for a month, but 10 kills with the highly manoeuvrable Dr.I during that short timeframe had likely contributed to his sense of invulnerability. Voss was lost in late September 1917 attempting to take on eight Royal Flying Corps SE.5a fighters single handedly.

Despite their fearsome reputation, the Dr.I had been suffering from serious build quality issues, the majority having been grounded for the month of November 1917 after some examples broke up in flight, one killing Udet's former commander at Jasta 15, Heinrich Gontermann (39 kills). The updated Triplane was little better as von Richthofen's brother Lothar (40 kills), squadron leader of Jasta 11, was lucky to survive an upper wing failure in 1918. There were other issues with the design, as the aircraft was only capable of approximately 100mph and its limited range (90 minutes) also required a forward operating base to be effective, closer to the front.

By the end of 1917, the balance had shifted well in favour of the Allies. The total production run of the Dr.I was only 320, certainly not enough to tip the balance of air

power even if it had lived up to all expectations, which it clearly didn't. By comparison, the production run for the new Sopwith Camel was closer to 5500. With a similar climb rate with the standard 130hp engine, its maximum speed was superior to the Dr.I, and its ceiling of 21,000 ft was marginally better. Unlike the Sopwith Triplane, the Camel was equipped with twin Vickers machine guns, and its firepower matched the twin Spandau units mounted on the Albatros and Fokker.

The Camel was a rotary design with its crankshaft fixed in place (like the Dr.I), and the rotating mass of the engine provided both its primary strength and weakness. It turned far more quickly to the right than left, out-turning anything in the sky, yet adding a level of predictability into dogfight tactics. Though challenging, unstable and dangerous to fly, the Sopwith Camel in the hands of an experienced pilot was unmatched. The flimsy Nieuport 28 was being replaced by the stout French SPAD S.XIII, which had entered service during the summer of 1917. Although not nearly as manoeuvrable as the Camel, the SPAD was faster than any other fighter of its day.

FIGHTER OF CHOICE

The Germans were forced into a position where they needed a superior design quickly; one that could be mass produced, simple to maintain, and could offset the Allied air supremacy of late 1917/early 1918. A competition was held with the aircraft evaluated by Germany's top pilots, to determine the successful design that would go into mass production.

Reinhold Platz had designed a new biplane, another of the V series of cantilever wing-style aircraft, the V.11. Without bracing wires, the fabrication of the aircraft, and more importantly the maintenance time for the wing structure was significantly reduced. As a result, the V.11 could be expected to spend more time in operation.

Initial testing was far from favourable, but the quickly revised design with an elongated fuselage and rudder modification was selected by Manfred von Richthofen as the best of the competition.

The initial aircraft had the inline six-cylinder Daimler-Benz engine, which was considerably more powerful than the Dr.I's, but was an insufficient leap forward, as some of the Camels were now being fitted with 150hp radials. By the time the new Fokker reached the front lines, it would likely be underpowered. The latest versions of the Daimler-Benz D.IIIa motor were developing closer to 180hp, and those were the chosen powerplant for the initial batch of what became known as the Fokker D.VII. Due to the severity of the situation on the Western Front and the lack of sufficient production facilities at Fokker, the type was also fabricated by two Albatros factories under licensing agreements with Fokker.

At the end of 1916, Daimler-Benz engine designer Max Friz, unhappy with reluctance by the firm to embrace his designs for an updated design for their overhead camshaft in-line six, moved to work for an emerging company 'Bayrische Motoren Werke' – or BMW. Friz' resume included such engineering gems as the engines the

> **"Göring's weapon of choice while leading the 'Flying Circus' was the Fokker D.VII(F)."**

Mercedes factory cars had used to sweep the French Grand Prix in 1914.

Now at BMW and free to develop his concepts, he set to work on a large bore version (150mm x 180mm stroke) of a similar water-cooled engine. The 19,058cc BMW IIIa was not only of larger displacement, it was of far higher compression (6.4:1) with an altitude compensating carburettor. Although the performance numbers for the D.VII seem unremarkable versus the Allied competition, at high altitude the performance of the 200hp BMW engine in the model D.VII(F) set it apart from anything in the skies over 1918 Europe.

The engine had been designed with the understanding that the powerplants of the day could not be fully exploited at higher elevations. Were the engine tuned for performance at high altitude, the increased density of air at low altitudes led to an overly lean engine easily wrecked by detonation. Friz' altitude-compensating carburettor technology of 1917 was essentially a butterfly which would open at higher elevations permitting a greater quantity of air, in theory allowing the proper air/fuel mixture throughout a larger range of altitude. The system clearly left much to be desired, but aircraft fitted with the BMW IIIa engine were unlike the others, left struggling with excessively rich fuel/air mixtures that seriously hampered performance in a climb.

The BMW engines were often tuned so that they were excessively lean at sea level as a baseline, which then enhanced the effective altitude range where the F model would maintain its full horsepower. The performance of the D.VII(F) at altitude was simply in a class by itself. Post-war testing confirmed approximately a 30hp advantage to the BMW over the Daimler-Benz engine. This engine put BMW on the map as a manufacturer of cutting edge engineering. The first D.VIIs were delivered to the Western Front in April 1918, only days after Manfred von Richthofen's loss in his Dr.I on the 21st. ➤

Cockpit of Fokker D.VII 4635/18.
Eric Long/NASM, National Air and Space Museum, Smithsonian Institution

Close up of The Vintage Aviator Ltd's airworthy Fokker D.VII replica used in the film *The Blue Max*, showing off its lozenge paintwork at Hood Aerodrome, Masterton, New Zealand, in November 2009. **Jarrod Cotter**

The D.VII which is now part of the National Air and Space Museum's collection pictured shortly after it was captured in 1918. **NASM via author**

BMW IIIa engine, serial number 1875, on display at the National Air and Space Museum. **Norm DeWitt**

Although the D.VII shared the Dr.I's limited 90-minute range, it was to have an immediate impact and upon the later arrival of the (F) BMW variant, it quickly became the fighter of choice, with its predictable handling and astounding rate of climb at altitude. The type was stable and solid in a dive, and would climb at higher angles than other aircraft of the day. It is believed that something in the area of 1700 D.VIIs were produced, and with a total production of approximately 700 BMW IIIas engine supply also spread across two other aircraft applications, such as the all-metal innovative monoplane, the Junkers D.I.

The F model of the D.VII was a highly sought after prize for the German aviator. However, the BMW-engined Fokker was not delivered to the front until June 1918, and in such limited numbers versus their Allied opposition, they were too little, too late.

Hermann Göring (22 kills), who later was the Commander of the Luftwaffe in World War Two, had been a highly decorated pilot in the 'Great War', and was awarded the Pour Le Mérite (Blue Max) for his success in combat. He was to become the last commander of Richthofen's Jagdgeschwader 1, the 'Flying Circus', in July 1918. Göring's weapon of choice while leading the 'Flying Circus' was the Fokker D.VII(F).

CAPTIVE 'BIRD'

On 9 November, Lt Heinz von Beaulieu-Marconnay took to the skies in his Ostdeutsche Albatros Werke (East German Albatros factory) assembled D.VII #4635/18, laden with the marking 'U-10', a tribute to his former cavalry unit, the 10th Uhlan Regiment. Giving literal definition to the term of being lost in 'the fog of war', the German pilot had landed at a small airfield, which was currently in American hands. Two days before the Armistice, the D.VII had been seized by the Allies, and eventually found its way to the US War Department for evaluation and testing. In 1920, the aircraft was given to the National Air and Space Museum on the Washington DC Mall, where it remains today.

TVAL pilot Gary Yardley starts up the Fokker D.VII. **Jarrod Cotter**

Across the aisle from the Daimler-Benz-powered D.VII sits an original BMW IIIa engine on display in front of a photographic mural of an aircraft assembly plant from the time. Sadly, it appears that no original D.VII(F) has survived, but with an original D.VII on display along with an original BMW IIIa engine, the two versions are well represented at the museum.

Anthony Fokker's company was immediately in siege mode after the signing of the Armistice on 11 November. Within the text of the agreement, it stated which items were to be surrendered to the Allies: 'especially all machines of the D.VII type'. No other aircraft type was so listed. Fokker hid all the D.VII assemblies he could in the barns and structures near the Fokker factory, eventually smuggling enough across the border to Holland so that he could restart his company there, selling the re-assembled D.VIIs. Anthony Fokker eventually moved to America to start an aircraft division there, and in 1939 he died in New York City.

The success story of Fokker as a Dutch aircraft company continued until 1996 when it filed for bankruptcy. The divisions that eventually emerged from the liquidation became known as the Fokker Aerospace Group. The Fokker name continues to this day.

BMW found itself under threat of liquidation at war's end in November 1918. Their only product at that time was the IIIa engine, such was the overwhelming military demand. Within a month of the Armistice, the factory was ordered closed. Facing an uncertain future; upon re-opening, the new focus of the company was to provide engines for any and all applications except for aviation. In this era, there wasn't much of a civilian aviation industry, yet despite these challenges facing the company, Max Friz stayed with BMW. Other manufacturing contracts kept the company viable, and in 1923 they were again allowed to enter the aviation engine business, and introduced their famous boxer twin engine R32 motorcycle.

Although BMW's circular logo is often incorrectly interpreted as an image of a spinning propeller, it is not; as those are the colours of and were meant as a representation of the Bavarian flag. Perhaps, in hindsight, it serves well as an unintended reminder of the Fokker D.VII(F), the dominant aircraft of World War One. ■

NATIONAL AIR AND SPACE MUSEUM

Perhaps without peer, the Smithsonian Institution's National Air and Space Museum holds the world's largest collection of aircraft and spacecraft. There are two display facilities, one on Washington DC's National Mall and the larger Steven F Udvar-Hazy Center on the grounds of Dulles International Airport.

Inside the Mall building, if your fancy turns to the early history, there is the original 1903 Wright Flyer, for which no introduction is necessary, as well as numerous aircraft from World War One and the 1920s and 30s, such as Charles Lindberg's *Spirit of St Louis*. Numerous fighters from World War Two are also displayed, such as the Lockheed P-38 Lightning.

Also displayed are two of the best-known rocket-powered X planes of the 1940s and 50s, Chuck Yeager's Bell X-1 and the North American X-15. Spacecraft such as John Glenn's Friendship 7 or the Apollo capsule used on the Skylab 4 mission, bring the story into the space age.

Some of the larger exhibits are at the Steven F Udvar-Hazy Center, where one finds a Concorde and Space Shuttle, along with *Enola Gay*, the B-29 used in the first atomic bomb attack. Special events are often remembrances of historic episodes, such as the recent reunion of the Apollo 13 crew on the 40th anniversary of their mission. It is a collection of the highest magnitude and quality, and not to be missed.
Photo: Norm DeWitt www.nasm.si.edu

The gods above must be crazy…

Ryan K Noppen describes the aerial adventures over Africa during World War One.

The African campaign of World War One was certainly one of the more adventurous of the conflict, pitting over half a million British, South African and other Commonwealth troops against small but spirited and well-trained German colonial forces. In a theatre of operations where the climate was just as deadly as bullets and shells, and where soldiers not only had to be wary of the enemy but also the carnivorous local wildlife; the African campaign also highlighted the use of modern technology and mobility such as motorcars, railways, radio, synthetic fuels, and aircraft to overcome the challenges posed by the landscape.

The reconnaissance capabilities of early aircraft provided combatants in this distant and often overlooked theatre with a scope of information that was extremely valuable in such a vast area crippled with limited resources. Despite being cut off from the Fatherland due to the British naval blockade, the Schutztruppen in German East Africa and German Southwest Africa set an innovative standard for the use of aircraft in their territories. Although heavily outnumbered, German aircraft and pilots made creative and innovative use of the machines they had available, prompting a similarly innovative response from the British and the South Africans. The result, demonstrated in the following episodes, was not only the beginning of military aviation in Africa but also the serious beginning of any aviation in sub-Saharan Africa.

DUEL IN THE DELTA

The first aerial campaign in Africa during the war had nothing to do with the movements or actions of large ground forces, but rather centred around the presence of a single warship. The SMS *Königsberg*, a 3400-ton light cruiser, was in Dar-es-Salaam, German East Africa, for the German Colonial Exhibition of 1914 as the storm clouds of war began to gather. Her mission, in the event of war, was to act as a commerce raider, sinking as many enemy merchant ships as possible while avoiding enemy warships that outclassed her.

The *Königsberg* did not have much luck locating enemy merchantmen in the Indian Ocean, but managed to sink the British protected cruiser HMS *Pegasus* off Zanzibar on 20 September 1914 before boiler trouble forced her to return to port. Since the main German port of Dar-es-Salaam was too exposed, Fregattenkapitän Max Loof sailed his cruiser into the nearby Rufiji River Delta, docking at a small inland settlement called Salale.

Also in Dar-es-Salaam at the outbreak of the war was a flying instructor named Bruno Büchner and his Pfalz-AGO pusher biplane. He had been sponsored by a German confectionery company to make demonstration flights at the colonial expositions in German Southwest Africa and German East Africa in an effort to promote aviation in the colonies. When the war began, Büchner offered his services to Oberstleutnant Paul von Lettow-Vorbeck, the Schutztruppe commander in German East Africa. Von Lettow-Vorbeck ordered Büchner to make a reconnaissance flight over Zanzibar, but the aircraft was hit by the fire of two British gunboats en route and upon landing, its nose stuck in sand, somersaulting over and sending Büchner flying.

After Büchner recovered from his injuries, he supervised the conversion of the aircraft into a floatplane in the railway workshops in Dar-es-Salaam; metal pontoons were attached under the fuselage and tail. The Schutztruppe decided to turn Büchner's aircraft over to the navy to serve as the aerial eyes for the *Königsberg*. Büchner made several taxi runs in the converted floatplane but the lack of high-octane fuel prevented the Germans' only aircraft in the colony from taking to the skies again. While the German experience with military aviation in East Africa was short-lived, that of the British was just beginning.

Short Folder No.121 at Durban, South Africa, with men of 4 Expeditionary Squadron RNAS.
IWM Q84144

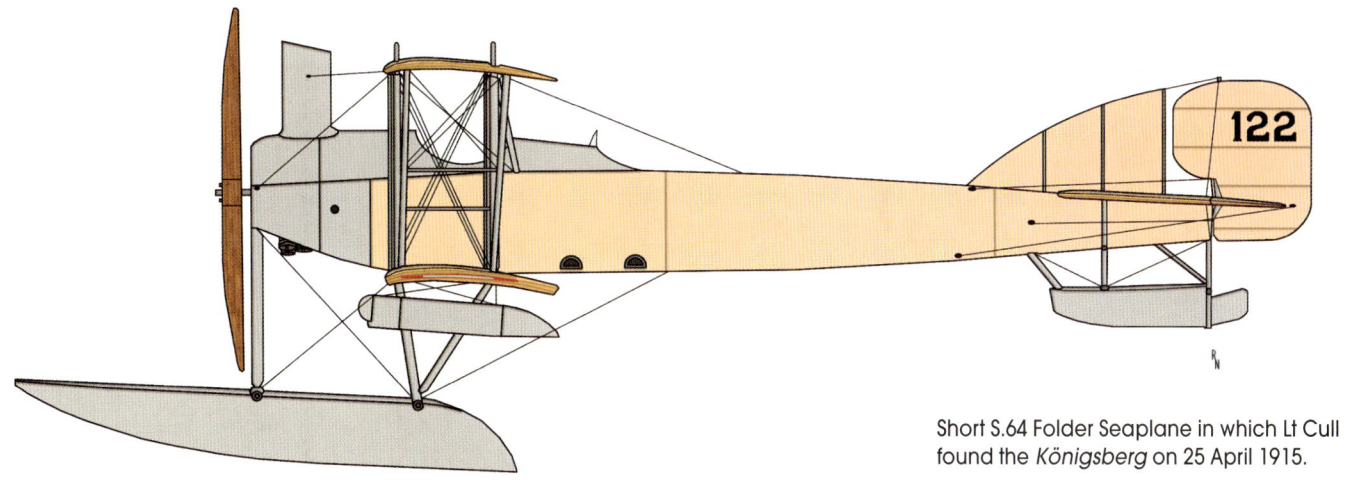

Short S.64 Folder Seaplane in which Lt Cull found the *Königsberg* on 25 April 1915.

"...the climate was just as deadly as bullets and shells..."

The presence of the *Königsberg* in German East Africa was a major concern for the British Admiralty; this solitary warship represented in theory a minute 'Fleet-in-Being' (Admiral Alfred von Tirpitz's strategy for employing the German High Seas Fleet in the North Sea), one whose very presence forced the British to maintain a significant naval force, which could have been used elsewhere, to keep her blockaded within the coastal waters of the German colony. The *Königsberg* further frustrated the Royal Navy forces in the area when she disappeared into the waterways and dense jungles of the Rufiji River Delta, especially since the British believed that a warship of her size could not navigate far inland due to the shallow waters.

In order to release Royal Navy assets off East Africa to more pressing theatres, the *Königsberg* had to be located and destroyed. Rear-Admiral Herbert G King-Hall, the commander of the Royal Navy's Cape Station, knew that his officers were unfamiliar with the Rufiji Delta, thus making the search for the *Königsberg* by water a risky and possibly fruitless venture. Since he could not get through the Delta, he decided to fly over it.

King-Hall contacted a civilian pilot, Mr Dennis Cutler, who had been giving aerial demonstration flights in two Curtiss F single-engine flying boats in South Africa before the war, leased one of his flying boats and commissioned Cutler into the Royal Naval Air Service; his mission was to reconnoiter the Rufiji Delta from the air and locate the *Königsberg*. Now Flight Sub-Lieutenant Cutler and his Curtiss were shipped from South Africa to the small island of Niororo, where a sandy beach was quickly converted into a makeshift seaplane base. The Curtiss had been damaged in transit so Cutler and his mechanic/observer Midshipman Arthur Gallehawk had to make improvised repairs, finally getting the small flying boat airborne on 22 November. ➤

Bruno Büchner's Pfalz-AGO biplane in the railway shops at Dar-es-Salaam. The native workers are preparing the metal pontoons that were attached to the aircraft.
Bundesarchiv, Bild 105-DOA5035, Walther Dobbertin

Aerial reconnaissance photo taken by Leutnant Fiedler during one of his bombardments of the South African encampment at Tschaubaib.

After a number of reconnaissance flights, the *Königsberg* was finally located; Cutler reported that the cruiser had steam up and King-Hall worried that she might make a break for the open sea, now having been located. Cutler was ordered to keep a constant watch on her but on 10 December an engine failure forced him down onto the Rufiji. Cutler tried to burn the aircraft but he was captured by the Germans before he could finish. Although the Curtiss was damaged beyond repair, its remains were recovered under fire by Midshipman Gallehawk and a British tugboat shortly after Cutler was captured. After the end of this first attempt at aerial reconnaissance, Admiral King-Hall requested reinforcements from Great Britain to deal with the *Königsberg*.

On 21 February 1915, 4 Expeditionary Squadron RNAS, comprising two Royal Naval Air Service Sopwith Type 807 floatplanes and their pilots, Flight Lieutenants JT Cull and HEM Watkins, arrived at Niororo Island at the entrance to the Rufiji. Much to the dismay of the British, however, the narrow air-intake systems of the 100hp Monosoupape-Gnome engines hampered the Sopwiths' performance in the dense tropical air to the extent that even unarmed, the aircraft could not reach an adequate scouting altitude. Furthermore, the heat caused the glue holding the canvas to the wings to melt, the wooden propeller to warp and the skin to peel off the floats.

It was not until 23 April, when three Short Folder floatplanes were delivered to Niororo Island, that the RNAS pilots received aircraft that could effectively operate in the tropical climate. But even the Short floatplanes presented difficulties of their own; the aircraft had previously been extensively used at the RNAS school on the Isle of Grain and they were damaged in transit, requiring extensive repairs before they were delivered to Niororo Island.

Native labourers carrying a Caudron G.III landplane to the RNAS aerodrome on Mafia Island in June 1915. **All author's collection unless noted**

Finally, on 25 April, Lt Cull made the first reconnaissance flight in a newly arrived Short Folder and located the *Königsberg* for the first time since Sub-Lt Cutler's last flight on 10 December 1914. The pilots made a number of reconnaissance flights over the *Königsberg* over the course of the next two months, encountering heavy ground fire on each mission. The stalemate in the Rufiji Delta was to shift in the favour of the British in late June when Admiral King-Hall's plan for the elimination of the *Königsberg* could effectively begin; two shallow draft monitors, HMS *Mersey* and HMS *Severn*, armed with 6-inch guns and capable of navigating the inlets of the Rufiji Delta arrived from Britain along with two Farman F.27 and two Caudron land-based aircraft. Anticipating the arrival of these, an airfield had been constructed on Mafia Island; their better performance would greatly enhance the scouting and attack capabilities of 4 Expeditionary Squadron.

The first attack on the *Königsberg* commenced on 6 July 1915 when the *Mersey* and *Severn* took up bombardment positions in the Delta with Lt Cull flying overhead in a radio-equipped Farman directing their fire. On this occasion, the *Königsberg's* fire was

> **"…the *Mersey* and *Severn* took up bombardment positions in the Delta with Lt Cull flying overhead in a radio-equipped Farman, directing their fire."**

more accurate, damaging the *Mersey* and forcing the monitors to withdraw. The British drew final blood on 11 July when the monitors again challenged the German cruiser with Lt Cull and FSL Arnold directing fire overhead; this time the monitors' fire was spot on and after a number of hits, explosions began to wrack the *Königsberg* and soon the whole ship was ablaze.

Ironically, in a last act of defiance, the *Königsberg's* gunners managed to shoot down Cull's Farman, which made a forced landing in the river but both Cull and Arnold survived. Upon the return to Mafia Island, the officers celebrated; Lt Cull and FSL Arnold each received the Distinguished Service Order, and in a tribal ritual that seemed like a fitting end to a long and frustrating campaign, Lt Cull set fire to the worn-out Short Folders on the beach.

GERMAN EAGLES AND SOUTH AFRICAN BOERS

On the opposite side of the continent, the British outlook for a quick victory in German Southwest Africa at the beginning of the war was initially pessimistic. Although the German colony was sparsely populated, much of the territory was dominated by the Kalahari and Namib Deserts, territory which required extensive logistic preparation to cross. Furthermore, in one of the great ironies of World War One, the Germans had unchallenged air superiority over German Southwest Africa for most of the campaign.

In April of 1914, the German Southwest African colonial administration requested two aircraft to be shipped from Germany for evaluation. On 19 May 1914, the first aircraft,

Aerial photo of the wreck of the Königsberg in the Rufiji Delta, taken in December 1916. Note the path on the shore adjacent to the ship: the Schutztruppe removed the Königsberg's guns and mounted them on carriages, using them as mobile artillery for the rest of the war. **IWM SP 989**

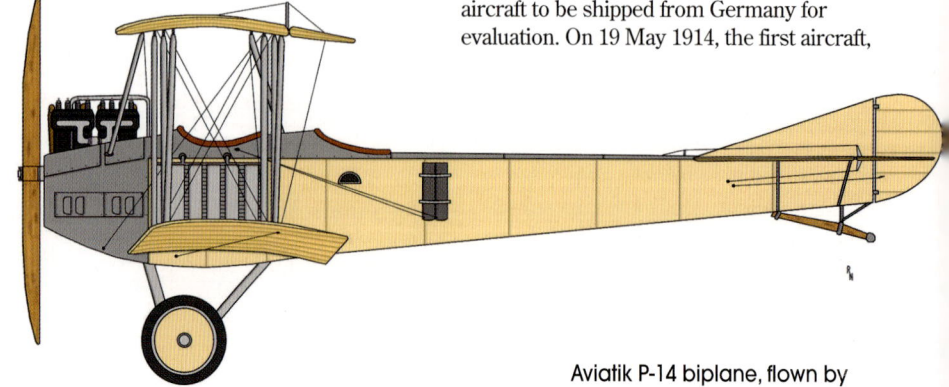

Aviatik P-14 biplane, flown by Leutnant Alexander von Scheele.

The Aviatik P-14 of Leutnant von Scheele being pushed by members of the Schutztruppe at Otjimbingwe, German Southwest Africa.

South African Pilots Powell, Carey-Thomas, Wallace, van der Spuy and Cripps at Karabib, 1915.
SANDF via SAAF Museum

an Aviatik P-14 biplane, arrived from Germany, while the second, an LFG-Roland Pfeil biplane, arrived in early June. The pilots of the fledgling German colonial air arm arrived in May as well; military pilot Leutnant Alexander von Scheele, Aviatik company pilot Willy Trück, and Austrian civilian pilot Paul Fiedler. The aircraft were assembled in the railway workshops in Karibib and Keetmanshoop and provisional airfields were made in those towns.

The pilots were not enthusiastic about the performance of their aircraft; the nearly all-wood construction of the Aviatik made it less than ideal for tropical conditions and both aircraft were thought to be underpowered. Scheele further asserted that they were handed the "leftovers" of the German aviation industry as pilots in Germany found the Aviatik already obsolete and the German Army had refused to purchase the LFG due to its sluggish performance. The Reichskolonialamt in Berlin responded that it could afford no other aircraft for the colony and the beginning of the war in August precluded any further deliveries from Germany. The aircraft were abruptly commandeered into the Schutztruppe and Trück and Fiedler were both given the rank of Leutnant. Along with von Scheele, they were to be the lone German eagles facing the numerical might of the British lion in the deserts of southwestern Africa.

The Aviatik and the LFG were quickly made ready for combat missions over the rugged terrain. Two tin tubes were attached to the side of the Aviatik from which bombs made from artillery shells could be dropped. Von Scheele also kept a horse's feed bag, filled with grenades, tied to the side of the cockpit. Fiedler's aircraft was similarly equipped and both machines carried a compass, signal mirror, emergency rations, water bags, a rifle, basic tools, and a telephone connector – a significant extra load necessitated by the rugged terrain and the relative unreliability of the engines.

One of the primary targets for aerial reconnaissance and bombing was the massive encampment at Tschaukaib in the Namib Desert, where the South Africans were forming an army to march inland to Windhoek. Fiedler, equipped with a camera with a telescopic lens and several bombs, made his first attack on Tschaukaib on 17 December. One of Fiedler's bombs hit an artillery piece, killing one artilleryman and wounding four others. This first raid caused a bit of panic among the South African troops; artillery was set up to fire on incoming aircraft, soldiers were instructed to fire their rifles, troops were ordered to take cover in trenches when an aircraft was approaching, and a number of bomb-proof shelters were constructed. ➤

Captain Kenneth van der Spuy in the uniform of the Royal Flying Corps. Van der Spuy was promoted to captain toward the end of the German Southwest Africa campaign. He also flew missions in German East Africa and northern Russia during and immediately after the war. **SANDF via SAAF Museum**

The antennas of the German radio station at Windhoek. These radio stations were the only means by which Germany's African colonies could maintain contact with the Fatherland, thus making them the prime campaign objectives of the British.

Kapitänleutnant Ludwig Bockholt, commander of the L 59 Afrika-schiff during Operation China Sache.

WS Rayner, a Reuters correspondent accompanying the South African troops, witnessed a number of the attacks made by von Scheele and Fiedler: 'Altogether the Germans sent their aeroplanes 13 times. Explosives were dropped on nine occasions – once at Haalenberg, once at Rothkuppe, four times at Tschaukaib and three times at Garub; the first time at Haalenberg on November 29, 1914, the last time at Garub on March 27, 1915. Through the wireless, 'Fritz' intimated that he would be visiting us on Christmas morn, and leaving a couple of cards, but he never did. And we all got up so early to make sure of seeing him – in time!

'... It was not bomb throwing, however, but in intelligence work that the German airman really scored. The position of our camps and their approximate strength were always known to him, and, of course, to his superiors; he generally returned with telescopically taken photographs. Lantern slides were made from the films, and, at illustrated lectures, were subsequently shown and explained to gatherings of officers.'

The South Africans committed a disproportionate amount of manpower and equipment on account of the two German aircraft, something which must have satisfied von Scheele and Fiedler. As the German air raids became more frequent, initial South African panic gave way to routine, or for some, excitement:

'... At first the airman was regarded as a terror; very shortly, and he was almost welcomed as an interlude. One young Afrikander was seen to jump from his trench trembling violently and full of rage. Shaking his fist at the retreating airman, he yelled: "You damned schelm; you aimed that at me!" But that was his first experience of aerial warfare. Later on, I saw the same young fellow showing quite another disposition... After the last explosion, he assured everybody that there were "No more for no more!" Then he joined in the general stampede for the scenes of the explosions, to be in at the inevitable search for souvenirs, in the form of shell splinters, which was prosecuted with great energy and thoroughness. I should be inclined to say that if all the finds were pieced together they would make the whole of 'Fritz's' thirty shells complete!'

SOUTH AFRICAN AVIATION

Although the South Africans grew more accustomed to the German air attacks, they must have wondered how with all its might the British Empire would allow the Germans to maintain complete control of the skies over South Africa. The answer lay thousands of miles away in England.

The South African military leadership had not completely neglected developments in aviation prior to the outbreak of the war. When the South African government created the Union Defense Force in 1912, it established the framework for a new military air arm, the South African Aviation Corps. The government hired a private pilot, Cecil Paterson, to train 10 students at his flight school in Alexandersfontein on two biplanes of his own design. Paterson trained his 10 students in late 1913 and in the spring of the following year, six were selected by the South African government for advanced flight training in Great Britain. In the summer of 1914, Captain Gerard Wallace and Lieutenants Gordon Creed, Edwin Emmet, Basil Turner, and Kenneth van der Spuy, whose Boer family had fought against the British less than 20 years before, completed their training at the Central Flying School at Upavon and became the first South African pilots to join the Royal Flying Corps.

Back in South Africa, the government, growing weary of the seemingly omnipresent German aerial activity, recalled the South African pilots back to Africa in November in order to activate the South African Aviation Corps. At that time, South Africa's air arm existed only on paper and now had pilots but no aircraft. The South Africans literally had to shop for their own aircraft, but quickly realised that most British aircraft were unsuited to the climate and terrain requirements of the southern African theatre of operations; low-horsepower engines could not achieve a high enough altitude to fly over mountains, wood and fabric would be made brittle by the desert sun and there was even a concern that the

A Farman F.27 outside the hangar at Walvis Bay. The first hangar built there proved to be too low to accommodate the Farmans. **SANDF via SAAF Museum**

The Royal Naval Air Service sent two BE.2 biplanes with the SAAC to German Southwest Africa. These aircraft, with their low-horsepower engines and wooden frames, were ill-suited for the desert terrain and were rarely used during the campaign.

timber aircraft frames would make a tempting target to wood-eating red ants.

Lt van der Spuy visited the Farman factory in France where he came across what at the time was the aircraft most suited to southern Africa's rigorous environment; the Henri Farman HF.27 had an all-steel framework and a powerful 150hp Canton Unné radial engine. The Royal Flying Corps and the Royal Naval Air Service had control over the distribution of the Farman airframes and Canton Unné engines; but through van der Spuy's organisational skills and a clever ruse, the South Africans were able to obtain six HF.27 airframes and six engines. Since South Africa had no aviation industries, mechanics were recruited from the Royal Naval Air Service and were sent along with ground equipment and spare parts to the front in March 1915.

Finally, in April, the first three Farmans were picked up from the factory and van der Spuy arranged their transport as well as that of the pilots to Walvis Bay, arriving on 30 April 1915. The ground crew had built a proper airfield at Walvis Bay and the Farmans were assembled. Since Lt van der Spuy was the pilot most familiar with the Farman biplanes, he made the first operational flight of the South African Aviation Corps on 6 May.

Lt van der Spuy and his comrades arrived rather late in the campaign for German Southwest Africa, however. Only six days after the Boer's first flight, the city of Winkhoek, capital of the German colony, surrendered to General Louis Botha's advancing forces. The Germans were retreating along their railway line deeper into the northern interior. Nevertheless, van der Spuy flew his Farman to the recently captured German airfield at Karibib and began to fly reconnaissance missions for the South African ground forces. ➤

LFG Roland Pfeil, built by Luft Fahrzeug Gesellschaft, flown by Leutnant Paul Fiedler.

Lt van der Spuy in one of the SAAC Henri Farman F.27s with ground crew at Walvis Bay. **SANDF via SAAF Museum**

Lt van der Spuy recalled the following: 'I recollect General Botha once jokingly saying to me at Omaruru, on my return from a long reconnaissance: "You are a good flyer, Ken – but an even better vêrkyker (binoculars)." Puzzled, I enquired as to what he meant. He replied: "…This morning, until you came back, I was able to see only so far" – he pointed – "now I can see for hundreds of miles… wonderful!"'

The South Africans were now reaping the benefits of aerial reconnaissance, something which the Germans had exclusively enjoyed for most of the campaign. The Germans also began to experience what it was like to be on the receiving end of an aerial bombardment. Lt Cripps joined van der Spuy at Karib on 15 June and on one mission where both aircraft were flying together, the two South Africans bombed and disabled a German locomotive on the railway near Tsumeb.

The German and South African aircraft were never to meet each other in skies during the campaign in German Southwest African. The Germans' LFG crashed on 17 April and repairs were not completed until the end of June in the railway workshops at Tsumeb. The Aviatik continued its reconnaissance and harassment duties until it had to make a forced landing on 1 May. Following repairs, it was test flown on 26 May but on that day Leutnant von Scheele crashed upon landing, destroying the aircraft.

The South Africans suffered from similar misfortunes; Lt Cripps crashed his Farman at Omaruru on 17 June while an attempted landing on an unsuitable airfield at Kalkfeld damaged Lt van der Spuy's Farman. Both pilots were injured and were out of the

> **"Two tin tubes were attached to the side of the Aviatik from which bombs made from artillery shells could be dropped."**

The SAAC at a forward base in German Southwest Africa with two Farman F.27s and ground support vehicles visible. **SANDF via SAAF Museum**

campaign. When the German colonial government and the Schutztruppe formally surrendered the colony on 9 July 1915, there were only two remaining Farmans left to the South Africans.

While the number of aircraft used during the campaign for German Southwest Africa was very small, their operations represented one of the first effective uses of aviation in a modern and highly mobile campaign. The ingenuity displayed by the Germans in their use of aerial reconnaissance to track the movements of the numerically superior South African forces allowed Schutztruppe units on several occasions to withdraw along the railway, thus avoiding being caught in a pitched battle or an enveloping movement. Likewise, the South Africans' aerial reconnaissance late in the campaign located the German units and enabled proper pursuit and encirclement.

Afterwards, most of the South African pilots and ground crew were reformed into the 26 Squadron (South African) of the Royal Flying Corps and they would see further service in German East Africa.

THE 'CHINA MATTER'

In November of 1917, British pilots in East Africa were interrupted from their routine reconnaissance patrols for a mission which they must have thought came from someone stricken with malarial fever: a message was received from the War Office in London instructing British forces in East Africa to be on the lookout for a German Zeppelin, and if possible to destroy it.

The most remarkable – and unique – aerial mission to take place over Africa during World War One did not have its origins on that continent but rather in Germany. In the fall of 1917, a plan was hatched between the Imperial German Navy and the Reichskolonialamt to circumvent the British naval blockade of the German ports and send ammunition and medical supplies to General von Lettow-Vorbeck's forces in German East Africa… via Zeppelin. Hoping that Germany would have at least one colony still in her position when peace negotiations began by maintaining von Lettow-Vorbeck's army in the field, the Reichskolonialamt recognised the General's desperate need for medical supplies from Germany.

The Navy staff, after observing the record 101-hour endurance flight of Zeppelin LZ120 in July of 1917, realised that a specialised Zeppelin could fly non-stop from Europe to German East Africa. Thus, the Admiralstab commenced Operation China Sache (China Matter) and ordered the conversion of the L57, then under construction, to enable it to fly 4350 miles at an average speed of 40mph while carrying an 11-ton cargo of ammunition, machine guns, medical supplies, radio parts, and other tools that the Schutztruppe might need. The airship would not be able to make the return flight to Europe, so much thought was given to how its structure could be used to make tents, radio antennas, etc. Von Lettow-Vorbeck's troops would rendezvous with the Zeppelin at a location in the Makonde Highlands, designated China Gebiet.

The L57 made her maiden flight on 26 September under the command of Kapitänleutnant Ludwig Bockholt; he found the ship to react sluggishly to the controls and also thought her to be significantly underpowered. On 7 October, however, Bockholt ordered the airship out of its shed at Jüterbog for a speed test but the high winds of an incoming storm blew the Zeppelin out of the control of the ground handlers and into the airbase's fence where the structure broke and the ship went up in flames.

A British military encampment in the Egyptian desert, photographed by the L 59.

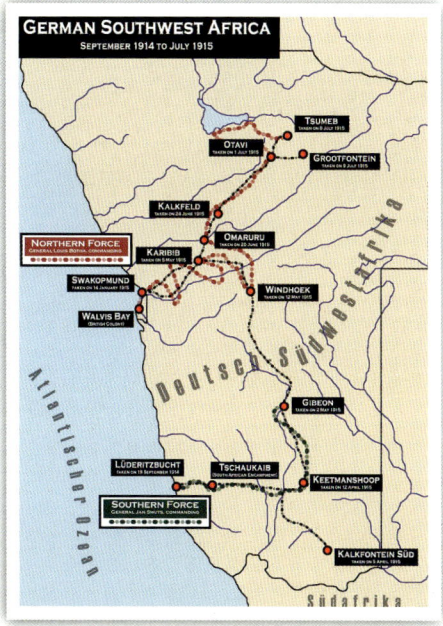

German Southwest Africa
September 1914 to July 1915

BIBLIOGRAPHY

Blake, Arthur. Vlieghelde van Suid-Afrika. Kaapstad: Nasionale Boekhandel Beperk, 1966.

Chapman, Peter. Dust on the Horizon: The Air War in German South West Africa 1914-1915, Part 1. Cross & Cockade International 34, No.3 (2003) : 152-164.

Dust on the Horizon: The Air War in German South West Africa 1914-1915, Part 2." Cross & Cockade International 34, No.4 (2003) : 207-216.

Davilla, James J and Arthur M Soltan. French Aircraft of the First World War. Stratford: Flying Machine Press, 1997.

Dye, Air Vice Marshal Peter. Royal Naval Air Service Operations in German East Africa 1914-1918: Part 1. Cross & Cockade International 37, No.3 (2006) : 157-185.

Farwell, Byron. The Great War in Africa: 1914-1918. New York: W.W. Norton & Company, 1986.

Goebel, Ing Johannes. Afrika zu unsern Füßen: Lettow Vorbeck-entgegen und ander geheimnisvolle Luftschiffahrten. Leipzig: Verlag von KF Koehler, 1925.

Heiss, Friedrich. Das Zeppelinbuch. Berlin: Volk und Reich, 1936.

Hoyt, Edwin P Jr. The Germans Who Never Lost: The Story of the Köningsberg. New York: Funk & Wagnalls, 1968.

Jones, HA The War in the Air: Being the Story of the part played in the Great War by the Royal Air Force, Vol. III. Nashville: Battery Press, Inc, 1998.

Mahncke, JOEO. "The Fliegertruppe of the Imperial German Army." South African Military History Society Journal 12 no. 2 (Dec, 2001).

Rayner, WS & WW O'Shaughnessy. How Botha and Smuts Conquered German South West. London: Simpkin, Marshall, Hamilton, Kent & Co, Ltd, 1916.

Robinson, Douglas H The Zeppelin in Combat: A History of the German Naval Airship Division, 1912-1918. Atglen: Schiffer Military/Aviation History, 1994.

Thetford, Owen. British Naval Aircraft Since 1912. Annapolis: Naval Institute Press, 1991.

van der Spuy, Kenneth Reid. Chasing the Wind. Capetown: Books of Africa, 1966.

Villard, Henry S Mission East Africa: The Flight of Zeppelin L59. Cross & Cockade International 23, No.2 (1992).

W.S. Rayner & W.W. O'Shaughnessy, How Botha and Smuts Conquered German South West (London: Simpkin, Marshall, Hamilton, Kent & Co., Ltd., 1916), 86-88.

Rayner, 87-88.

Kenneth Reid van der Spuy, Chasing the Wind (Capetown: Books of Africa, 1966), 82.

Ing. Johannes Goebel, Afrika zu unsern Füßen: Lettow Vorbeck-entgegen und ander geheimnisvolle Luftschiffahrten (Leipzig: Verlag von K.F. Koehler, 1925), 96.

The Admiralstab did not give up on the Africa mission despite this setback; it ordered the conversion of the L59, then under build in Staaken, to the same specifications as the L57. The new Afrika-schiff was commissioned on 25 October and arrived at the Central Powers' southernmost aircraft base at Jamboli in Bulgaria on 4 November. The first two attempts made by the L59 to fly to German East Africa ended in failure due to miscalculating the amount of ballast required for the flight. Finally, on 21 November, the L59 set out again, made it over Anatolia without incident and set a southerly course over the Mediterranean.

As the L59 cruised over the Mediterranean during the night of 21/22 November, a storm forced the radio operator to retract the airship's radio antenna, which meant she was now out of contact with Berlin. Kapitänleutnant Bockholt would have to navigate without any meteorological or navigational updates from the Admiralstab.

On the morning of the 22nd the L59 crossed over the African coast near Mersa Matruh and headed into the Egyptian desert. The climate soon made things miserable for the crew; the intense heat was draining, the glare of the sun off the sand made it difficult to see and the turbulent desert winds kept the underpowered airship from maintaining a smooth flight, causing many to become airsick. As day gave way to evening, the L59 crossed the Nile north of Wadi Halfa and the air grew increasingly humid and heavy, causing the airship to lose buoyancy. The crew had to drop most of the ballast just to keep it aloft. After making a sweep to the west to avoid flying near Khartoum, the Zeppelin's radio, which had been damaged in the storm over the Mediterranean, was finally repaired and after midnight on the 23rd a disturbing message was received from the massive Nauen radio station outside of Berlin.

The onboard radio was again ready after a while; the machine parts which were damaged had been removed with the ship's tools. There! – a radio message from the Admiralty – "Last military base of Lettow-Vorbeck, Revala,

has been lost. Entire Makonde Highlands in possession of the English. Part of Lettow's forces captured. The rest hard-pressed to the north. Return immediately!"…

One of the crewmen aboard L 59, Ingenieur Johannes Goebel, noted the following: "The distance from Nauen to Khartoum amounts to 4500 kilometers. The Nauen radio waves had finally located a single particular grain in a vast air ocean.

From here on, everyone concerned had to consider the fate of our comrades in German East Africa as inevitable. Even before the beginning of these last fateful events, the territory still held by the Schutztruppe was so small that a landing in the area could no longer be taken into consideration. One had also to think about the time-consuming unloading of the cargo, or the reaction of enemy aircraft – which our own aircraft could not counter – and, what lastly was out of the question, to think about the difficulties of the landing in particular. No meteorologists or radio stations could broadcast the wind on the ground, no landing crew waiting there for a completely unexpected airship."

Reluctantly, Bockholt reversed course and headed north back to Europe.

From 15-18 October, von Lettow-Vorbeck had fought and won the last major battle of the African campaign at Mahiwa. In doing so, however, he lost nearly a third of his strength and was running out of ammunition. To remedy this, he withdrew his forces deeper into the interior, eventually invading Portuguese Mozambique on 25 November in

Zeppelin L59, the Afrika-schiff.

order to capture weapons, ammunition and medical supplies from the ill-defended Portuguese garrisons.

Ironically, if the L57 had not been destroyed, she would have arrived at the rendezvous point when von Lettow-Vorbeck's forces still controlled the area. The morale of the crew was low, as they had yet again to cope with the blistering heat of the day and the freezing cold of the night in the desert, more storms over the Mediterranean and the realisation that they were not able to complete their mission.

After over 95 hours in the air and having travelled over 4200 miles, the L59 finally came down over Jamboli in the early morning of 25 November. While its intended mission had not been a success, the L59 and its crew had achieved a significant endurance record. For years after the war, European travellers in the Egyptian desert would hear of Bedouin stories about a great spirit that appeared in the sky in 1917, witnesses to a top secret German mission in the skies above Africa. ∎

Nottingham's aerial warrior

Captain Albert Ball VC DSO ** **MC became one of Britain's first air aces to gain celebrity status.**

Albert Ball was born in Nottingham, and as a teenager enlisted in the 7th (Robin Hood) Battalion of the Sherwood Foresters (Nottinghamshire and Derbyshire Regiment) after the outbreak of World War One. By October 1914, he gained a commission as a 2nd Lieutenant. He was given a posting in England, but was keen to get to France. Albert took private flying lessons at Hendon and qualified for Royal Aero Club Certificate No.1898 on 15 October 1915 and then requested a transfer to the Royal Flying Corps.

He began his military flying training that same month and flew solo during the first week of December. Completing his training at the Central Flying School, Albert was awarded his RFC wings on 26 January 1916.

On 18 February 1916, his first operational posting was to 13 Squadron in France, mostly flying Royal Aircraft Factory BE.2cs on reconnaissance duties. While flying 4070 on 29 March, Albert experienced his first aerial combat when he attacked a German scout. A second enemy aircraft joined in the combat hitting Albert's aircraft before they both made off for their lines.

Albert Ball receives a few final words before departing London Colney for France in SE.5 A4850 on 7 April 1917. **Courtesy Nottingham City Museums and Galleries**

Portrait of Captain Albert Ball VC DSO** MC, painted by Edward Newling c1921. Note that the famous pilot is portrayed wearing the crimson ribbon of the Victoria Cross, which in reality was awarded posthumously. **Courtesy Nottingham City Museums and Galleries**

On 7 May 1916, Albert was posted to 11 Squadron, which was selecting 'experienced' pilots to fly Nieuport and Bristol Scouts for fighting patrols – a role met with much eagerness by the daring pilot who had been known to regularly engage flights of enemy aircraft in his slow and steady BE.2c. He was billeted in a nearby village, but instead opted to move to a tent on the flight line and later built his own wooden hut stating that he wanted to be closer to his aeroplane in case the enemy came looking for a fight. While flying a Bristol Scout on 15 May 1916, Albert scored his first outright aerial victory when he shot down an Albatros C while flying 5313. He soon achieved ace status after shooting down four more enemy aircraft in the squadron's Scouts.

FIRST AWARD

As his aerial victories and achievements grew, the *London Gazette* of 27 July 1916 cited the award of the Military Cross to 2nd Lt Albert Ball: 'For conspicuous skill and gallantry on many occasions, notably when, after failing to destroy an enemy kite balloon with bombs, he returned for a fresh supply, went back and brought it down in flames. He has done great execution among enemy aeroplanes. On one occasion he attacked six in one flight, forced down two and drove the others off. This occurred several miles over the enemy's lines.'

Albert requested a period of rest but was instead posted to 8 Squadron to fly the BE.2 again. On 14 August, which was Albert's 20th birthday, he received welcome news that he was to return to 11 Squadron. Once again flying Nieuports, he was soon rapidly increasing his tally. On the 22nd, he was engaged in a dogfight with 14 German aircraft 15 miles behind enemy lines, during which he scored a triple victory. His aircraft was damaged, but he managed to get it back to Allied occupied territory within just a mile before running out of petrol. His windscreen had been hit and spars were damaged, so he set about repairing them before going to sleep beside the Nieuport. A party took fuel out to him the following day and he flew the field-repaired machine back to base, only to receive news that he was to be transferred to 60 Squadron which was to become a Scout unit. Albert was given A201 as his personal mount, and this aircraft's propeller 'spinner'

Away from the ferocious aerial combat over the Western Front, Albert takes time out to play with Goff at the family home. **Courtesy Nottingham City Museums and Galleries**

was painted bright red. The enigmatic pilot would shoot down 16 enemy aircraft in that machine alone.

At this point, Albert was given some leave, and hadn't realised that his achievements had received so much publicity back home that he had gained 'celebrity' status. While just walking the streets of Nottingham, he would be continually stopped and congratulated.

BACK TO IT

On his return to France, the victories kept coming; on several separate occasions during September he scored multiple 'kills' in a day. His actions of this period had not gone unnoticed, as there were simultaneous citations noting that Albert had achieved the rare distinction of being awarded the Distinguished Service Order and Bar. His citation for the DSO appeared in the *London Gazette* of 26 September, and the same day that for his Bar read: 'For conspicuous skill and gallantry. When on escort duty to a bombing raid he saw four enemy machines in formation. He dived on to them and broke up their formation, and then shot down the nearest one, which fell on its nose. He came down to about 500 feet to make certain ➤

Family portrait taken in the garden of Sedgley House while Albert was on leave in October 1916. His parents are at left, and his sister Lois is seated right. The family's pet collie was called Goff. **Courtesy Nottingham City Museums and Galleries**

CAPT. BALL. V.C. D.S.O. M.C.
SAVY 1916.

Albert Ball poses in front of a Nieuport Scout at Savy in 1916 while he was serving with 60 Squadron.

A wing-strut pennant flown on the aeroplane of Captain Albert Ball, which was purchased by His Grace the Duke of Portland at a sale at Sotheby's and was then presented to the Lord Mayor of Nottingham, Sir Albert Ball, father of the late pilot. He then handed it over to the city. **Jarrod Cotter**

Splendid studio portrait of Albert Ball. **Courtesy Nottingham City Museums and Galleries**

On display in Nottingham Castle is this Avro-manufactured windscreen pierced by enemy gunfire and removed from an aircraft flown by Albert Ball. **Jarrod Cotter**

it was wrecked. On another occasion, observing 12 enemy machines in formation, he dived in among them, and fired a drum into the nearest machine, which went down out of control. Several more hostile machines then approached, and he fired three more drums at them, driving down another out of control. He then returned, crossing the lines at a low altitude, with his machine very much damaged.'

HOME AGAIN

On October 1, Albert was in combat again, downing three more German aircraft. On his return to Savy, he received news that he was to have a period of leave, followed by a posting to the Home Establishment. He arrived at Nottingham railway station on 5 October and was met by his sister Lois who drove him to the family home, Sedgley House.

There he was not only met by his loving parents, but also by a gathering of local journalists and photographers all eager to get his story. A local photographer had been asked to take pictures of the heroic pilot with his family in the garden of Sedgley House, some of which are included within this article. On 18 November, Albert was invested with his Military Cross and DSO and Bars at Buckingham Palace by King George V. The second Bar to his DSO was gazetted on 26 November, making him the first officer in the British Army to receive three DSOs.

Albert's new posting saw him take up instructional duties with 34 (Reserve) Squadron at Offordness. Being an instructor was not to his liking, and he looked for a return to France. He even persuaded a contact to approach General Sir David Henderson through the 'old boy' network

with his request, but it was quickly rebuffed. He continued his attempts to get back to operational flying, and success came in February 1917 when news came that he was posted as a Flight Commander to 56 (Training) Squadron at London Colney, Hertfordshire, which was in the process of working up for France.

On 19 February, he received a tribute from his home city when he was made an Honorary Freeman of Nottingham. The ornate casket containing his script appropriately featured a silver biplane on its lid. A few days later he eagerly joined his new squadron to prepare for a return to France. On 13 March, Albert went to Farnborough to collect and deliver the unit's first SE.5.

On 25 March, he met 18-year-old Flora Young. The two had an immediate attraction with each other, and having only just met, Albert invited her to go flying with him in an Avro 504. That night he wrote the first of regular notes to her and spent all the off-duty time he could with the beautiful young lady. At the end of the month, 56 Squadron received orders to deploy to France, so on 5 April, Albert proposed to Flora. The dashing young pilot gave his bride-to-be his ID wrist bracelet instead of an engagement ring.

On the 7th, Albert set off to cross the Channel in SE.5 A4850. Even though Albert had personally modified his new aircraft, he disliked the SE.5 and gained permission from Major General Sir Hugh Trenchard to instead fly a Nieuport 17, receiving B1522 in time for 56 Squadron getting its authorisation for operations on 22 April.

The following day, Albert engaged German aircraft several times in his Nieuport, claiming 56 Squadron's first victory. He then

> "A young French woman pulled Albert from the wreckage, and he died in her arms..."

set about an Albatros but overshot, and the German observer returned fire hitting the Nieuport's wings numerous times. Albert nursed his preferred mount back to base for repairs, and then immediately returned to battle in an SE.5. He shot down one enemy aircraft in flames and forced a second to land.

On 26 April, his tally rose further with a double victory while flying A4850, plus one more on the 28th. A4850 became so badly damaged as a result of combat that it was sent away for repair. Into early May his victories continued, with Albert persisting with his preferred lone patrols. He was fortunate to survive on more than one occasion, as the multiple German aircraft he engaged had resulted in much damage to his aircraft.

DEATH OF AN ICON

On the evening of 7 May 1917, near Douai, Albert led 11 SE.5s from 56 Squadron into combat with aircraft of the notorious Jasta 11. Deteriorating visibility was hampering the fight, and Albert was last seen giving chase to the Albatros D.III of Lothar von Richthofen near Loos. Albert hit the young von Richthofen's aircraft fuel tank, which forced him to land. The German pilot was unhurt, and is thought to have observed Albert's SE.5 disappear into thick grey cloud. A German officer on the ground then watched Albert Ball's aircraft exit inverted from the bottom of the dark cloud in a shallow dive, at an altitude of only a few hundred feet, with its propeller stopped. It crashed close to a ruined farmhouse near the village of Annoeullin. A young French woman pulled Albert from the wreckage, and he died in her arms before German officers arrived on the scene. ➤

Above: Scene from Albert Ball's funeral held by the Germans with full military honours on 9 May 1917. Also present are some Allied airmen prisoners of war. **Courtesy Nottingham City Museums and Galleries**

Silver gilt casket containing the Freedom of the City of Nottingham conferred on Albert Ball on 19 February 1917. An extract from the minutes relating to this reads: 'Flight Commander Captain Albert Ball, DSO, MC, being a person of distinction within the meaning of the Honorary Freedom of Boroughs Act, 1885, be admitted an Honorary Freeman of the City of Nottingham, in recognition of the great services rendered by him as an Officer of the Royal Flying Corps in connection with the operations of the British Expeditionary Force in France, and as a mark of the appreciation of his fellow citizens for his bravery in the face of the enemy.' **Jarrod Cotter**

Far left: Albert Ball's khaki tunic with RFC wings and medal ribbons at left breast, RFC collar badges and three Captain's pips on the shoulders. The silk moiré medal ribbon bars are those of the Distinguished Service Order with two rosettes, a faded Military Cross and the Russian Order of St George. Along with other items of the famous pilot's uniform, this was once on display in 56 Squadron's crew room at RAF Coningsby. Nowadays it is kept in controlled and secure storage for preservation, and rarely sees the light of day. **Jarrod Cotter**

Top left: Albert's original forage cap with RFC badge. **Jarrod Cotter**

Left: Cylindrical iron canister with a cork stopper which was dropped by the Germans with a blue pennant attached over the British lines in late May 1917. A piece of paper inside read that Captain Albert Ball had been killed during an air fight over Annoeulin on 7 May 1917. **Jarrod Cotter**

This is another incident involving a famous aviator of World War One where the exact circumstances are unknown to this day. The Germans credited Lothar von Richthofen with shooting Albert Ball down; however, there is much scepticism regarding that as there was no evidence that the aircraft was brought down by hostile fire and Albert was reported by a German doctor to have died solely from injuries as a result of the crash. It is thought likely that the propaganda generated by crediting von Richthofen could have led to the claim, and the most likely reason for the crash is that Albert became disorientated in the cloud and by the time he exited had no chance to recover control. Such an early example of an SE.5 would have been powered by an engine that would not have been able to maintain inverted flight for more than a matter of seconds, which perhaps explains the report that the aircraft's propeller had stopped.

On 9 May 1917, Albert Ball was buried by the Germans with full military honours. Messages were sent home saying he was missing in action, and it was only at the end of May that the Germans dropped a canister behind Allied lines containing a note stating that the young pilot had been killed.

VC AND LEGACY

On 8 June, Albert Ball was posthumously awarded the Victoria Cross for his actions from 25 April to 6 May 1917 as cited in the *London Gazette*: 'For most conspicuous and consistent bravery from the 25th of April to the 6th of May, 1917, during which period Capt Ball

took part in twenty-six combats in the air and destroyed eleven hostile aeroplanes, drove down two out of control, and forced several others to land.

'In these combats Capt Ball, flying alone, on one occasion fought six hostile machines, twice he fought five and once four. When leading two other British aeroplanes he attacked an enemy formation of eight. On each of these occasions he brought down at least one enemy.

'Several times his aeroplane was badly damaged, once so seriously that but for the most delicate handling his machine would have collapsed, as nearly all the control wires had been shot away. On returning with a damaged machine he had always to be restrained from immediately going out on another.

'In all, Capt Ball has destroyed forty-three German aeroplanes and one balloon, and has always displayed most exceptional courage, determination and skill.'

His parents were devastated at the loss of their much-loved eldest son and his father, Albert Ball Snr, bought the field in France where he had died. A memorial stone was placed at the crash site. Albert's loss was mourned throughout the nation, and was a severe blow to morale.

Within Nottingham Castle is the Sherwood Foresters Regimental Museum, which has on display several items relating

Dedication of the memorial by Air Marshal Sir Hugh Trenchard on 8 September 1921. **Courtesy Nottingham City Museums and Galleries**

to the pilot. These include his medals, a windscreen from one of his aeroplanes shattered by a hostile bullet and the casket that contained his Freedom of the City scroll. In the grounds of the castle is a large memorial, which was dedicated by Sir Hugh Trenchard on 8 September 1921. On top is a statue of Albert Ball, which looks out over the city, with an angel on his shoulder pointing skywards. The city of Nottingham has by no means forgotten its most famous aerial warrior. ■

With many thanks to Judith Edgar, Keeper of Community History, Nottingham City Museums and Galleries, for her time allowing the editor access to the Albert Ball collection of documents, photographs and other artefacts.

Reverse of Albert Ball's VC, showing that it was awarded 'For most conspicuous and consistent bravery' from 25 April to 6 May 1917. **Jarrod Cotter**

Memorial to Albert Ball within the grounds of Nottingham Castle. **Jarrod Cotter**

CAPTAIN
ALBERT BALL VC

1st Robin Hood Battalion Sherwood
Foresters attached Royal Flying Corps
D.S.O. Two Bars M.C.
Croix de Chevalier Legion d'Honneur
Order of St George Russia

Hon. Freeman of the City of
Nottingham

PER ARDUA AD ASTRA

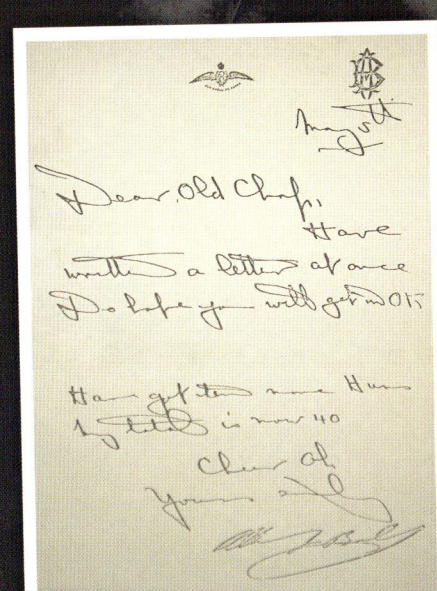

Letter written by Albert Ball addressed to one of his fellow pilots in Brighton dated 5 May 1917, just two days before he was killed.
Courtesy Nottingham City Museums and Galleries

"...he was engaged in a dogfight with 14 German aircraft 15 miles behind enemy lines, during which he scored a triple victory."

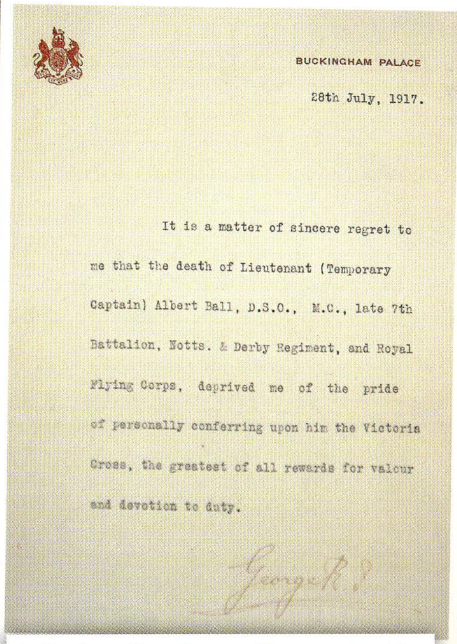

BUCKINGHAM PALACE

28th July, 1917.

It is a matter of sincere regret to me that the death of Lieutenant (Temporary Captain) Albert Ball, D.S.O., M.C., late 7th Battalion, Notts. & Derby Regiment, and Royal Flying Corps, deprived me of the pride of personally conferring upon him the Victoria Cross, the greatest of all rewards for valour and devotion to duty.

George R.I.

Letter from King George V expressing his regret at the death of Albert Ball and his wish to have been able to personally present him with the Victoria Cross.
Courtesy Nottingham City Museums and Galleries

On others' wings
The infancy of American air power

Douglas C Dildy, Colonel, USAF Ret'd, details how the US Air Service came to be and looks at its early operations.

'Flying the flag', a French-built Salmson 2A.2 observation aeroplane of the USAS 1st Aero Squadron cruises above the Western Front. The young American flying service selected the Salmson as their 'standard corps observation aircraft'. **All Official US Air Force photos via author**

In April 1916, the revolutionary Fokker E.IIIs of the German Fliegertruppe (flying force) were sweeping the skies over the Western Front with their synchronised Spandau machine guns. That same month, seven wealthy young expatriate American volunteers (with a French commander and executive officer) formed Escadrille de Chasse Nieuport (N) 124, equipped with Nieuport 17 C.1s. Meanwhile, in Mexico, the nascent American air power, represented by one squadron of fragile, underpowered communications aircraft, was virtually wiped out without a shot being fired.

THE PUNITIVE EXPERIENCE
By the spring of 1916, the Mexican Revolution – in which several vicious warring caudillos wrestled for control of their country – had been going on for six years. Most of the struggle occurred in central Mexico where a 'constitutionalist' coalition led by the Primer Jefe, General Venustiano Carranza, were eventually victorious and drove the leading

'revolutionary', a bandit chieftain called Francisco Pancho Villa (actually named Doroteo Arango), back into the wasteland of northern Mexico. In October 1915, the US government recognised Carranza as the legitimate ruler of Mexico and actively supported the de facto regime in its attempt to rid Villa as a threat.

Incensed, Pancho Villa turned his vengeance upon the Americans and on 9 March 1916 he led some 500 'Villistas' in a raid upon Columbus, New Mexico – home of the US Army's 13th Cavalry Regiment – killing 18 American citizens. The 13th Cavalry rallied quickly, chasing the raiders out of the town and back into Mexico, killing 60 in the process.

President Woodrow Wilson also reacted swiftly, the next day authorising Brigadier General John 'Black Jack' Pershing to lead a 'Punitive Expedition' into northern Mexico to locate and eliminate the outlaw bandito. To do so, Pershing was assigned elements of four cavalry and two infantry regiments, supported by two artillery batteries – and a squadron of aeroplanes.

On 15 March 1916, the 1st Aero Squadron joined Pershing's forces, detraining at Columbus. Under the command of Captain Benjamin D Foulois, the unit consisted of 11 pilots, 82 enlisted men and was equipped with eight unarmed Curtiss JN-3s. As an element of the US Army Signal Corps' Aviation Section, the 1st Aero Squadron was a communications – not a combat – unit.

Flying dispatches and mail between Pershing's rear echelon and the advanced headquarters (HQ) and keeping contact with the expedition's far-flung cavalry columns, the early Curtiss 'Jennies' of the 1st Aero Squadron were put to their first field test – and failed. The Punitive Expedition chased Villista forces some 380 miles into the state of Chihuahua, Mexico, advancing steadily until clashing with Carrancista forces at Parral on 15 April. By this time, the harsh climate and rough terrain had taken their toll on the fragile and underpowered (90hp Curtiss OX engine) JN-3s; all eight aircraft had been crashed, abandoned or condemned as unsafe for further service.

Two and a half years before, the 1st Aero Squadron consisted of eight Curtiss JN-3s participating in the 'Punitive Expedition' against Mexican revolutionary Pancho Villa. The dry, hot environment caused the aircraft's wooden propellers to warp and split, so between flights they were removed and placed in a humidor to preserve the glue holding their laminated layers together.

Two products of the American aircraft industry in 1918: a Dayton-Wright DH-4 (one of 4846 built by Dayton-Wright, Fisher Body, and Standard Aircraft – this one most likely is one of the 140 DH-4 trainers built by Standard Aircraft) parked alongside a Hispano-powered Curtiss JN-6H trainer.

They were replaced by a dozen Curtiss R-2s (JN-type airframes with the 160hp Curtiss VX engine) arriving 1-25 May. Adapted as reconnaissance machines, the R-2 was more capable – able to carry a shoulder-fired Lewis machine gun, a Brock automatic camera, a Dodd-Scott bombsight and small bomblets, or a 180 Watt wireless – but was just as frail.

While Pershing's forces occupied a large swath of northern Mexico, the 1st Aero Squadron provided communications and reconnaissance support operating from its base at 'Aviation Field' at Columbus with a four-aeroplane detachment with Pershing's HQ. Over the summer months, the unit flew 540 missions, logging 346 hours, covering 19,553 miles of forbidding territory.

However, the 'Punitive Expedition' was unsuccessful in locating Pancho Villa, and on 28 January 1917, Pershing began his final withdrawal from Mexican soil – because a much larger crisis loomed upon the American horizon.

JOINING THE WAR AGAINST GERMANY

Nine days before, the US government had learned of the infamous 'Zimmerman Telegram' – a message from German foreign minister Arthur Zimmermann to Ambassador Heinrich von Eckhardt instructing him to 'inform the President of Mexico... as soon as it is certain that there will be an outbreak of war with the United States... [that] we shall make war together and... Mexico is to reconquer [sic] the lost territory of New Mexico, Texas and Arizona.'

This of course caused an outrage in Washington, underscored by Germany's initiation on 1 February of 'Unrestricted Submarine Warfare'. In the next five weeks, 10 American merchant ships – six freighters, two tankers and two schooners – were sunk with the loss of 63 American lives. Infuriated, the US Congress passed a joint resolution announcing that a 'state of war' existed with Germany, and on 6 April 1917, President Woodrow Wilson declared war upon the Kaiser's Empire.

On that day, the Signal Corps' operational air strength consisted of two squadrons in the US (1st Aero at Columbus, NM, and 3rd Aero at San Antonio, Texas) and another (2nd Aero) in the Philippines, with six more organising at various locations. Some 132 aircraft were on strength: 42 operational reconnaissance machines and 90 trainers. The command had 131 officers – including 56 pilots and 51 students – and 1087 enlisted men.

Placing huge faith in America's immense industrial potential, the French were especially anxious to realise the benefits of the US joining the Allies as an 'Associate Power'. Premier Alexandre Ribot

telegrammed Wilson requesting 'a flying corps' of 4500 aircraft, 5000 pilots and 53,000 mechanics – with a total production of 16,500 aircraft and 30,000 engines – be available by July 1918, which 'would allow the Allies to win the supremacy of the air'.

The proposal was studied by the Joint Army and Navy Technical Aircraft Board, headed by now-Major Benjamin Foulois, and recommended meeting this requirement by mass-producing Curtiss trainers, De Havilland 4s and SPAD, Sopwith and SE.5 pursuit planes. The Board forwarded their determination to the government's six-member Airplane Production Board the next month. This panel quickly found that – except for Curtiss trainers – the US lacked an aircraft industry capable of meeting these goals. Fortunately only five days after the declaration of war, the Dayton-Wright Airplane Company was established, planning from the outset to use automobile manufacturing techniques to license-produce French and British designs.

Nonetheless, in an ambitious initiative, on 24 July the US Congress appropriated $640 millions with the naively unrealistic goal of producing '22,625 aeroplanes plus 80 per ➤

cent spares and 44,000 engines'. This programme was intended to equip 345 combat squadrons, of which 263 were planned to be in-theatre by June 1918.

Additionally, on 29 May, the Aircraft Production Board tasked two automotive engineers, one from the Detroit-based Packard Motor Car Company, to design an aero engine that had a high power-to-weight ratio and was adaptable to mass production. Five days later, the famous 'Liberty' engine was born. The modular, water-cooled 27-litre 12-cylinder L-12 produced 400hp and was soon being manufactured by seven automobile companies. By the end of the war, daily production exceeded 150 motors per day – a total of 13,574 were made before the Armistice.

'THE YANKS ARE COMING…'

On 27 May 1917, Major General John J Pershing and his staff – including Major Townsend F Dodd (second commander of 1st Aero Squadron) as Aviation Officer – boarded the SS *Baltic* for an uneventful voyage across the Atlantic. Arriving in Paris on 20 June, Dodd joined Lieutenant Colonel William 'Billy' Mitchell (former Assistant Chief of the Aviation Section) and four other officers (all of whom had served with Dodd in Mexico).

Arriving 12 days later was Major Raynal C Bolling, who had been commissioned by the Aircraft Production Board to purchase foreign aircraft for the American training facilities in Europe and to select the type of aircraft and motors to be produced by American factories. Bolling soon learned that British aeronautical factories were operating at near maximum capacity, but was pleased to find production potential in France as long as the US provided raw materials and additional machine tools.

Also, Bolling's Commission very quickly saw that the pace of technological development of pursuit aircraft far outstripped any American ability to compete in this arena. Consequently, Bolling let $65-million in contracts for France to provide 6600 aircraft and 8500 engines – 2000 SPAD XIIIs; 1500 other pursuit aircraft, type to be determined; 1500 Breguet 14 bombers; and 1500 Nieuport and 100 Caudron trainers. These would fill the immediate needs of the expanding air arm while indigenous production of combat types was organised.

While Dodd favoured the Salmson 2 A.2 for American production, Bolling selected the De Havilland 4, primarily because it could more readily accommodate the 400hp Liberty L-12. The DH-4, powered by a 375hp Rolls-Royce Eagle VIII, was judged 'particularly effective' in both reconnaissance and bombardment, but Rolls-Royce's production rate was limited, so replacing it with an American equivalent was an elegant solution.

Based on these agreements, on 11 July, Pershing approved an updated 'General Organisation Project' that planned to have 296 aeronautical squadrons in-theatre by 30 June 1919 – a far more reasonable goal now that the limiting factors were known.

Salmson 2 A.2 'No.4' of the 90th Aero Squadron in flight. Arriving at the front on 16 June 1918, the 90th Aero was one of the ten USAS squadrons eventually equipped with the Salmson observation aircraft. The sturdy Salmson was a favourite because its fuel tank was enclosed in a 3.5mm thick rubber shield, virtually eliminating the airmen's worst fear: in flight fire.

Milestones included having 60 squadrons in France by the end of June 1918, and 100 by the end of that year. In the event, knowing that the Russian armistice in mid-December 1917 freed huge quantities of German soldiers for renewed offences on the Western Front, the priority of trans-Atlantic shipping was naturally given to divisions of American 'doughboys' instead of aero squadrons.

To implement the aviation programme, on 27 November, now-Brigadier General Foulois, with a staff of 112 officers and 300 enlisted men, arrived at the American Expeditionary Force (AEF) General Headquarters (GHQ) at Chaumont. Mitchell was made the Air Commander, Zone of Advance (forward area) and began designing the tactical organisation and employment of the American air force and Bolling was named Foulois' Assistant Chief and Head of Supply. Unwilling to have these dynamic, aggressive and sometimes maverick pilots run his air service, Pershing eventually named his staid West Point classmate Brigadier General Mason M Patrick to be his Chief of the Air Service, AEF, with Foulois as his deputy. ➤

Initially the 1st Aero Squadron was just a Signal Corps communications unit. On 7 April 1916 two of the unit's JN-3s flew dispatches from Pershing's HQ to the US consul in Chihuahua City, Mexico. While squadron commander Capt Benjamin D Foulios went into town to deliver the dispatches, Lt Herbert A Dargue guarded their aircraft (#43). He was confronted by a stone-throwing mob of angry Mexicans that burned holes in the wing fabric with their cigarettes and attempted to slash fuselage fabric with knives. Dargue purposely kept the photographer busy posing him at various angles to keep the crowd away from the aeroplane until a detachment of Mexican soldiers arrived to keep them at bay.

TIMELINE OF US AIR SERVICE UNITS DECLARED OPERATIONAL IN FRANCE, 1917-1918

1917

6 April	US declares war on Germany
27 May	Major General John Pershing and the staff of the AEF departs USA for France
24 July	US Congress authorises $640-million to produce a force of 22,625 aircraft, planning on establishing 263 squadrons in France by 30 June 1918.
27 November	Brigadier General BD Foulois and his staff arrive in France to establish the US Air Service for the AEF.

1918

DATE	UNIT DESIGNATION	UNIT TYPE	AIRCRAFT	NOTES
18 February	103rd Aero Sqn	Pursuit	SPAD VII C.1	Former Esc SPA.124 'L'Escadrille Lafayette' Assigned to 3rd Pursuit Grp Re-equipped with SPAD XIII
9 March	95th Aero Sqn	Pursuit	Nieuport 28 C.1	Assigned to 1st Pursuit Grp Re-equipped with SPAD XIII
19 March	94th Aero Sqn	Pursuit	Nieuport 28 C.1	Assigned to 1st Pursuit Grp Re-equipped with SPAD XIII
5 April	1st Aero Sqn	Observation	Dorand AR.I A.2	Assigned to 1st Army Obs Grp Re-equipped with SAL2A2
9 May	12th Aero Sqn	Observation	Dorand AR.II A.2	Assigned to 1st Army Obs Grp Re-equipped with SAL2A2
30 May	88th Aero Sqn	Observation	Dorand AR.II A.2	Assigned to 1st Army Obs Grp Re-equipped with SAL2A2
2 June	27th Aero Sqn	Pursuit	Nieuport 28 C.1	Assigned to 1st Pursuit Grp Re-equipped with SPAD XIII
	147th Aero Sqn	Pursuit	Nieuport 28 C.1	Assigned to 1st Pursuit Grp Re-equipped with SPAD XIII
3 June	91st Aero Sqn	Observation	Dorand AR.II A.2	Assigned to 1st Army Obs Grp Re-equipped with SAL2A2
12 June	96th Aero Sqn	Bombardment	Breguet 14 B.2	Assigned to 1st Day Bomb Grp
16 June	90th Aero Sqn	Observation	Sopwith 1½ B.2, SPAD XI, Breguet 14 A.2	Assigned to IV Corps Obs Grp Re-equipped with SAL2A2
22 June	99th Aero Sqn	Observation	Sopwith 1½ B.2	Assigned to V Corps Obs Grp Re-equipped with SAL2A2
30 June	139th Aero Sqn	Pursuit	SPAD XIII C.1	Assigned to 2nd Pursuit Grp
1 July	148th Aero Sqn	Pursuit	Sopwith Camel	with RAF 65 Wing, based at Capelle airfield, near Dunkirk
	13th Aero Sqn	Pursuit	SPAD XIII C.1	Assigned to 2nd Pursuit Grp
15 July	17th Aero Sqn	Pursuit	Sopwith Camel	with RAF 65 Wing, based at Petite Synthe, near Dunkirk
	49th Aero Sqn	Pursuit	SPAD XIII C.1	Assigned to 2nd Pursuit Grp
8 August	135th Aero Sqn	Observation	US-made DH-4	Assigned to IV Corps Obs Grp
10 August	93rd Aero Sqn	Pursuit	SPAD XIII C.1	Assigned to 3rd Pursuit Grp
18 August	28th Aero Sqn	Pursuit	SPAD XIII C.1	Assigned to 3rd Pursuit Grp
	213th Aero Sqn	Pursuit	SPAD XIII C.1	Assigned to 3rd Pursuit Grp
21 August	22nd Aero Sqn	Pursuit	SPAD XIII C.1	Assigned to 2nd Pursuit Grp
12 September	8th Aero Sqn	Observation	US-made DH-4	Assigned to IV Corps Obs Grp
	24th Aero Sqn	Observation	Salmson 2 A.2	Assigned to 1st Army Obs Grp
	50th Aero Sqn	Observation	US-made DH-4	Assigned to I Corps Obs Grp
	104th Aero Sqn	Observation	Salmson 2 A.2	Assigned to V Corps Obs Grp
14 September	9th Aero Sqn	Night Observ'n	Breguet 14 A.2	Assigned to 1st Army Obs Grp
	11th Aero Sqn	Bombardment	US-made DH-4	Assigned to 1st Day Bomb Grp
	20th Aero Sqn	Bombardment	US-made DH-4	Assigned to 1st Day Bomb Grp
5 October	168th Aero Sqn	Observation	US-made DH-4	Assigned to IV Corps Obs Grp
18 October	166th Aero Sqn	Bombardment	US-made DH-4	Assigned to 1st Day Bomb Grp
	185th Aero Sqn	Night Pursuit	Sopwith Camel	Assigned to 1st Pursuit Grp
23 October	141st Aero Sqn	Pursuit	SPAD XIII C.1	Assigned to 4th Pursuit Grp
28 October	354th Aero Sqn	Observation	US-made DH-4	Assigned to VI Corps Obs Grp
	638th Aero Sqn	Pursuit	SPAD VII C.1	Assigned to 5th Pursuit Grp
31 October	258th Aero Sqn	Observation	Salmson 2 A.2	Attached to French VII Armee
	278th Aero Sqn	Observation	US-made DH-4	Assigned to 2nd Army Obs Grp
5 November	163rd Aero Sqn	Bombardment	US-made DH-4	Assigned to 2nd Day Bomb Grp
	186th Aero Sqn	Observation	Salmson 2 A.2	Assigned to 2nd Army Obs Grp
10 November	25th Aero Sqn	Pursuit	SE.5a	Assigned to 5th Pursuit Grp
	100th Aero Sqn	Bombardment	US-made DH-4	Assigned to 2nd Day Bomb Grp
	155th Aero Sqn	Bombardment	US-made DH-4	Assigned to 2nd Day Bomb Grp
11 November	41st Aero Sqn	Pursuit	SPAD VII C.1	Assigned to 5th Pursuit Grp
	85th Aero Sqn	Observation	US-made DH-4	Assigned to 2nd Army Obs Grp
	138th Aero Sqn	Pursuit	Sopwith Camel	Assigned to 5th Pursuit Grp

THE FRENCH CONNECTION

The first US combat unit was not American at all, but the French Escadrille SPA.124, the famous 'L'Escadrille Lafayette', now equipped with SPAD (Société Pour Aviation et ses Dérivés) VII C.1s. Some 38 Americans had been members of the popular wartime unit; of these nine had been killed, two wounded and retired, and another captured, while the escadrille was credited with 42 victories.

The survivors provided a wealth of combat experience to the blossoming American air service. Seven became commanders of new USAS pursuit squadrons, four more became flying instructors and one a test pilot, and two were assigned to headquarters (AEF/GHQ and Washington DC). The longest surviving member, Major William Thaw, became the

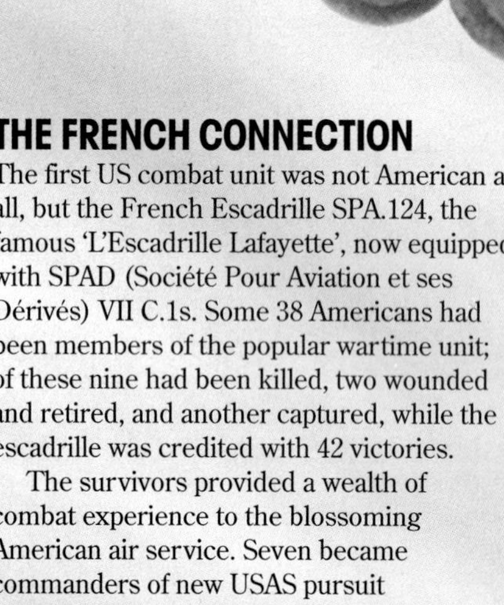

Close up of a Salmson 2 A.2, looking in such pristine condition that it is most likely a brand new example being held at the 1st Aero Depot awaiting assignment to a unit.

103rd Aero Squadron commander when it joined the USAS on 18 February 1918. Meanwhile four others – including 16-victory 'ace' Major G Raoul Lufbery – were transferred to the 94th Aero Squadron, helping the fabled 'Hat-in-the-Ring' squadron become the highest scoring USAS fighter unit with 67.5 victories total.

Additionally, there were another 162 American aviators in 93 different French units, loosely organised in what was known as the 'Lafayette Flying Corps' (LFC). While 38 of these were casualties in French service, 60 of the survivors transferred to the USAS (although 20 remained with their French escadrilles) and provided another treasure of operational experience, six becoming USAS squadron commanders.

Meanwhile, the first all-American unit to deploy to France was, fittingly, the 1st Aero Squadron. Still based at Columbus, NM, on 5 August 1917 it packed up and boarded a train, then the SS *Lapland*, arriving at the USAS's expansive 3rd Aviation Instruction Center at Issoudun, France, five weeks later.

Once the pilots were proficient on French machines, the 1st Aero moved to Amanty, where they were joined by observers graduating from the 1st Corps Aeronautical School and were issued 22 Dorand-designed Armeé Renault (AR) I A.2s. Sent to Ourches to gain combat experience operating over the front with the French XXXVII Corps, the 1st Aero Squadron flew its first mission on 7 April 1918.

The decrepit Dorands – called 'Antique Rattletraps' by the crews – were replaced with 18 SPAD XI two-seaters (that also proved unsatisfactory) while awaiting the arrival of the highly desired Salmson 2 A.2s. The following month, they were joined by the 12th and 88th Aero Squadrons, and in June by the 91st Aero – all initially equipped with AR II A.2s – forming the I Corps Observation Group (COG) under Major John Reynolds, a 1st Aero veteran of the Punitive campaign.

The neophyte fighter pilots of the 94th and 95th Aero Squadrons completed their initial training at Issouden on some of the 598 Nieuport 23/24/27s purchased as pursuit trainers, then moved to Villeneuve-les-Vertus in February/March 1918. The USAS did not yet have the priority to obtain their 'standard pursuit' aircraft – the SPAD XIII C.1 – so the French provided 36 Nieuport 28 C.1s, a type which they had rejected in favour of the SPAD. These two new fighter units established the 1st Pursuit Group at Toul, France, on 5 May 1918 with Major Bert M Atkinson, another 1st Aero member who flew in Mexico, as its first commander.

Two additional units, to 'flesh out' the 1st Pursuit Group, came by way of the 'British contribution' discussed later. These were the 27th and 147th Aero Squadrons. Trained on JN-4s in Canada and Texas, these formations arrived at Issoudun in March for 'top off' training on French types, before being issued Nieuport 28 C.1s and moving to Toul to join the premier American fighter group on 2 June. ➤

USAS ORDER OF BATTLE 14 SEPTEMBER 1918

AIR SERVICE, US FIRST ARMY – 1ST PURSUIT WING

2nd Pursuit Grp	13th Aero Sqn	Pursuit	SPAD XIII C.1	Gengoult Afl'd, Toul
	22nd Aero Sqn	Pursuit	SPAD XIII C.1	Gengoult Afl'd, Toul
	49th Aero Sqn	Pursuit	SPAD XIII C.1	Gengoult Afl'd, Toul
	139th Aero Sqn	Pursuit	SPAD XIII C.1	Gengoult Afl'd, Toul
3rd Pursuit Grp	28th Aero Sqn	Pursuit	SPAD XIII C.1	Vaucouleurs
	93rd Aero Sqn	Pursuit	SPAD XIII C.1	Vaucouleurs
	103rd Aero Sqn	Pursuit	SPAD XIII C.1	Vaucouleurs
	213th Aero Sqn	Pursuit	SPAD XIII C.1	Vaucouleurs
1st Day Bomb Grp	11th Aero Sqn	Bombardment	Dayton-Wright DH-4	Amanty
	20th Aero Sqn	Bombardment	Dayton-Wright DH-4	Amanty
	96th Aero Sqn	Bombardment	Breguet 14 B.2	Amanty

AIR SERVICE, US FIRST ARMY – CORPS OBSERVATION WING

I Corps Obs Grp	1st Aero Sqn	Observation	Salmson 2 A.2	Dommartin-les-Toul
	12th Aero Sqn	Observation	Salmson 2 A.2	Dommartin-les-Toul
	50th Aero Sqn	Observation	Dayton-Wright DH-4	Dommartin-les-Toul
III Corps Obs Grp	88th Aero Sqn	Observation	Salmson 2 A.2	Souilly
IV Corps Obs Grp	8th Aero Sqn	Observation	Dayton-Wright DH-4	Ourches
	90th Aero Sqn	Observation	Salmson 2 A.2	Ourches
	135th Aero Sqn	Observation	Dayton-Wright DH-4	Ourches
V Corps Obs Grp	99th Aero Sqn	Observation	Salmson 2 A.2	Souilly
	104th Aero Sqn	Observation	Salmson 2 A.2	Souilly

AIR SERVICE, US FIRST ARMY – ADDITIONAL UNITS

1st Pursuit Grp	27th Aero Sqn	Pursuit	SPAD XIII C.1	Eriza-la-Petite
	94th Aero Sqn	Pursuit	SPAD XIII C.1	Eriza-la-Petite
	95th Aero Sqn	Pursuit	SPAD XIII C.1	Eriza-la-Petite
	147th Aero Sqn	Pursuit	SPAD XIII C.1	Eriza-la-Petite
1st Army Obs Grp	9th Aero Sqn	Night Obs	Breguet 14 A.2	Amanty
	24th Aero Sqn	Observation	Salmson 2 A.2	Gondreville
	91st Aero Sqn	Observation	Salmson 2 A.2	Gondreville

OTHER ADDITIONAL UNITS – ATTACHED TO THE RAF

	17th Aero Sqn	Pursuit	Sopwith F.1 Camel	Petite Synthe and
	148th Aero Sqn	Pursuit	Sopwith F.1 Camel	Capelle, Dunkirk
	183rd Flt Detachment*	Observation	Sopwith 1½ Strutter	Luxeuil-les-Bains

(A Flight of 258th Aero Sqn, formed 10 Sep 1918, but not yet operational)

Left: Two of the 2915 JN-4Ds (these with earlier model wings) practising formation flight in the Texas skies. While American military aviation officials planned and prepared for the enormous expansion of the air arm to meet the demands of going to war with Germany, the Signal Corps Aviation Section 'ramped up' the pilot training programme to provide many of the aviators needed by the new squadrons.

Col Billy Mitchell was very much a hands-on, on-scene air commander. Using one of the six SPAD XVI A.2s (most were sent to the USA for evaluation), he toured the front from Switzerland to the Channel, with repeated sorties to closely observe the American sector, from Soissons to Nancy, and he frequently visited each of his group and squadron commanders. Here his SPAD is seen at a Salmson observation unit's base.

PREPARING FOR THE OFFENSIVE

Bombardment featured prominently in the American aviator's vision of air power, even from the earliest days. During the 'Punitive Expedition', the young airmen of the 1st Aero had a local Mexican railroad shop fabricate 400 three-inch bombs while waiting for the Ordnance arsenal to make 240 more (plus 25 practice bombs). Eschewing 'dropping bombs by hand', Lts Dodd and Scott invented a 'bomb carrier and release' device and designed a functional bombsight for their R-2s.

The first real opportunity for these visions to take flight was when the USAS acquired the small Clermont-Ferrand bombing school – near the Michelin munitions factory – and 10 well-used Breguet 14 B.2 bombers. This, the 7th Aviation Instruction Center, struggled to provide a bombardment training programme, graduating only one quarter of that planned.

The 96th Aero Squadron arrived at Clermont-Ferrand in mid-November 1917, and spent six months learning the altogether new trade of bombardment. Moving to Amanty in May with their 10 Breguets, the 96th was the sole USAS bombing squadron until mid-September when the first DH-4 equipped units arrived.

Meanwhile, in June, the Nieuports of the 1st Pursuit Group were finally beginning to be replaced with the long-awaited SPADs, 208 survivors being passed to the pursuit training school at Issoudun. Fortunately, enough SPADs were arriving to outfit another four squadrons – the 13th, 22nd and 139th, as well as the famed 103rd – and, on 30 June, these formed the 2nd Pursuit Group under Major Davenport Johnson, another 1st Aero/Punitive Expedition veteran. One

America's first bombing unit, the 96th Aero Squadron, arrived at the front with ten Breguet 14 B.2s. This aircraft – #4012 – along with five others, was lost on a disastrous raid on 10 July 1918 when they became disoriented above an undercast and landed in German territory, all being taken prisoner. Eleven new Breguets were obtained from the factory and inexperienced crews were drawn from three training centres, but the unit had to learn their trade all over again.

month later, the 3rd Pursuit Group was formed, headed by Major William Thaw. Given the 28th, 49th, 93rd and 213th squadrons, Thaw traded the 49th to Johnson so his 103rd Aero could be part of his group.

Similarly, in late July, sufficient Salmson 2 A.2s became available to begin equipping the USAS observation units. As more of these arrived at the front, each US Army Corps was provided a group. As an interim, the 88th Aero was issued 18 Sopwith 1½ Strutters and transferred to the new III COG. Additionally, the 90th Aero arrived with another 18 Sopwiths to form the IV COG and the similarly equipped 99th established the V COG.

Crated in Dayton, Ohio, and shipped across the Atlantic, the first American-built

DH-4 arrived at the large USAS assembly plant at Romorantin on 8 May 1918. The first 'Liberty' DH-4 unit was the 135th Aero Squadron, called the 'All American Squadron' because it was the first to have American crews flying US-built aircraft. On 7 August, 15 DH-4s roared off on the unit's first operational mission, taking off with great fanfare and press coverage, into poor weather.

As General Mitchell's plans for supporting Pershing's St Mihiel offensive took shape, five additional observation units were hurried to the front: two with DH-4s, two with Salmsons and one (night observation) with Breguet 14 A.2s. Since the USAS was receiving both Salmsons and DH-4s, aircraft deliveries now outpaced aircrew training resulting in many observation units showing up with only 12 crews.

On 10 September, the 1st Day Bombardment Group was established with the 96th Aero Squadron being hastily joined by the 11th and 20th squadrons, which arrived at Amanty with only 24 aeroplanes and crews between them. Delays in obtaining bomb racks and ordnance meant they were not operational for another four days.

THE BRITISH CONTRIBUTION

While British aircraft production provided only modest numbers of aircraft to the USAS – 258 aeroplanes versus 4881 purchased from the French – the RFC/RAF provided several vital training opportunities, nearly doubling the number of fighter squadrons the USAS was able to field in 1918.

In an exchange programme with the RFC, 300 American aviation cadets and 800 'other ranks' went to Camp Borden, near Toronto, Canada, for training on 680 Curtiss JN-4Ds built by Canadian Aero. In exchange, each winter the RFC used two airfields at Taliaferro, Texas. Additionally, another 204 cadets originally detailed to be trained at Foggia, Italy, were given flight training at Oxford.

Graduates from these two programmes formed seven fighter squadrons – five of

Lieutenant Arthur J Coyle, commander of the 1st Aero Squadron, and his observer-gunner Arthur Beaverbrook, with their Salmson 2 A.2 'Gertrude A'. The twin Lewis machine guns were French-made 7.7mm calibre and the small 'Maltese crosses' are patches over holes caused by German bullets and shrapnel. After the St Mihiel and Meuse-Argonne offensives Coyle was promoted to become commander of the I COG on 16 October 1918.

which went directly to the USAS pursuit groups – and a flight of bombers. Two fighter squadrons – the '17th American' and '148th American' (predominantly Toronto graduates) were issued Sopwith Camels and joined the RAF's 65 Wing at Dunkirk, flying with much success – 123 victories for 33 losses – against the Germans over Flanders.

In late October, these were transferred to the USAS command and, with the 25th Aero (mostly Oxford graduates issued 24 SE.5as) and 141st (a former base squadron near Dover) with SPAD XIIIs, formed the 4th Pursuit Group under Major Charles J Biddle, an experienced former LFC member.

Finally, in addition to the 231 pilots trained in the Toronto and Oxford programmes (another 41 had been killed in training and 77 elected to join RAF squadrons), another 65 Americans who were members of RFC/RAF units transferred to the USAS. Like their LFC counterparts, these too provided a wealth of operational experience to the new units being formed monthly on the American front.

THE GREAT AMERICAN AIR OFFENSIVE

After the 'Great War' was won, before Congress, in his 1926 memoirs and in Winged Defense, General Billy Mitchell boasted 'we had the greatest air force ever employed under one command' – some 1476 warplanes. Of these over half – approximately 711 French, 84 British (Independent Air Force bombers) and 30 Italian (Caproni bombers attached to the French Division Aerienne) – were in Allied units attached to Mitchell's command – Air Service, First US Army – for the campaign.

The ground offensive began on 12 September with most of General Pershing's 19 American divisions battering the 'St Mihiel salient' – a bulge in the front pointed towards Paris resulting from the German spring offensives. The salient was held by General der Artillerie Max von Gallwitz's 10-division strong Armee Gruppe C.

Initially, the planned bombing missions were stymied by bad weather but beginning on the 14th, the USAS took command of the air over the salient and harried the retreating Germans. Bombing missions interdicted the German railway network and strafing attacks by pursuit units harassed enemy troop columns.

Nevertheless, the Germans fell back in good order, straightening and tightening their defensive lines, and when the fighting diminished, Mitchell moved his air forces 40 miles north to support Pershing's next phase – the Meuse Argonne Offensive – set to begin on 26 September. This would be the last great battle of the 'Great War' and the Armistice would follow in November, finally ending the 'War to end all wars'.

While the American build-up of air power in World War One failed to realise its ambitious goals or its advocates' expectations, it presaged the massive expansion – and global reach – of the US Army Air Forces in World War Two, only 25 years hence. ∎

USAS AIRCRAFT IN EUROPE

DATE REC'D	AIRCRAFT	NUMBER	FROM	NOTES AND REMARKS
PURSUIT AIRCRAFT				
Dec 1917	SPAD VII C.1	170	France	Includes Esc SPA.124 aircraft
Unk'n 1918	SPAD VII C.1	19	Britain	Sent to USA for familiarisation
Mar 1918	Nieuport 28 C.1	297	France	Replaced by SPAD XIII
Mar 1918	SPAD XIII C.1	893	France	Equipped 13 USAS Sqns
Jun 1918	Sopwith F.1 Camel	143	Britain	Equipped 4 USAS Sqns
Jul 1918	SPAD XII Ca.1	1	France	Cannon-equipped; service evaluation at front then to USA
Oct 1918	RAF SE.5a	38	Britain	Equipped 1 USAS Sqn
Oct 1918	Packard LUSAC-11	2	USA	Experimental Two-Seat Pursuit
Oct 1918	Sopwith Dolphin	5	Britain	Four to USA for evaluation
BOMBARDMENT AIRCRAFT				
Feb 1918	Sopwith 1½ B.2	130	France	Obsolete; replaced by Bre14/DH-4
Mar 1918	Breguet 14 B.2	47	France	Equipped 1 USAS Sqn
Mar 1918	Farman 50 Bn.2	2	France	Experimental Night Bomber
May 1918	Dayton Wright DH-4	1,440	USA	Equipped 13 USAS Sqns
OBSERVATION AIRCRAFT				
Feb 1918	SPAD XI A.2	35	France	Unsuitable; replaced by SAL2A2
Apr 1918	Salmson 2 A.2	705	France	Equipped 10 USAS Sqns
Jun 1918	Breguet 14 A.2	229	France	Equipped one USAS Sqn
Jul 1918	Acft Mfg Co DH.9A	2	Britain	Sent to USA for evaluation
Aug 1918	RAF FE.2b	30	Britain	Night Observation Aircraft
Aug 1918	SPAD XVI A.2	6	France	Most to USA for evaluation
Oct 1918	Caudron R.11 A.3	2	France	Experimental Artillery Observation
TRAINING AIRCRAFT				
Sep 1917	Nieuport 80/81/82E.1	564	France	Primary Trainers
Sep 1917	Nieuport 17 C.1	75	France	Pursuit Trainers; plus one Nieu 17bis C.1 sent to USA for evaluation
Sep 1917	Nieuport 21 C.1	198	France	Pursuit Trainers
Oct 1917	Morane 21.R2	138	France	"Rouleur" Ground Trainer
Nov 1917	Nieuport 24 C.1	121	France	Pursuit Trainers
Nov 1917	Nieuport 24bis C.1	140	France	Pursuit Trainers
Nov 1917	Nieuport 28 C.1	297	France	Pursuit Trainers
Nov 1917	Caudron G.3/4 A.2	192	France	Twin Engine Bomber Trainers
Dec 1917	Dorand AR. I A.2	22	France	Observation Trainer
Jan 1918	Breguet 14 E.2	100	France	Advanced Trainers
Jan 1918	Nieuport 23 C.1	50	France	Pursuit Trainers
Feb 1918	Farman 40 A.2	30	France	Photo Trainers; operated in UK
Feb 1918	Dorand A.R. II A.2	120	France	Observation Trainers
Feb 1918	Sopwith 1½ A.2	384	France	Observation Trainers
Feb 1918	SIA (FIAT) 7B-1	19	Italy	Observation Trainers
Apr 1918	Voisin 8/10 Bn.2	10	France	Night Bombardment Trainers
Jun 1918	Morane 30 C.1	51	France	Pursuit Trainers
Jul 1918	Avro 504K	52	Britain	Advanced Trainers
Aug 1918	RAF BE.2e	12	Britain	Primary Trainers

Note: Numbers acquired include those accepted after the Armistice.
Source: US Army Aircraft (Heavier-than-Air) 1908-1946, James C Fahey, editor (Ships and Aircraft: NY, 1946).

Left: A Dayton-Wright DH-4 of the 8th Aero Squadron at the USAS 1st Air Depot, Colombey-les-Belles, after the Armistice. Some 628 DH-4s saw service at the front, equipping 13 American bombing and observation squadrons. USAS DH-4s were coated with an aluminiumised dope oversprayed with dark green on the fuselage and wing upper surfaces.

Britain's first aerial defenders

Martyn Chorlton takes a brief look at the Royal Flying Corps Home Defence squadrons and their fight against the Zeppelin.

Up to late 1915, Great Britain had no official defensive infrastructure with regard to an attack from the air. Ever since the first Zeppelin attack over Norfolk on the night of 19/20 January 1915, it was clear that something needed to be done to combat this aerial menace. The problem was not confined to the Zeppelins either – enemy aircraft had been attacking the south-east of England since 24 December 1914 when a single bomb was dropped on Dover.

As the war progressed the quality and amount of aircraft would increase and their attacks would cause considerably more casualties and damage than the airship did. However, because of the distance it could travel, the Zeppelin was feared much more than any bomber so the formation of the Home Defence (HD) squadrons was seen as a morale exercise to bolster the civilian population.

The main weapon of choice for the fledgling HD squadrons was the Royal Aircraft Factory BE.2c which, by early 1916, was relegated to second line duties and was effectively obsolete. While serving over the trenches in France, the aircraft was nicknamed 'Fokker Fodder' owing to its poor performance. Its 90hp RAF engine propelled the BE.2c along at just 72mph and the aircraft's maximum ceiling was 10,000ft, which it took 45 minutes to reach. This ceiling, even for the early marks of Zeppelin, was easily surpassed once ballast was released to escape the attacker and this applied to almost all other Allied aircraft available at the time. In its favour was the fact

that it was easy to fly and very stable, making it a good gun platform which was essential, especially while operating at night.

The BE.2c went on to serve with 12 HD squadrons and the first success came on 31 March 1916 when Lt A de Brandon of 19 (Reserve) Squadron from Hainault Farm attacked L15 east of Brentwood. The airship had already been damaged by shrapnel from anti-aircraft guns at Purfleet before Brandon began his attack. Several explosive darts were dropped without apparent effect followed by an unsuccessful attempt to drop an incendiary bomb before Brandon lost sight of the airship. The combined ground and air attack on L15 eventually took effect as the airship broke its back while off the Kent coast and plunged into the sea from 2000ft.

IN FULL PUBLIC VIEW

Many months passed before the first sole victory came – but importantly it took place in full public view and on British soil. On the night of 2/3 September 1916, Lt WL Robinson took off from Suttons Farm in his 39 (HD) Squadron BE.2c 2092. After patrolling at 10,000ft since taking off at 23:05hrs, Robinson spotted a Zeppelin over north-east London which was under heavy but inaccurate ground fire. Having climbed to nearly 13,000ft, Robinson pushed the nose of the BE.2c down towards the Zeppelin and, at a range of 800ft, emptied a drum of Brock and Pomeroy bullets plus tracer into the airship. This seemed to

have no effect, but after firing a second drum at just 500ft a fire quickly broke out and within seconds the rear of the airship was engulfed in flames. The Schütte-Lanz SL11, under the command of Cdr W Schramm, nosed earthwards, eventually crashing at Cuffley with the loss of all on board. Witnessed by hundreds of thousands of people, the event was just what was needed to show that the HD squadrons were an effective defence.

The publicity and adulation that Robinson received was followed with the award of the ultimate accolade, the Victoria Cross. The award was not seen as justified by the aircrew fighting over the Western Front. They had little respect for HD operations and this remained the case for the rest of World War One. As if to emphasise the point, newly promoted Capt Robinson was posted as a Flight Commander with 48 Squadron only to get shot down by Richthofen's 'Flying Circus' on his first operation.

The founding HD Squadrons were all equipped with the much maligned RAF BE.2c.

As new aircraft became available, priority, understandably, was always given to those units operating in France and even training units gained preference over the HD squadrons. By the end of 1916, the RAF BE.12 was beginning to be introduced. Its main advantages over the BE.2c were a larger fuel capacity and a more powerful 150hp RAF 4 engine. It still only had a service ceiling of 12,500ft and this would prove useless against enemy bombers as by mid-1917, the German Gotha V was capable of reaching over 21,000ft. The RAF FE.2 which was being removed from front line service also started to equip several HD squadrons by the end of 1916, but this was also lacking a good service ceiling.

MORE EFFECTIVE FORCE

While the workload of the HD squadrons was steadily declining, 14 squadrons were still in existence when the RAF was formed on 1 April 1918. It was only by this late stage in World War One that the HD squadrons were equipped with more capable aircraft. Although 33, 37, and 75 Squadrons were still operating the FE.2 and BE.12, the remainder could now boast the capable F.2b, 1½ Strutter, Camel, 504NF and the SE.5a. Priority was still given to front line squadrons and training units, but with so many aircraft now available, thanks to high production, better equipment was available for all.

By the time the Armistice arrived, there were still 13 HD squadrons operating across the country, more than half of them now equipped with the Sopwith Camel. The majority of these were disbanded in 1919 along with their landing grounds which were little more than 90-acre grass squares with a tent or two along the edge.

The effectiveness of the HD squadrons against the Zeppelin during World War One is open to debate. However, the fact that the RFC was seen to be doing something about the airship attacks was actually more valuable in raising civilian morale than it was in shooting down Zeppelins. Of the 53 occasions when Zeppelins, individually or in groups, operated over Britain, 5751 bombs were dropped, killing 556 people and injuring a further 1358. Of the 115 Zeppelins built, seven were brought down or shared by HD squadrons out of the 77 lost by the Germans during World War One. ■

Above: Hainault Farm located in north-east London was a perfect location for accommodating HD squadrons in defence of the capital. It was a brief home for 39, 151 and 153 Squadrons, but it was 44 (HD) Squadron which served there the longest firstly with the 1½ Strutter followed by the Camel.

Exceptionally rare shot of an RAF FE.2b serving with 51 (HD) Squadron at Tydd St Mary, Lincolnshire, in 1917.

An example of a Sopwith Camel night-fighter of 112 Squadron, which served at Throwley, Kent, during the later stages of World War One. **All via Time Line Images**

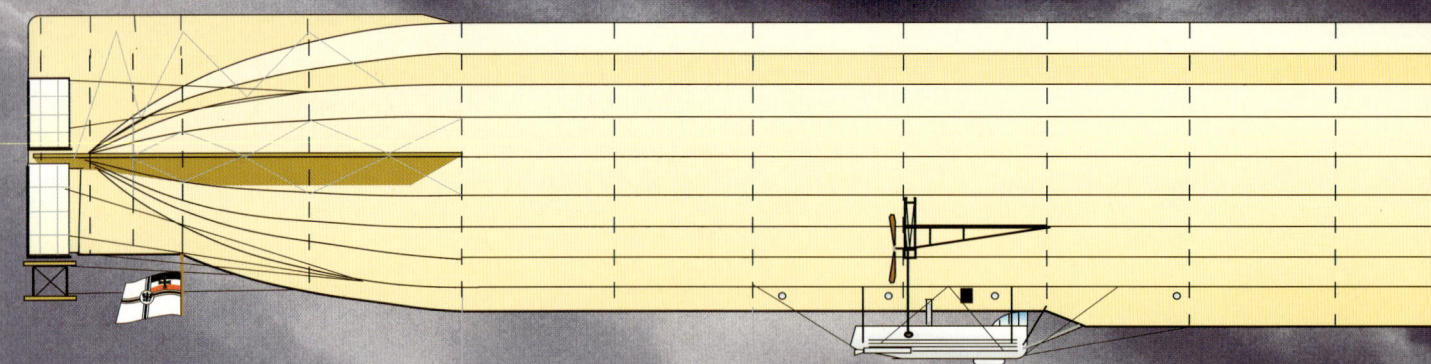

First Zeppelin raid on the British Isles

DG Ridley-Kitts MBE details how the first aerial bombardment on Britain by Zeppelins took place in error on towns along the North Norfolk coast.

Before the 'Great War' there was a widely held belief among the British public that in the event of a conflict with Germany, within hours of a declaration of war fleets of giant Zeppelin airships would launch bombing attacks on our major cities.

heightened on 26 August when two German Army Zeppelins attacked Antwerp at night, causing widespread damage, killing 12 persons and bombing a hospital – an act that outraged British and international public opinion alike.

Count Zeppelin's first airship had flown

Alternative targets including Dover, Portsmouth, Manchester, and the port facilities on the Humber were also suggested for consideration in this plan. These areas were considered to be legitimate military targets, being 'Defended places' as defined in the Hague Convention of 1899 that governed

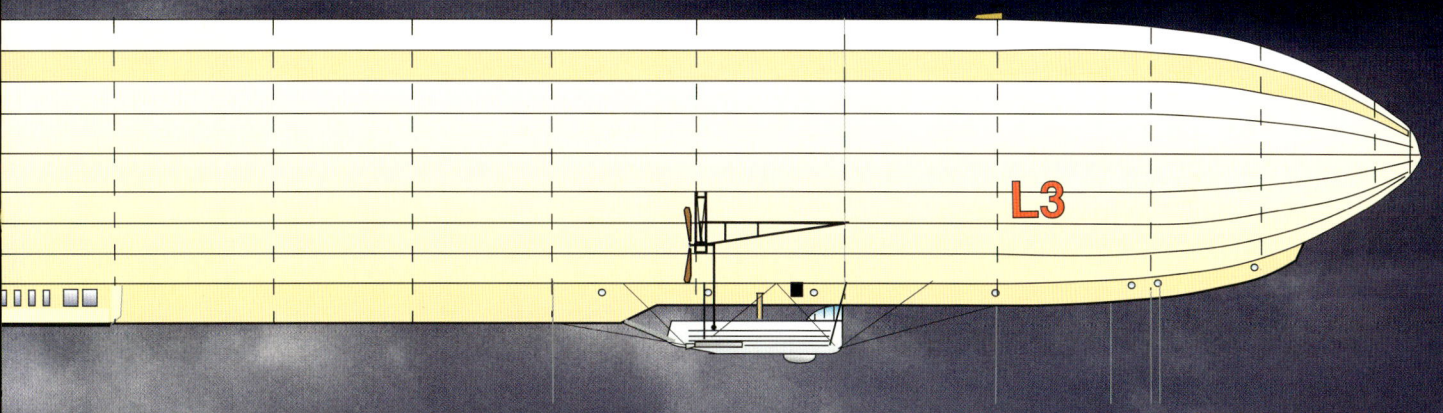

blast of fire from the German battlecruisers *Seydlitz*, *Von der Tann*, *Moltke*, with the armoured cruiser, *Blucher*, and three accompanying light cruisers. Against these overwhelming odds, *Halcyon* pluckily returned fire with her two 4.5-inch guns before seeking shelter in a smoke-screen laid by the destroyer *Lively* that allowed the gunboat to turn away with minor damage and escape to the south-west. The German squadron standing off Great Yarmouth then proceeded to bombard the town for 30 minutes, causing extensive damage from their 11-inch high explosive shells before retiring unmolested to their base at Wilhelmshaven.

In December, the German battle-cruisers again dashed across the North Sea to bombard Hartlepool, Whitby and Lowestoft in a daring attack. This once more took the defences by surprise.

The shock effect of these raids was to raise the fear of an imminent full-scale landing on the East Coast. Indeed, it required the Army to permanently station two divisions of troops in the eastern counties purely to oppose the threat. Also, early in 1915, a squadron of 'Pre-Dreadnoughts' were anchored at Sheerness to protect the Southern approaches, and hopefully to counter any further incursions by the German Fleet.

AIR RAIDS

An initial attempt to raid the British Isles by air was made on 13 January 1915 by the naval airships L5 and L6 (from Nordholz), together with L3 and L4 (from Fühlsbuttel near Hamburg). The airships flew westward into deteriorating weather conditions until at 3:00pm, flying in heavy rain over the Friesian Islands, the air fleet was ordered to abandon the undertaking and return to base.

Six days later, on 19 January, a second attempt was made with the L3 (Kapitanleutnant Fritz) and L4 (Kapitanleutnant von Platen Halemund) taking off from Fühlsbuttel at 10:50am, while L6, with Oberleutnant von Buttlar Brandenfels in command, departed Nordholz at 9:38am. Korvettenkapitan Strasser, the charismatic Leader of Naval Airship Service, who was to earn the unswerving loyalty of his crews by his example and courage, and who developed the Zeppelin airship into a formidable weapon of war in the four-year struggle, was also aboard the L6, anxious to take part in this epoch making raid.

The instructions from the Commander in Chief of the High Seas Fleet ordering the raid included the instruction 'Distant scouting mission to the west only H.V.B. to be carried'. HVB, or 'Handelsschiffsverkersbuch', was the German merchant service signal code book. This had already been compromised and passed on to the British when a copy had been captured by the Russians after sinking a German cruiser in the Baltic. British Intelligence soon realised that any reference ➤

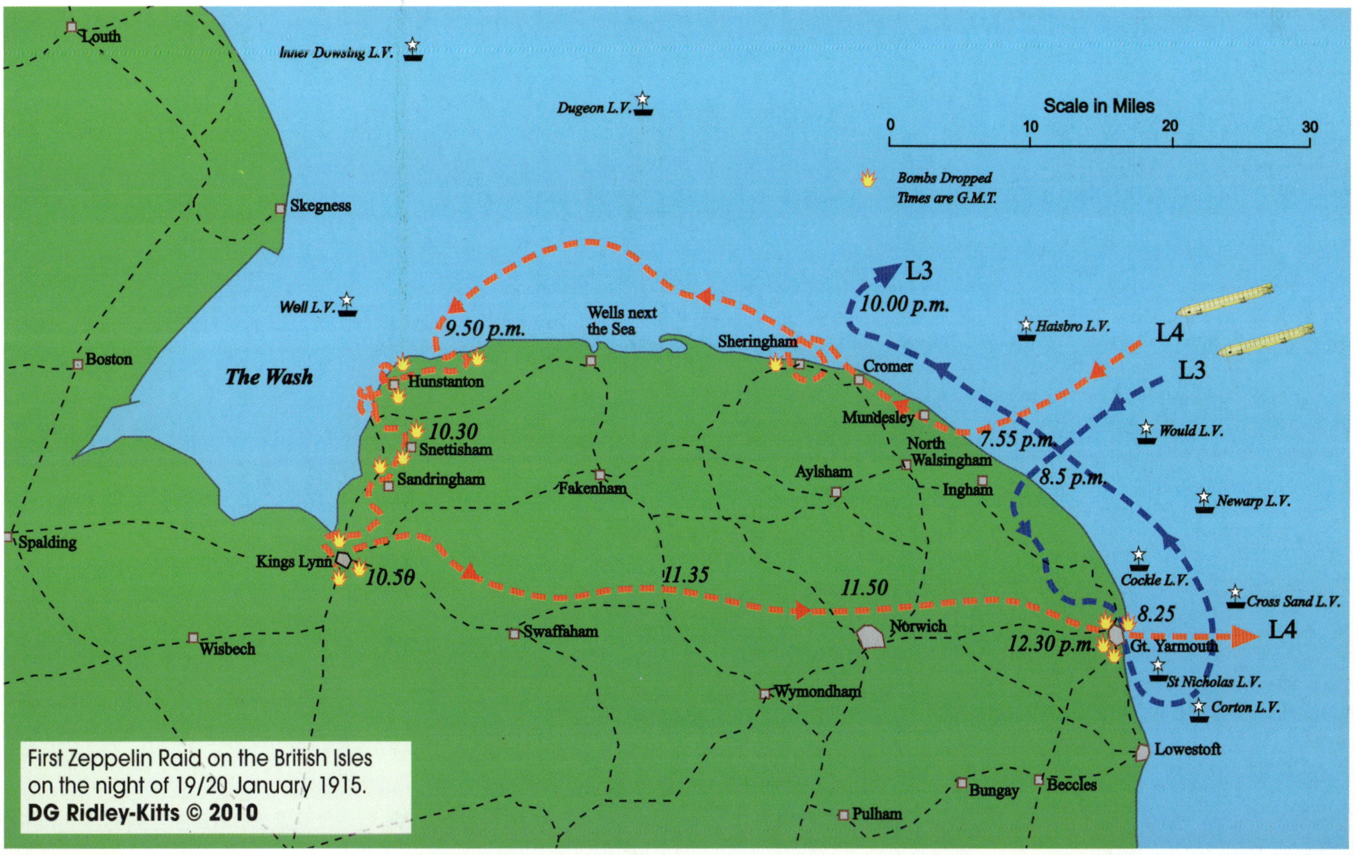

First Zeppelin Raid on the British Isles on the night of 19/20 January 1915.
DG Ridley-Kitts © 2010

in a wireless message from an airship indicating 'only H.V.B. on board' indicated that its purpose was to attempt a raid on the British Isles.

With air temperature at take-off two degrees below freezing, the airships were able to carry a maximum bomb load of high explosive and incendiaries. L3 and L4 carried up to 1100lb of bombs each, while the L6, starting from its base nearer the English coast, had a heavier load of 1450lb.

The L3 represented the latest development in airship design and was 518ft in length, with a diameter of 48ft and a capacity of 794,500 cubic feet of hydrogen gas. This gave a gross lift of 23 tons, of which 9.2 tons was available for useful load. Useful load consisted of fuel, water ballast, munitions and crew, while three Maybach CX engines of 200hp were capable of driving the craft through the air at a top speed of 47mph with a theoretical range of 1000 miles.

Strasser, flying aboard the L6, detailed her commander to raid "England south and the Thames," while L3 and L4 were ordered to attack the "Midlands and the Humber area." The L6, taking the more southerly route, encountered severe icing and rain and after four hours flying, when she was north-east of the Dutch island of Terschelling, 100 miles short of the English coast, the crankshaft of her port rear engine broke. This forced the airship to return to base, much to Strasser's chagrin.

Meanwhile, the L3 and L4 headed west in clear icy weather on a bearing of 287° magnetic which should have brought them to the mouth of the Humber. But unknown to their commanders, the wind had gone about and a north-easterly had set them to the southward over the sea. In the open gondolas in sub-zero temperatures, the crews struggled to keep the motors running and prevent the radiator water from freezing, while both ships

Later in the war, Home Defence squadrons were established to counter the threat of aerial attacks on Britain, and this photo shows the remains of Zeppelin L32 which was shot down in flames on 24 September 1916 by Lt F Sowrey of 39 Squadron which was based at Suttons Farm. This was the second of three Zeppelin victories by the pilots of 39 Squadron and all were achieved flying the BE.2c. **Via Time Line Images**

had to drop nearly a third of their water ballast just to maintain altitude and counter the build-up of ice on their envelopes.

At 6:40pm on the Norfolk coast at Ingham, a village a mile and a half from the sea, a man walking down a hill in the dark sighted "two bright stars low down out to sea apparently 100 feet apart" and they were moving slowly towards him. Unknown to him, he had sighted the navigation lights of the L3 and L4 as they came in over the *Ower Bank* light vessel.

At 8:05pm, the L3 crossed the Norfolk coast near Ingham, while the L4 made landfall some 10 minutes earlier in the vicinity of Mundesley. On board the L3, Kapitanleutnant Fritz immediately realised that his airship had been driven far south from his intended target, and after dropping parachute flares to orient himself and recognising Happisburgh and the *Winterton* light vessel, he changed course to head down the coast towards Great Yarmouth, rising to an attack altitude of 5000ft.

FIRST CASUALTIES

Bearing down on the town, the L3 began her bomb run at 8.20pm. Fritz claimed to have been fired on by a battery and responded by dropping nine high-explosive bombs and seven incendiaries, which caused £7000 worth of damage to buildings over a wide area, killing and wounding a dozen or so residents. Two of the bombs fell in the St Peter Plain area and killed a 72-year-old woman, Martha Taylor, who was returning home from shopping, and a 53-year-old man, Sam Smith, a shoemaker who had been working in his shop. They were the first

"...the thunderous roar of the motors added to the sense of panic and the helplessness felt by many as the aerial visitants cruised unmolested across the darkened countryside on that icy cold night."

civilians ever killed by aerial bombardment in Great Britain.

After crossing the town, Fritz turned the L3 out to sea, passing over the *Corton* light vessel and then steering up the coast between the *Cockle* and *Newarp* light vessels until he came abeam of Cromer at 10:00pm. Here, Fritz stood about to the north-east returning across the North Sea bringing the L3 safely back to her base after a flight of 23 hours.

On the ground, as the raid progressed, confusion reigned. Even the number of raiders was in doubt; coastguards at Cromer reported seeing six airships, while some members of the public said the attackers were aeroplanes. One woman who had seen the raider overhead later said it was "the biggest sausage I have ever seen," while another described it as "a church steeple travelling sideways." Additionally, many people commented on the thunderous roar of the motors that added to the sense of panic and the helplessness felt by many as the aerial visitants cruised unmolested across the darkened countryside on that icy cold night.

Meanwhile, Kapitanleutnant von Platten-Hallermund aboard the L4 initially believed he had reached the southern shore of the Humber in accordance with his orders, and he followed the coast northward passing over Cromer. It lay in darkness and was undetected by the airship crew. Continuing along the coast, the airship circled over Sheringham where a salvo of bombs and incendiaries were released. These caused some slight damage before L4 turned out to sea, presumably in the belief that she would there find the north bank of the Humber

AIRSHIP HERITAGE TRUST

The Airship Heritage Trust is a registered charity dedicated to the preservation of Britain's airship history. It was established at RAF Cardington next to the historic airship sheds in 1985 by relatives and friends of those involved in the 1921-1936 airship programme.

Membership is open to anyone with an interest in lighter than air travel, and members receive the AHT's in-house magazine *Dirigible* three times a year. For more information, contact the AHT membership secretary: Brian Harrison, 9 Quaggy Walk, Blackheath, London SE3 9EL. Alternatively, go online at: www.airshipsonline.com

IT IS FAR BETTER TO FACE THE BULLETS THAN TO BE KILLED AT HOME BY A BOMB

JOIN THE ARMY AT ONCE & HELP TO STOP AN AIR RAID

GOD SAVE THE KING

which would lead her to the city of Hull. However, realising that his navigation must be in error, Von Platten-Hallermund again turned south, this time crossing the Norfolk coast at 9:50pm near Hunstanton. Bringing the airship down to 800ft, he dropped flares and then, at 10:15pm, aimed two bombs at the Hunstanton wireless station but both missed.

After circling the town uncertainly for 15 minutes, the L4 passed over the village of Heacham where two more bombs were dropped, then she flew on to Snettisham where her eighth bomb badly damaged the church. Continuing southwards, the L4's next bombs fell on the Sandringham estate, which caused Queen Mary, who was in London at the time with the King, to be convinced that the royal couple were the objective of the raid, rather than a chance of fate. At 10:50pm, attracted by the lights of King's Lynn to the south-west, the L4 bore down at speed on the city while the by-now-alerted authorities frantically attempted to impose a blackout.

Here, Von Platten-Hallermund, after claiming to have been illuminated by searchlights and also to have been fired upon, released seven 110lb high-explosive and six incendiary bombs on the streets below in retaliation. His fourth bomb fell in the narrow Bentinick Street and exploded with great violence, causing extensive damage to houses, trapping and injuring many in the rubble and killing a 14-year-old boy.

A further tragedy occurred a few streets away when a 26-year-old widow, Alice Gazley, whose husband had been killed in December in the fighting in France, died after being struck in the street by shrapnel from a bomb while she was running for shelter. Leaving a total of two dead and 13 injured and much material damaged, the L4 turned eastwards, overflying Norwich at 11:50pm – being fully blacked out it did not attract the Zeppelin's attention.

Finally, at 12:30am, L4 stood out to sea above Great Yarmouth, from where her commander reported by wireless that he had "successfully attacked several fortified places between the Tyne and the Humber." He then set course for L4's home base at Fuhlsbüttel, Hamburg, where the airship landed within five minutes of the L3. The returning crews were hailed as heroes and received decorations for their bravery in their own country, while they were condemned as murderers and 'aerial pirates' in Britain.

In the wake of the raid, assertions were made that the Zeppelins had been guided to their targets by a network of spies signalling out to sea, and many innocent motorists driving at night through the Eastern Counties were stopped and questioned over the coming months as possible enemy agents. These stories were so widespread that the Member of Parliament for King's Lynn, Holcombe Ingleby, was so convinced

that such activities were true that he asked questions in the House, and even wrote a book to expose the 'Spy scandal'.

Although the material damage and casualties incurred were minimal compared to later events, the significance of the raid was that in spite of being protected by the world's most powerful navy, aerial warfare now exposed the civilian population of our islands to new dangers that the authorities seemed powerless to counter.

As a footnote, in a raid on 17 February 1915, the L3 and the L4 at Fuhlsbüttel (again under the command of Fritz and Von Platten-Hallermund) were detailed at 4:00am to attack British warships reported off the Skagerrak. Both Zeppelins reached the search area successfully but they did not sight the reported warships and turned for home against a rising southerly wind.

Fighting against the increasing force of the wind, the L3 suffered engine failure off the Danish island of Lyngvig. Still struggling south, at 5:45pm, a second engine broke down so that Fritz had no option but to put

the L3 down on the Danish island of Fanoe, near Esbjerg. With all the 16-man crew safe, Fritz then set fire to the ship and his secret papers before surrendering to Danish troops, and internment.

Aboard the L4, Von Platten-Hallermund was also in trouble with two engine failures over 200 miles from his base, and he was also obliged to make a forced landing on the Danish coast, this time at Blaavands Huk. In fierce winds, the airship crashed into the raging surf, with the crew leaping for their lives. This caused the lightened craft to whirl away on the storm, carrying four of their companions to a lonely death far out in the North Sea. Von Platten-Hallermund and the bedraggled, exhausted survivors then gratefully allowed the Danish police to lead them also into internment; their part in the air war was over. ∎

This article has been reprinted with kind permission from The Airship Heritage Trust journal, Dirigible. With thanks to Dr Giles Camplin, DG Ridley-Kitts MBE and John Cutler.

Battle for the Suez Canal

Desmond Seward describes some of the actions of 14 Squadron RFC in the Sinai Desert in the period 1915 to 1916.

In 1915, the troops of the Entente occasionally left their trenches on the Western Front to fight the Germans, at hideous cost for some small scrap of ground. In Eastern Europe, Austro-Hungary and Germany waged a less static war against Russia and Serbia, with equally dreadful casualties. Italy joined the Entente, establishing a new front, while Bulgaria joined the Central Powers and created yet another. Everywhere the struggle became siege warfare on a massive scale, with neither side making progress.

During the first half of 1916, France and Germany inflicted terrible losses on each other at Verdun. Britain suffered appalling casualties at the Somme. Her attempt to seize the Dardanelles at Gallipoli had by now ended in a humiliating failure. Romania declared war on the Central Powers in August; but by the end of the year, the Germans had occupied three-quarters of her territory, including Bucharest.

From the start, the Central Powers had seen the Suez Canal (running from the Mediterranean to the Red Sea through the Sinai Desert) as the British Empire's jugular vein; since it was Britain's route to India, along

which passed not only Indian but Australian, New Zealand and South African troops.

So important was the Canal for merchant shipping that during the war, vessels were moored 15 or 20 miles up it. Even if they could not capture the Canal, a small Turkish army could at least tie down large quantities of troops and munitions needed elsewhere by the Allies. However, the enemy would have to attack across the Sinai.

'AS TERRIBLE AS ANY SEA'

The heart of the Sinai was a triangular waste of sand, crossed by three camel routes, which met at El Arish near the Mediterranean Sea where the Turks established their advance headquarters. In The Australian Flying Corps in the western and eastern theatres of war, 1914-1918, FM Cutlack described it as follows: 'It is mostly inhospitable desert, made the more hideous by great sand-hills heaped up by scorching winds – a vast waste of land whose dangers and loneliness are to the unsophisticated European as terrible as any sea. The tracks which reach out over it are routes that must often be followed rather by compass or stars than by landmarks.'

Along the coast, a series of 'hods' – small oases amid palm trees – possessed surface wells which held a very limited supply of brackish water. This lack of water ruled out a British advance into enemy territory.

No troops were better suited to desert warfare than the Turkish infantry. While TE Lawrence dismissively called the 'askers' an army of serfs, John Buchan (in his novel Greenmantle) thought they were 'as fanatical as the hordes of the Mahdi'.

Able to campaign for months on a few biscuits and a handful of dates, covering ground almost as fast as cavalry, they seemed to need much less water than their opponents. They had the good fortune to be commanded by a succession of gifted officers on loan from the German Army – Friedrich Freiherr Kress von Kressenstein, Erich von Falkenhayn and Otto Liman von Sanders – every one of whom led from the front.

The first of these commanders was a tall, skeletally thin, Bavarian gunner with a fleshless face adorned by pince-nez and a perpetual cigarette, in no way inhibited by lack of troops and weaponry. His attack on the Canal in February 1915, intended to bring about a pro-Turkish Egyptian revolt, was a

The author's father is in the pilot's seat of this BE.2c at Ismailia being briefed by Capt Albrecht, 14 Squadron's adjutant, cNovember 1916. At this point, the main danger, apart from the perennial hazards of engine failure and a forced landing without wireless or water, was attack by Fokker Eindeckers.

Above: Stuart Reid in typical flying gear of the period. At this stage of the war, pilots generally dressed like this, in very light helmets, long leather overcoats and field boots. The clothing was rather warm for low altitudes in the desert heat, and offered little protection against the extreme cold when flying high.

Opposite page: Taken from another aircraft, this picture shows the author's father flying a Martynside scout over the Judean Hills. It was taken on 25 February 1918 in terrain west of the Dead Sea, which by then was well inside British territory. **All author's collection.**

failure, but no reverse ever dismayed him. Despite being heavily outnumbered, his 'Desert Force' continued to menace the border.

In contrast to Kress von Kressenstein, General Sir Archibald Murray, a former CIGS, who had taken over as Commander-in-Chief, Egyptian Expeditionary Force (EEF) at the beginning of 1916, was essentially a desk soldier. In his late fifties, a veteran of the Zululand campaigns, white-haired and with a lined, peevish countenance, he looked older than he was. TE Lawrence described him in *Seven Pillars of Wisdom* as 'all brains and claws, nervous, elastic, changeable'. On one occasion, Murray's Chief of Staff told Lawrence: 'Now you're not to frighten him: don't forget what I say!'

No doubt he was a gifted organiser who laid the foundations for his successor's triumph – camps, food stores and reservoirs, trailways, signal stations and ammunition depots. But he was no good at winning battles.

His GHQ was originally at Ismailia, the port at the mouth of the Canal that supplied fresh water and was the centre of his new rail network. Here, he sat down to plod on with his preparations. As Lawrence put it in *Ibid*: 'Sir Archibald's army, probably the most

cumbersome in the world, had to be laboriously pushed forward on its belly.'

But the Allies' evacuation of Gallipoli at the end of 1915 intensified the Turkish threat to the Canal, and even Murray was stung by Lord Kitchener's sneer that troops were supposed to defend the Canal and not the Canal the troops. Ponderously, he began to set in motion what he intended to be a methodical advance across the northern Sinai.

SWELLING RANKS

Early in autumn 1916, Murray moved his GHQ from Ismailia to the Savoy Hotel at Cairo in the Sharia Kasr-el-Nil, the city's most expensive hotel. (Crowned by a domed turret, it looked a bit like Harrods in London.) His staff grew to a size that many observers thought ludicrously inflated. Whenever he went to the front on a tour of inspection, which did not happen too often, he travelled in an armoured train, insisting that three aircraft fly overhead, just in case the enemy – no doubt well informed of his movements by Egyptian spies – should send aircraft to 'strafe' him. This infuriated the RFC who, in Seward's words, regarded their Commander-in-Chief at the Savoy Hotel as 'a damned old woman'. ➤

"Lt Van Ryneveldt was forced to land on the shore amid the sand dunes after a bullet hit his engine sump… another aircraft came down to his rescue, cramming him into the forward cockpit with the observer."

There had been a more or less token RFC presence in Egypt since 1915, half a dozen Maurice Farmans and Henry Farmans, clumsy pushers, supported by French seaplanes from ships just off the coast. They were replaced in February 1916 by 14 Squadron of the RFC's Fifth Wing. (A squadron was three flights of four machines.) It consisted of BE.2cs with a few Bristol Scouts, operating from a headquarters aerodrome at Ismailia and three auxiliary aerodromes on the Canal. Their main activity at this stage was reconnaissance and photography by BE.2cs, an aircraft whose range was 100 miles at most – only made possible by loading one of its cockpits with several cans of fuel.

The other half of the wing was 1 Squadron of the Australian Flying Corps, many of its personnel being former cavalrymen from the legendary Australian Light Horse, such as a certain Lt Ross Smith. They were determined to do better than the 'Poms' and there was keen rivalry between the two squadrons, the British making jokes about the plumed headgear of Anzac cavalrymen as a sly dig at their neighbours. ('I think that hat would suit very well even a woman, don't you think so?' teased 'Major AD Fuze' in *The Gnome*.) But nobody ever laughed about the fighting qualities of the Australians. Confusingly, until

the creation of the Royal Air Force in 1918, No.1 Squadron was known as 'No.67 Squadron, RFC'. Arriving in Egypt in the summer of 1916 with no machines and no trained pilots, within just a few weeks it was making a valuable contribution.

PATROLLING THE CAMEL ROUTES

Meanwhile, the aircraft of 14 Squadron flew on a daily routine of reconnaissance and survey work. They also patrolled the three camel routes across the Sinai Desert over an area that extended 60 miles in front of the British lines, watching for any sign of an enemy advance. In addition, they made weekly bombing raids on Turkish strongpoints – notably on Hassana, Maghara and Rodh Salem. The object of these raids was to eliminate, or at the very least to diminish the enemy's water supply.

Lt Hill was particularly successful at Hassana, dropping a 20lb bomb as a sighting shot within a few yards of the water tank, then following it up with a hundred-pounder, which exploded in the middle of the tank and destroyed the pumping machinery. After photographing the damage, Hill flew back to his aerodrome at Qantara. (The war diary thought it worthy of note that he covered a distance of 180 miles.)

Next time, Hill was not so lucky, failing to return from a reconnaissance over Bir El Mazar and the Bardawi Lagoon. The aircraft that went to look for him could find no trace of pilot and machine. Eventually, secret agents discovered what had happened. Forced by engine trouble to land on the coast, for three hours he had used his machine-gun to hold off the Turkish patrols sent to capture him, until his ammunition ran out and he was taken prisoner.

The RFC's aircraft were backed up by the East Indies and Egypt Seaplane Squadron of the Royal Navy, which carried machines that until recently had been supporting the forces in Gallipoli and were flown by members of the Royal Naval Air Service.

Led from May by the bearded Cdr CR Samson, they too carried out reconnaissance and bombing missions. The 'Corps', including my father, disliked the RNAS, whom they regarded as pretentious and on the whole ineffectual, irreverently referring to the garrulous, boastful Samson as 'Flying Christ'. Even so, they were forced to co-operate closely since life was becoming much harder for both services.

In March, two of the seaplanes had spotted half a dozen new aircraft hangars at Beersheba near the enemy headquarters

DH.1a 4609 of 14 Squadron while based in Palestine, circa late 1916. This under-powered 'pusher' was only used operationally by 14 and the last in service with the unit was shot down in March 1917. (Please note, this artwork is for illustrative purposes of this publication and does not appear in *Wings over the Desert* from where the article is extracted.)
Juanita Franzi/Aero Illustrations © 2010

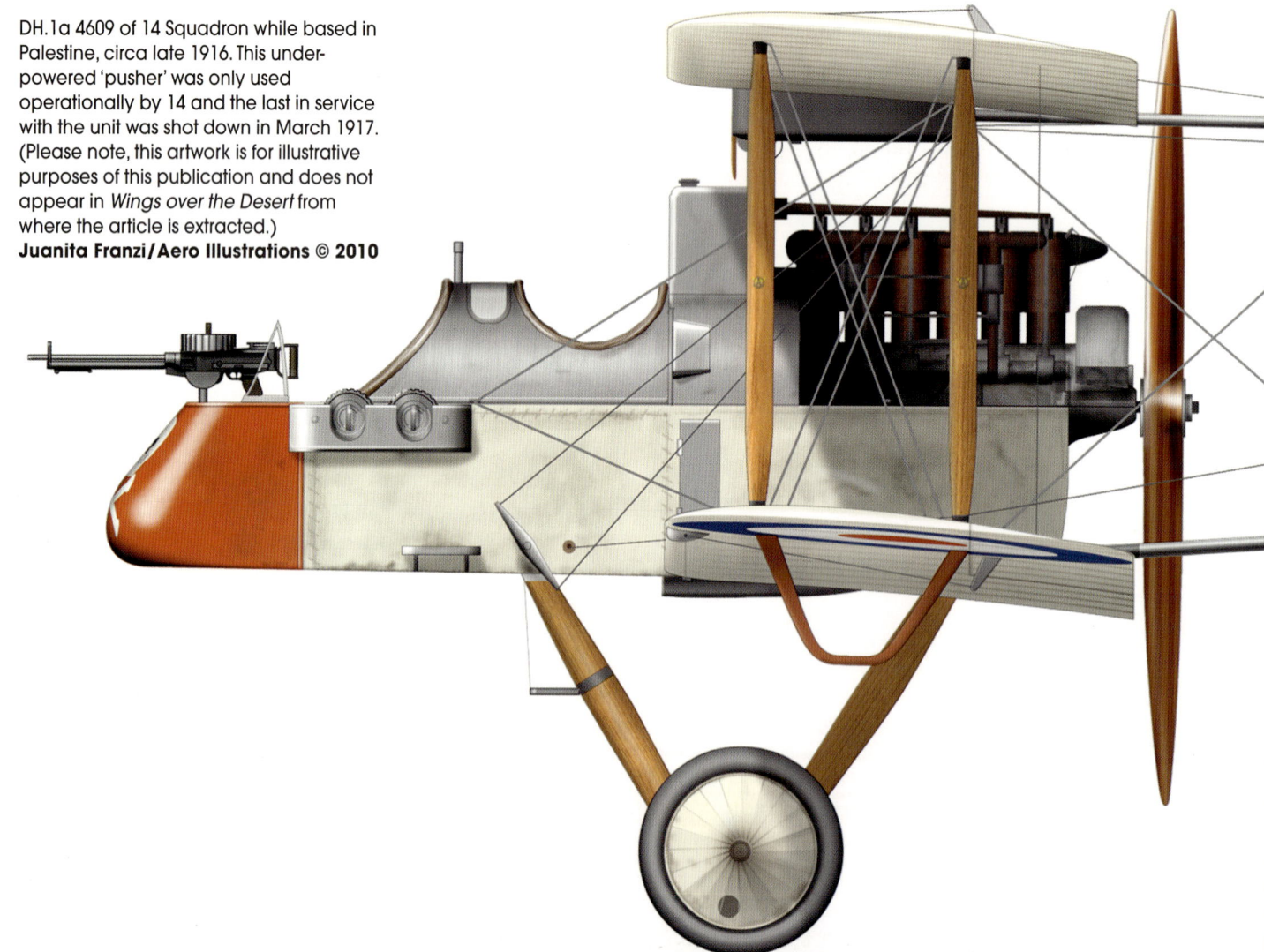

and at El Arish on the coast. These hangars announced the arrival in Palestine of what in October 1916 would become known as the 'Luftstreitkräfte' (the German Imperial air service), in the form of Fliegerabteilung 300.

Commanded by Hauptmann von Heemskerck, the airmen of this squadron seem to have been a very decent lot, as well as remarkably good pilots. The war diary and photographs in *The Gnome* show that among them were one or two Austro-Hungarian officers from the Imperial and Royal air troops (K und K Luftfahrtruppen), who were probably regulars with a knowledge of Turkish picked up during garrison duty in the Balkans. Like the British and Australians, they were all convinced that their side was going to win the war.

TECHNICALLY SUPERIOR FOE
Their machines included 14 Rumpler C.1 reconnaissance aircraft, two-seater biplanes that outpaced most of the British types in the Sinai and climbed much faster. Since they could fly higher, they were often able to do their work unmolested. They also possessed several single-seater Pfalz E.II scouts, which were armed with twin Spandau machine-guns firing through the propeller, and could dive at unusually high speed. This was the start of a

depressing technical superiority of enemy machines over British ones on the Sinai Front. 'It was not the German policy to relegate obsolete aeroplanes to subsidiary theatres of war', drily observe the authors of *The War in the Air*. The Pfalz scouts were soon joined by Fokker monoplanes – the 'Eindecker', that scourge of the Western Front. Luckily for the British, the Germans in Palestine had comparatively few machines and were to remain outnumbered until October 1917.

Unlike the Western Front, there were few dogfights at this stage of the campaign. Most hostile activity was confined to bombing, the British raiding El Arish and Beersheba while the Germans attacked Port Said. The RFC's missile was a 20lb Spencer bomb, aimed by hand over the side of the cockpit, and the Hun version was about the same size. The British also dropped leaflets in Turkish and Arabic encouraging the enemy's troops to desert, although Turkish officers shot any soldier found reading them.

On 13 June 1916, on a probing skirmish on El Arish as a preliminary to a full-scale raid, 14 Squadron ran into one of the much-feared Fokker monoplanes. But instead of a BE.2c, the Eindecker attacked a DH.1a 'pusher', which had no propeller in front to

prevent its Lewis gun from firing forward while he attacked from the wrong angle. 'Our machine', says the diary, 'manoeuvred [so] as to keep above and behind the Fokker with the nose of the machine firing towards him, so that he could be ranged by our fire. This combat, which took place at 7000 feet and for part of the engagement at a distance between the machines of 50 to 70 feet, was finally terminated by the German... using his superior diving speed to escape.' The diarist adds proudly, 'Our one "Pusher" De Havilland two-seater fighter was always a terror to the enemy.'

Whatever the diarist may say, the DH.1 was far from Fokker-proof and the crew were lucky to survive. Underpowered, with a top speed of 80mph, it was alarmingly vulnerable to attack from behind; but fortunately the Eindecker pilot – probably unaccustomed to his new aircraft – did not use the tactic of diving out of the sun that proved so effective on the Western Front. London had such a poor opinion of DH.1s that none were sent to France and only a very few to the Middle East. Eventually, this sole surviving example was shot down by enemy aircraft fire in March 1917, during a bombing raid on the Turkish railhead at Tel el Sheria. ➤

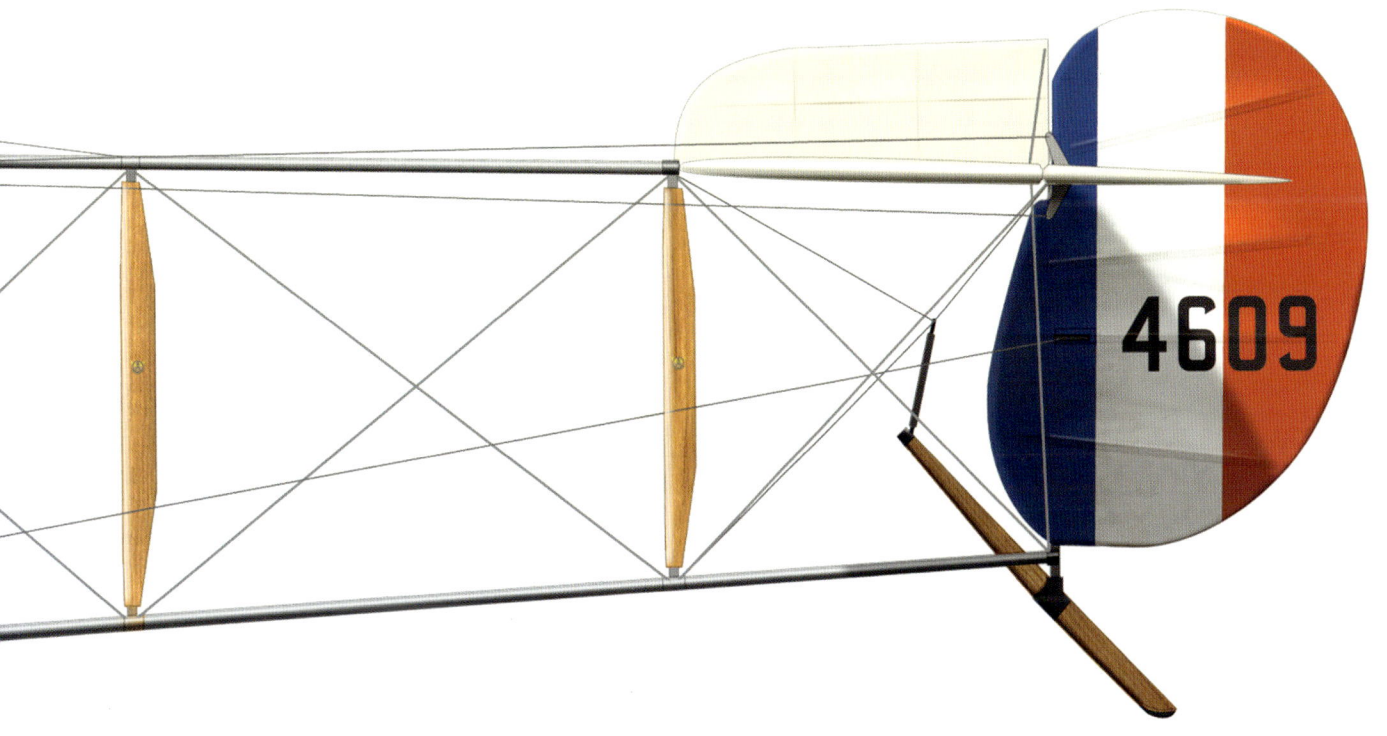

"Forced by engine trouble to land on the coast, for three hours he had used his machine-gun to hold off the Turkish patrols sent to capture him, until his ammunition ran out and he was taken prisoner."

AIRFIELD ATTACK

The RFC's main attack, a week later, caught the enemy off his guard. A total of 11 BE.2cs from Qantara (some used as single-seaters to carry heavier bombs) flew 10 miles out to sea before flying inland at a height of 7000ft and passing over the enemy aerodrome at El Arish. Then they circled back, coming down to 600ft to drop their bombs – 76, according to German sources. Lt Tipton went even lower, blowing to pieces an enemy machine, together with the mechanics frantically trying to get it into the air. In addition, two other enemy aircraft were destroyed, including a Pfalz and a Rumpler that had just taken off and already reached 100ft. Also, six out of ten hangars were set on fire, two or three being burned to the ground, while seven ground crew were killed or badly injured. One of the British aircraft, descending to 200ft, wound up this unusually successful attack with machine-gun fire.

The raiders did not escape unscathed. Three BE.2cs – flown as single-seaters – were brought down by anti-aircraft fire. Tipton was taken prisoner, but managed to escape. Lt Van Ryneveldt (later the first man to fly from Egypt to the Cape) was forced to land on the shore amid the sand dunes after a bullet hit his engine sump and burned his machine. However, another aircraft came down to his rescue, cramming him into the forward cockpit with the observer. Overloaded, soft sand clogging its wheels, it had trouble taking off, but somehow returned safely to base.

Defiantly, Fliegerabteilung 300 responded to the raid on the same day. That evening its undamaged Rumplers flew over Port Said and dropped 43 bombs.

> **"It was not the German policy to relegate obsolete aeroplanes to subsidiary theatres of war."**

In the summer of 1916, wireless (Morse code) was first used by the RFC during an operation by troops to destroy the wells at Wadi Muksheib. On one of the three main routes across the Sinai to Ismailia, these were about 40 miles away, the object was to prevent the Turks attacking across the desert from this direction. Squadron wireless personnel were attached to the column, and reconnaissance aircraft patrolling in front of its advance made regular reports by wireless or by dropping messages – handwritten notes jotted down in the air.

The RFC had by now been reorganised. Fifth Wing's HQ was still at Ismailia, with the headquarters flight and one-and-a-half flights of 14 Squadron. Another flight was at Qantara, while the remaining half-flight was at Port Said. Qantara used 80 camels to bring up its petrol, sand carts (sledges) hauling its spare parts and tents. In addition, under Fifth Wing's command were one-and-a-half flights of 1 Squadron of the Australian Flying Corps, the other half-flight being at Kharga in the Western Desert.

The first full-scale battle in Palestine in which the RFC and the AFC took part was at Romani in the summer. Both played a vital role in the build-up, reporting the approach of enemy forces as early as 19 July. When the enemy pushed their line forward on the night of 27/28 July, preparing for the offensive, every available machine – 17 in all – bombed them, breaking up their formations and hampering their communication and supply lines.

The Turks finally attacked on 3 August. However, Kress von Kressenstein could only muster 18,000 combat troops, who were driven off next day after some very hard

fighting at bayonet point among the sandhills where our men had dug in. By the night of 5 August, the enemy were in full retreat, losing 4000 prisoners. Nevertheless, they fell back so fast to El Arish, 50 miles behind, that the pursuit was unable to catch them. But the Suez Canal would never again be under threat.

During the engagement, Capt Grant-Dalton, flying a Bristol Scout, was attacked by three Aviatiks. Although badly wounded in a most unequal combat, he managed to land safely behind the British lines at Romani.

GALLANT DUTY

On 11 August, a BE.2c of 14 Squadron was not so lucky. Brigadier-General Chaytor, commanding the Anzac division, was reconnoitring Bir el Abd on horseback when he saw enemy aircraft guns shooting at a British aircraft. He said: "Suddenly the anti-aircraft fire was switched off and an enemy aeroplane swooped down on ours which was apparently badly damaged, but shortly steadied and came down about three-quarters of a mile south-east of my headquarters.

"Captain Rhodes, my aide-de-camp, went off to locate the plane to give first aid, and I to headquarters to send an ambulance. On finding the plane, Captain Rhodes found that the pilot, 2nd-Lieut EW Edwards, who was very badly wounded – I think seven bullets had hit him, one of which broke his lower jaw on both sides, another his shoulder – had gone off to get help for the observer who was shot in the chest and could not move. The observer, 2nd-Lieut J Brown, though in great pain, refused to have his wounds attended to until he had made his report, as he said they had some important information and he was afraid he would faint if his wound was touched. He very gallantly held himself

Canvas hangar at an advanced airstrip. Along with tents, fuel, oil and other supplies, hangars like this were brought up on camels under the cover of darkness.

together until he had dictated his report and verified it and then, his duty done, fainted and died two hours later."

The information seems to have been that the Turkish rearguard was withdrawing from Bir el Abd. The war diary provides further details. After the BE.2c was attacked by two Aviatiks, the pilot became unconscious from his wounds, only recovering when the aircraft was within 500ft of the ground. The diary adds that Brown had been on his way back to England to train as a pilot when he learned that the enemy was advancing and immediately telephoned for permission to return and take part in the battle.

Several other men had been seriously wounded, one mortally, while the Germans lost only a single machine, which was driven down out of control by an RFC scout over Salmana.

Another British aircraft, a BE.2c operating from Suez, nearly became a casualty during a reconnaissance after the battle, when its engine cut out while flying over a mountain range in the southern Sinai. The pilot, Lt Kingsley, spotted a flat surface on a mountain at the eastern end of the range where he could land, but which was opposite a Turkish outpost. He landed, nonetheless. While he repaired the engine trouble – a faulty magneto – his observer kept the Turks at bay with the Lewis gun when they climbed up a ravine to try and capture them. As soon as he had fixed the magneto, he dived the aircraft off the side of the mountain until its engine picked up, returning safely to base. ➤

Above: Another example of the War Office sending inferior aircraft to the Middle East was the Bristol Monoplane, of which just 125 were ordered and, similar to the DH.1a, none were sent to France. Later in the war, the author's father gained unofficial test pilot status, and despite its looks was unimpressed after flying this type.

Below: A captured German Albatros seen under close examination by Allied personnel in September 1918. By then, the superiority of the Bristol F.2b Fighter meant that German pilots reportedly seldom dared leave the ground in this theatre.

When Seward joined 14 Squadron on 17 August, shortly after the battle of Romani, the Egyptian Expeditionary Force was grinding forward along the coast, across the Sinai Desert. Troops were concentrated at points commanding the main routes: while large-scale defensive works were under construction, lightly held front-line positions were taken up, cavalry and camel columns patrolling the area in front of the enemy. Since half a million gallons of water a day were needed for Murray's forces, filtering, pumping and storage machinery had to be built to bring it from the Nile, together with a metal pipeline and a railway. The pipeline and railway ran from Qantara which, from a small 'native village' became a huge military base, canal port and depot.

On 4 September, Capt Muir of 1 Squadron (and formerly of the Australian Light Horse) dropped 12 bombs with devastating effects on the Turks at Bir el Mazar, destroying enemy tents and silencing several anti-aircraft guns. The Australian airmen were certainly beginning to pull their weight. A few days later they co-operated with Anzac cavalry in an attack on Bir el Mazar that forced a Turkish withdrawal.

FLYING IN THEIR PYJAMAS
Fliegerabteilung 300 fought back. When six RNAS machines appeared over El Arish on 17 September at 05:24, with the object of directing naval guns on to the aerodrome, they were speedily chased away by two Rumplers flown by Oberleutnant Gerhard Felmy and Leutnant von Bülow-Bothkamp, and by a Pfalz scout flown by Leutnant von Hesler – all three still in their pyjamas.

Nevertheless, by mid-November 1916, the EEF was halfway to the Palestinian frontier. The objective was Kress von Kressenstein's headquarters at El Arish, which has been described as the 'strategic pivot of the eastern Sinai'. With its oases and sea port, in easy reach of enemy bases, it was not only the best possible position from which to defend Egypt and the Suez Canal, but also offered a springboard from which to invade Turkish Palestine. As the war diary comments: 'This pushing forward of our line necessitated the establishment of forward landing grounds, if contact with our advanced troops was to be effectively kept.'

By the end of October, 14 Squadron found itself operating from a forward aerodrome at Salmana. Within much closer range, on 11 November they bombed the German airbase at Beersheba and the adjoining railway station, causing extensive damage. (I think this must have been when my father scored his first 'hit' – which he recalled as dropping a bomb between two locomotives and blowing them off the track.) Turkish troop camps at Maghdaba were also bombed. During the last week of November, the squadron's forward aerodrome was again moved – north, to Mustabig. They were accompanied by the Australians.

By 10 December, the railway was within 20 miles of El Arish and ten days later, the squadron's reconnaissance machines reported that the Turks were evacuating the town. Expecting a British attack from the sea, when none was planned, Kress von Kressenstein had decided to withdraw his army to Maghdaba and Rafa. General Sir Philip Chetwode's Desert Column marched into El Arish on 21 December. Maghdaba fell the following day, but Rafa held out stubbornly until 8 January 1917. Kress von Kressenstein had wanted to pull back the troops defending Maghdaba, but since it was one of Turkey's last footholds in the Sinai, Djemal Pasha, who was the overall commander in the region, would not let them withdraw.

TURNING THE TIDE
No.14 Squadron and 1 Squadron distinguished themselves during what the Staff quaintly called 'The Affair of Maghdaba' – 13 BE.2cs dropped 120 16lb or 20lb bombs on the beleaguered Turks, together with six 100lb bombs. If ludicrously small by later standards, these 'hundred-pounders' were monsters for the period. On the day before, 21 December, 14 Squadron had attacked and seriously damaged a railway bridge just north of Beersheba.

One foggy morning at the end of the month, the visibility suddenly improved and, about 20 miles south of El Arish, from his BE.2c, a pilot suddenly saw two Turkish battalions withdrawing. After he had flown back to report, 11 aircraft returned to strafe them with bombs and machine-gun fire. Suffering heavy casualties, the enemy force disintegrated, survivors fleeing into the desert.

Kress von Kressenstein regrouped the Turks at Rafa, a knoll in front of which he began to dig in. His work parties were bombed daily by British aircraft, which took photographs of the trenches, providing a map to direct artillery fire. On the night of 8/9 January 1917 in 'The Action of Rafah', the

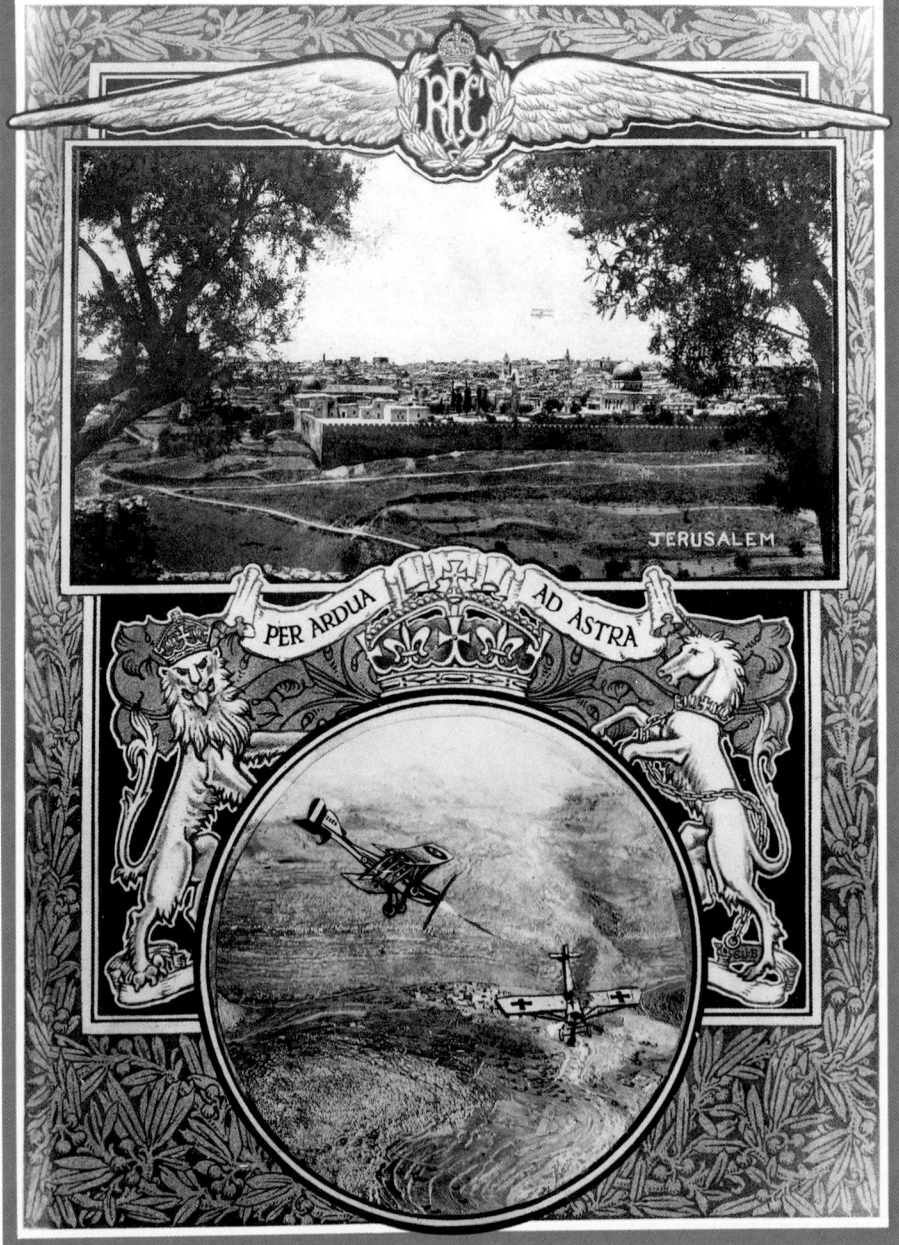

The RFC Middle East Brigade's Christmas card for 1917. Above it shows Jerusalem in a photo taken on 9 December, while below it depicts a BE.2c shooting down a Fokker Eindecker.

A picture taken by the author's father on 30 May 1917, which had 'Country in front of our lines near El Mendur' written on the reverse. The location is just south of Gaza and shows the Wadi Ghazi. At the time, there was a stalemate and British troops were bogged down in a situation similar to the trench warfare on the Western Front.

Australian Light Horse surrounded the position, then stormed it at bayonet point. No.14 Squadron helped by bombing and directing artillery fire. The enemy aerodrome at Beersheba was under constant attack, while attempts were made to intercept any German machine that appeared in the sky.

These attempts were not always successful. Lt Kingsley of 14 Squadron, apparently in a Martinsyde scout, flew up with suicidal bravery to engage two Fokker monoplanes and an Aviatik two-seater. Within minutes, he had been wounded twice, while another bullet went through his petrol tank. Making for the coast before his fuel leaked away, he dropped his bombs on any Turkish encampments he flew over and then ditched his aircraft in the sea north of Rafa. Trying to reach the British lines, he was captured by a group of Bedouins, who stripped him naked. Luckily, he was rescued by a patrol of Australian cavalry.

Throughout the engagement, British aircraft attacked the enemy from a low altitude, using bombs and machine-guns. Turkish troops on the march were shot up and motor convoys destroyed. Infantry in the trenches and gun crews in the batteries were similarly strafed from a height of only 200 or 300ft. The Turks became so fearful that their patrols and front-line troops were ordered to send up smoke signals as soon as they

spotted a British aircraft. The enemy also enlisted the help of the Bedouin, but British aircraft machine-gunned any found signalling, which put an end to the practice.

After the fall of Rafa, Fifth Wing's aeroplanes attacked Beersheba railway station and aerodrome incessantly, both by day and – when the moon was full – by night. Bombing parties generally consisted of three Martinsydes escorted by three Bristol Scouts. The Germans were forced to abandon the aerodrome, using it only as an occasional landing ground, and had to establish a new base 30 miles behind, at Ramleh. This, too, was soon under constant attack. Later, the Luftstreitkräfte moved back for a time to Beersheba, but was again forced to evacuate.

The other main bombing target was Junction Station. Here the railway from Jaffa to Jerusalem joined the line running south to Beersheba, along which travelled all Turkish reinforcements and munitions. It was also the starting point of a new line that the enemy was building in order to supply the eastern section of the Gaza-Beersheba Front.

In the meantime, British Sappers had been laying the tracks for the EEF's own railway from Ismailia, which now extended as far as Rafa. The logistic infrastructure was in place. Even General Sir Archibald Murray was ready to advance into Turkish Palestine. ∎

WINGS OVER THE DESERT

Similar to the article on pages 52-53, this feature is extracted from the recently published book *Wings over the Desert – In action with an RFC pilot in Palestine 1916-1918* (ISBN 978 1 84425 672 3) by Desmond Seward and is used by kind permission of the author and Haynes Publishing. Just to recap, this fascinating book is based around the experiences of the author's father, WEL Seward MC, who was a pilot with 14 Squadron RFC. Priced at £25, it can be ordered from Haynes by calling 01963 442030 or online at www.haynes.co.uk

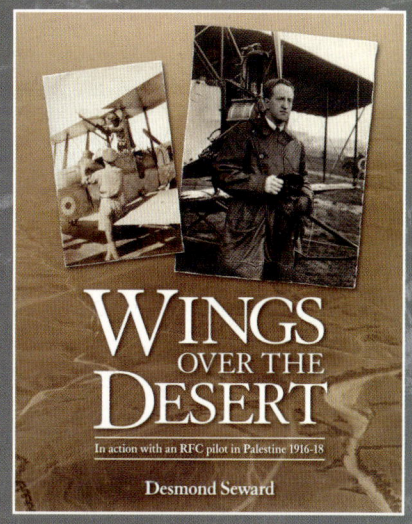

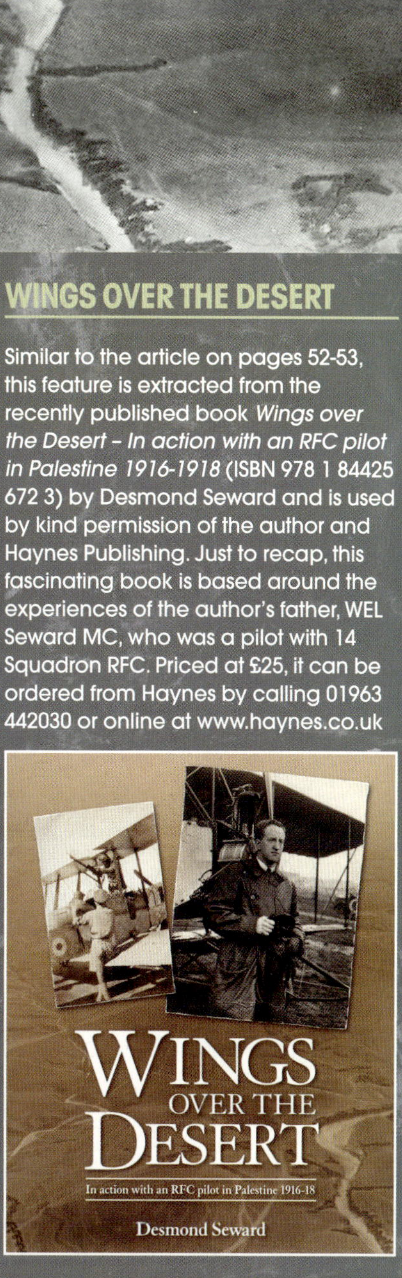

Shuttleworth's
World War One 'squadron'

The Shuttleworth Collection has numerous examples of airworthy World War One aircraft which are variously flown at the regular flying displays held during the summer season each year. Here we take a pictorial look at them to give a flavour of some of what can be seen at this fantastic venue.

Left: The second reproduction project built for the Shuttleworth Collection by the Northern Aeroplane Workshops created this Bristol M.1C. The monoplane fighter wears the colours of C4918 of 72 Squadron Royal Flying Corps, c1917. The reproduction was delivered to Old Warden in October 1997 and fitted with an original 110hp Le Rhone rotary engine, making its first flight on 25 September 2000. Old Warden's curved display line is especially popular with photographers, as it allows for such superb shots as this topside view of 'C4918'. Northern Aeroplane Workshops is currently constructing a Sopwith Camel for Shuttleworth. Many parts for this aircraft have been completed and the airframe is being assembled. This latter project highlights what an interesting future lays ahead with even more World War One types at this venue. **Nick Blacow**

Opposite: Sopwith Triplane 'N6290' is a reproduction aircraft built for the Shuttleworth Collection by the Northern Aeroplane Workshops and fitted with an original 130hp Clerget engine. It wears the paint scheme of an aircraft that was adorned with the prominently applied name *DIXIE*, which flew with 8 Squadron Royal Naval Air Service. The Triplane was delivered to Old Warden in June 1990, where the engine was then fitted. Its first flight took place on 10 April 1992. Sir Thomas Sopwith, founder of the original Sopwith Aviation Company, supported the project throughout his later life. He even decreed that Northern Aeroplane Workshops' newly built Sopwith Triplane should be considered as a 'late production example', therefore it is fitted with a manufacturer's plate in the cockpit bearing No.153. 'N6290' is seen here during take-off from Old Warden on 15 April 2010. **Jarrod Cotter**

Right: Another view of Sopwith Triplane 'N6290', this time making a turn in the skies over Old Warden on 15 April 2010. The picture again emphasizes the good photo opportunities available at this venue due to the display line and direction of light. **Jarrod Cotter**

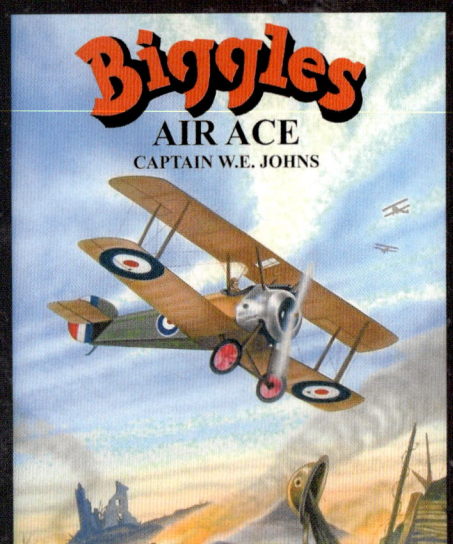

Generations of young boys have grown up reading with excitement the escapades of pilot and adventurer 'Biggles' in the famous book series by author Captain WE Johns. The character's full name was James Bigglesworth, who began his adventures as a teenage fighter pilot in the Royal Flying Corps during World War One.

Biggles first appeared in print in the story The White Fokker, published in the first issue of *Popular Flying* magazine in 1932. The first collection of Biggles stories, *The Camels are Coming*, was published the same year. The series eventually reached nearly a hundred volumes.

WE Johns, who died in 1968, was himself a pilot during World War One. On 16 September 1918 he was shot down in his DH.4 while on a bombing raid. He survived the crash and was taken prisoner of war, and post-war remained in the RAF until 1927.

WE Johns was a friend of Richard Shuttleworth, and it has been said that he and the town Biggleswade, close to Old Warden, provided the inspiration for the name of the heroic character. Bigglesworth supposedly takes the 'Biggles' from Biggleswade, and the 'worth' from Shuttleworth.

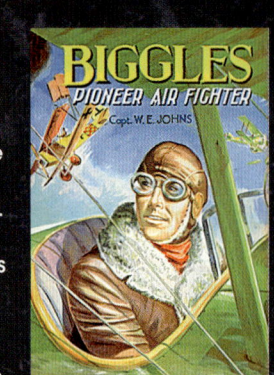

Right: William Beardmore was contracted to build 50 Pups under licence, which were to be armed with Le Prieur rockets for use against observation balloons. The rockets were fired from about 200 yards, then the sharp edge in the nose cone pierced the fabric and the escaping gas was ignited by the rocket. Some of the Pups had transparent areas fitted to the centre section of the upper wings to improve visibility for the pilot. The Shuttleworth Collection aircraft are on display throughout the year in the hangars, and outside of the flying season 9916 can often be seen fitted with representative Le Prieur rockets to give an idea of this aspect of aerial fighting in World War One. It is seen here with the rockets in place during December 2009, but the aircraft is not authorised to fly with them fitted. **Jarrod Cotter**

Below: The Sopwith Pup entered service with the RNAS in September 1916. It was a highly manoeuvrable scout with a good rate of climb and excellent handling qualities – it has often been described as one of the best 'pilot's aeroplanes' of World War One. However, its single gun armament was not a match for the more heavily armed German scouts that were arriving in 1917 which meant that by the autumn of that year it was being replaced by Sopwith Camels. The RNAS used the type for pioneering deck trials and in August 1917 a Sopwith Pup made the first ever landing on a ship at sea. The Shuttleworth Collection's Pup is 9917, which served for a time on HMS *Manxman*. It was acquired by Richard Shuttleworth in 1936. It is seen here about to take-off from Old Warden on 15 April 2010. **Jarrod Cotter**

Above: Royal Aircraft Factory SE.5a F904 is an original aircraft which didn't see operational service. Post-war it was purchased by Major JC Savage for his skywriting business and registered G-EBIA. Years later, in 1955, it was rediscovered in the Armstrong Whitworth flight shed at Whitley. It was restored for the Shuttleworth Collection by staff and apprentices at RAE Farnborough, flying again in August 1959. After mechanical problems with the original geared Hispano-Suiza, in 1975 it was instead fitted with a 200hp Wolseley Viper engine – recalling the type's teething troubles with engines when it entered service in 1917. **Rob Leigh**

Above: One of the original World War One aircraft flown by the Shuttleworth Collection is Avro 504K H5199. Avro 504s were used in various military roles, including observation, as bombers and especially as trainers. H5199 was built in 1918 as a K, but was converted to a radial-engined N while in RAF service. It later passed into civilian hands, but in 1940 was impressed back into military service. Following World War Two it was returned to civilian use and converted back to its original Avro 504K configuration by Avro apprentices for the film *Reach for the Sky* telling the story of Douglas Bader. Afterwards it became part of the Shuttleworth Collection. **Nick Blacow**

Below: Bristol F.2b Fighter D8096 was built in 1918, just too late to see service during World War One. It was, however, on the strength 208 Squadron in Turkey during 1923. In 1936 it was acquired by Captain CPB Ogilvie who stored it, along with many other aircraft, in Watford. The 'Brisfit' later became part of the Shuttleworth Collection and was restored by the Bristol Aeroplane Company, flying again in February 1952. **Nick Blacow**

HISTORY OF THE SHUTTLEWORTH COLLECTION

Richard Ormonde Shuttleworth inherited the Old Warden Estate on his 23rd birthday and took a keen interest in farming and estate management as well as in motor racing and aviation. After his inheritance he built up a sizeable collection of old cars and later, aeroplanes, restoring them to working order. Some of these still form the nucleus of the Shuttleworth Collection at Old Warden Aerodrome. When World War Two was declared in 1939, Richard joined the Royal Air Force and was posted to RAF Benson for night-flying experience. On the night of the 1/2 August 1940, aged 31, he was killed in a Fairey Battle which crashed into a hill while on a cross-country training flight.

Dorothy Shuttleworth was devastated by the loss of her son and set up the mansion as a Red Cross convalescent home for injured airmen and created a small chapel, dedicated to Richard. In 1944 she decided to place the estate in a Charitable Trust in memory of Richard; she wanted to ensure that it would continue as one entity to be used for the purpose of agricultural and aviation education, two interests that her son was especially keen on. Old Warden Park is therefore owned by the Richard Ormonde Shuttleworth Remembrance Trust.

The Shuttleworth Collection opened to the public in 1963, and over the years has increased significantly and its regular air displays draw crowds from all over the world. Its aircraft depict the history of flight from the early 1900s to the 1950s and shows how aeroplanes operated in the pioneering years, were rapidly developed through necessity during World War One, then used for sport, pleasure and business in the 1920s and 30s and once again became fighting machines during World War Two.

The Collection is situated at Old Warden, near Biggleswade in Bedfordshire, and is a traditional all-grass aerodrome situated in the grounds of the Old Warden Park Estate. The aircraft are displayed in eight hangars, which include a workshop facility giving the visitor a chance to view restoration and maintenance in progress. There is also a vehicle section, displaying vintage and veteran cars and motorcycles among other forms of transport.

The Shuttleworth Collection is open to view every day except for the Christmas to New Year week and is, of course, famous for its regular flying displays. Also to be seen on flying days and evenings are the Collection's vintage motor cars and motorcycles. It is located 50 miles north of London and is easily accessible from the A1. For more details and a list of the flying displays visit: www.shuttleworth.org

With thanks to Marketing Manager Andrew Ogden and photographers Nick Blacow and Rob Leigh for their help with this article. Historical information courtesy of the Shuttleworth Collection.

Highlighting the variety of types which form the Shuttleworth Collection, one of the star performers at flying displays is its superb World War Two era Westland Lysander which has been restored to represent V9367 MA-B of 161 Squadron, as flown by Plt Off Peter Vaughan-Fowler on Operation Apollo during the winter of 1942. This sees it painted all-over black and fitted with a dummy long range fuel tank and ladder, which would have been used by Special Operations Executive agents to climb in or out of an aircraft quickly after it had landed in enemy occupied territory. The beautiful aeroplane is seen being put through its paces at Old Warden on 15 April 2010. **Jarrod Cotter**

Short Admiralty Type 184

Martyn Chorlton profiles the world's first successful torpedo bomber.

In early 1915, Short Brothers unveiled their latest in a long line of naval seaplanes built in response to a requirement of the Admiralty. This requirement was simply for a torpedo-carrying seaplane capable of being stored and operated from the Royal Navy tenders of the day. Drawing on the valuable experience already gained, the new Short Admiralty Type 184 was destined to be built in large numbers and achieve great operational success.

The Type 184 was, for the day, a fairly large aircraft; it spanned over 63ft and was 40ft 7½ inches in length. To solve the problem of the large wingspan, the machine's wings could be folded back neatly along its length allowing it to fit in a seaplane tender's hangar with ease. The aircraft was produced with a variety of engines giving an average speed of 85mph at 2000ft. Its strength lay in the fact that it was the first of the breed that was capable of carrying a 14-inch torpedo between its floats.

Orders were hesitant at the start with only ten being requested by the Admiralty direct from Shorts. However, it was not long before the potential of the new aircraft was realised and Shorts received so many orders that it had to introduce several companies in as sub-contractors, virtually all of them without any

Short Admiralty Type 184 N.842 is carefully winched aboard HMS *Ben-my-Chree* in May 1915 before embarking for the Turkish theatre. **Stuart Leslie**

aircraft construction experience. These included future famous aircraft producers like Westlands, Fairey, Saunders and Supermarine. Fortunately, the Type 184 was not a complicated aircraft and its manufacture was relatively easy. As no production drawings were available for distribution these

were made 'from life'. Each of the contractors provided a draughtsman who, working from an actual Type 184, produced drawings of a group of components. Each firm made enough sets of its draughtsmen's drawings to send copies to the other contractors; in this way, each firm received a full set of drawings.

EMBARKATION

The Type 184 first entered service with the seaplane carrier HMS *Ben-my-Chree* on 21 May 1915. Under the command of Sqn Cdr CJ L'Estrange Malone, the ship set course for the Dardanelles 'with the unofficial intention of torpedoing the *Goeben* and the *Breslau*' (a German battlecruiser and light cruiser respectively). The ship arrived at Iero Bay, Mitylene, on 12 June 1915 with the first two Type 184s built; Numbers 841 and 842.

Success would come exactly two months later when the vessel was in the Gulf of Zeros. On 12 August 1915, a Short 184, flown by Flt Cdr CHK Edmonds, was despatched across the Isthmus of Bulair to attack a Turkish supply ship spotted off Injeh Burnu. The aircraft was designed for a pilot and observer, but Edmonds elected to fly alone as the Type 184 only had enough fuel for a 45-minute flight and the weight of the torpedo restricted his height to just 800ft, aggravated by the hot climate.

Type 184s of 'C' Flight at rest on the breakwater at RAF Cattewater, Devon, which was renamed Mount Batten in 1928. Note the railed crane which made handling this large aircraft in and out of water considerably easier.

> **"This small but significant operation did prove that it was possible to drop a torpedo from an aircraft to strike a selected target."**

As well as launching the careers of some of the future large British aircraft manufacturers, several lesser know companies such as Frederick Sage of Walton, Peterborough, also built the Short Type 184. **All via Time Line Images unless noted**

On spotting the enemy ship, Edmonds glided down to just 15ft above the surface and dropped his torpedo at a range of 350yds. The torpedo hit the target amidships and, as Edmonds turned away, he saw the vessel settling lower in the water by the stern. It is unfortunate that Edmonds' achievement was slightly tarnished by the fact that the ship had already been torpedoed by the British submarine E.14 and left beached in shallow water. This small but significant operation did prove that it was possible to drop a torpedo from an aircraft to strike a selected target.

It was not long before further success was achieved. A seaplane reconnaissance flight revealed that Ak Bashi Liman on the Gallipoli Peninsula was being used as an enemy supply base. On 17 August 1915, two Type 184s were sent out from the *Ben-my-Chree* to torpedo the transports being unloaded at the base. One was flown by Flt Cdr Edmonds and the other by Flt Cdr GB Dacre DSO, once again, neither carried an observer in order to save fuel and slightly improve performance. On approach to Ak Bashi Liman, Edmonds descended towards the supply base sighting three Turkish steamers. He selected the middle one for his attack, his torpedo accurately striking the vessel leaving it burning and sinking behind him. En route, Dacre had suffered engine problems and had to alight on the sea but was still able to taxi. He spotted an enemy tug and began to taxi towards it, receiving unfriendly rifle fire in

the process. Closing in, Dacre launched his torpedo at the tug which exploded and quickly sank. With the absence of the torpedo, the Type 184 was just able to get airborne, flying back to *Ben-my-Chree* at just 200ft above the sea.

Despite these early successes, even with its faults, it is surprising that the Type 184 was never used again for torpedo attacks. As more powerful engines were developed, its performance would have improved in the Turkish theatre and it could have influenced the whole campaign. The Type 184 also proved itself as a bomber which was, once again, first demonstrated by Edmonds and Dacre on 8 November 1915. The pair flew 120 miles to bomb a railway bridge south of Kuleli Burgas with two 112lb bombs each.

IN ACTION AT JUTLAND

Westland-built Type 184 No.8359 gained fame when it became the only aircraft of any type to take part in a major naval action during World War One. On 31 May 1916, the Grand Fleet headed towards Jutland to begin the greatest sea battle of the war. Two seaplane carriers were meant to have been involved,

but only HMS *Engadine* was able to take part, departing from Rosyth. At 14:20hrs the light cruiser HMS *Galatea* signalled 'enemy sighted' and Admiral Sir David Beatty ordered *Engadine* to despatch its Type 184. At 15:08hrs, Lt FJ Rutland and his observer, Assistant Paymaster GS Trewin, were airborne managing to pass four messages back to the *Engadine* before a petrol pipe broke, forcing the aircraft down onto the sea. Rutland managed to repair the pipe with a piece of rubber from his own lifejacket before returning to his ship. Unfortunately, the flight did nothing to assist Beatty as the *Engadine* was unable to pass on Rutland's reports.

A total of 936 Type 184s were built during World War One, 282 of which were still in service on 31 October 1918 and several served into the early 1920s. While its design and success was achieved as a torpedo bomber, it was more suited in its secondary role of bombing and reconnaissance. ∎

'Bloody Paralyser' Type Os

Martyn Chorlton presents a brief history of the Handley Page O/100 and O/400 in RNAS and RAF service.

HP O/100 No.1458 while serving with the RNAS Training Flight at Manston in October 1916. Virtually the same size as an Avro Lancaster, the Type O had the added advantage of folding wings which neatly slotted above and below the bi-tailplane. **Via Stuart Leslie**

Unfortunately the third O/100 to be delivered to the 3rd Wing at Luxeuil-les-Bain fell into enemy hands on 1 January 1917. No.1463, which was 'kindly' delivered to the enemy by Lt HC Vereker, was quickly repainted in German markings but crashed not long after. **Via Time Line Images**

'A bloody paralyser to the stop the Hun in his tracks' was the straight to the point signal sent by Cdr Charles Rumney Samson in 1914. The message, which was sent to the Admiralty Air Department, sowed the seeds which led to the development of the Handley Page O/100 and O/400 bombers. Thanks to Capt Murray Sueter, Handley Page was approached and commissioned to build an aircraft that could comply with Samson's message.

Up to this date, Frederick Handley Page had only built a few unconventional large aircraft, but this did not deter him and by mid-1915 plans were progressing well on a new large bomber. One of the designs that the new aircraft would draw from was the Type L or L/200 but, despite reaching an advanced stage of construction, it was not ordered by the RNAS. The new design was initially known as the Handley Page Type O (letter not numeral), but as it was designed with a 100ft wingspan, this was quickly changed into the slightly more imaginative Type O/100 and designated HP.11.

The first aircraft, No.1455, was built at Cricklewood and assembled at Kingsbury before being transported to Hendon on 15 December 1915 ready for its first test flight. With Lt Cdr John Tremayne Babington (who took part in the Avro 504 attack on Friedrichshafen on 21 November 1914) at the controls, the giant machine first took to the air on 17 December having only been conceived

The second prototype Handley Page O/100 No.1456 during early trials at Eastchurch in 1916. **Via Stuart Leslie**

No.216 Squadron, having operated the O/100 since October 1917, converted to the O/400 the following year. From May 1919 the squadron moved from France to the Middle East where it was destined to remain for the next 36 years. This O/400 is pictured at Amman in 1921 only months before the type gave way to DH.10. **Via Time Line Images**

just 12 months earlier. Powered by a pair of 150hp Sunbeam engines, the bomber could carry 200 gallons of fuel and despite its size, the incorporation of folding wings meant that it could be housed in a 70sq ft building. Four prototypes were built in various configurations with regard to crew, defensive armament and armour, all of which were later included in the production variants. The Sunbeam engines were never man enough for the job and were later replaced by the more powerful Rolls-Royce Eagle IIs, developing 260hp each. This had the marked effect of raising the bomb load from 600lb to over 1600lb.

The first aircraft were delivered to the RNAS Training Flight at Manston in the spring of 1916. Operational deliveries began not long after to a unit simply known as the Handley Page Squadron which was attached to the 3rd Wing at Luxeuil-les-Bain under the command of Capt Babington. The first two aircraft arrived safely but No.1463, being flown by Lt HC Vereker, became lost while above cloud on 1 January 1917. After breaking cloud, Vereker landed at the first airfield he encountered, which unfortunately turned out to be Chalandry, 12 miles behind enemy lines! The aircraft was later flown to Germany where, luckily for the British, it was destroyed in a crash a few weeks later before a serious evaluation could be made.

BOMBING BEGINS

The first raid by an O/100 took place on 16/17 March 1917 when Capt Babington bombed a railway junction at Metz in No.1459. After transfer to the 5th Wing at Coudekerque, daylight operations were flown against U-boat bases at Bruges, Ostend and Zeebrugge. No.7 (Naval) Squadron was the first official front line unit to operate the O/100 successfully, beginning operations against a group of German destroyers on 25 April 1917, when they sunk one of them.

A total of only 46 O/100s were eventually built, including the four prototypes, while

> **"A bloody paralyser to the stop the Hun in his tracks…"**

development of the more powerful HP.12 or O/400 progressed. All changes revolved around the powerplant where there was a severe shortage of Eagle engines. The main misguided problem was that the O/100's engines were built in right and left-hand versions as it was thought this would alleviate control asymmetry problems caused by torque. This had been holding up the output of the Eagle II and IV and it was not until tests were carried out on No.3138 at the Aeroplane Experimental Station at Martlesham Heath that the misconception was discovered. Now fitted with a pair of 360hp Eagle VIIIs, the original directional instability problems were eliminated with identical engines and propellers and the central fin adjusted. The structure of the new model was no different from its predecessor, so the internal bomb load was still no more than 1600lb, despite the aircraft's fuel system being moved from the engine nacelles to inside the fuselage. However, the increase in power and reduced drag of the engines increased the cruising speed from 76 to 97.5mph. Endurance was still eight hours as per the O/100, but range was increased by 100 miles with the same bomb load. New bombs allowed for different configurations including the 520lb light case rising up to the 1800lb SN(Mod) which was specifically designed to be dropped by the O/400. Production began quickly and the first of the 554 aircraft built arrived to equip the newly formed RAF from April 1918.

Nos.207 and 215 Squadrons were the first units to receive the new O/400 at Netheravon. Almost simultaneously, the type entered service with 216 Squadron at Cramaille, going on to serve with ten front line units before the end of World War One. The aircraft was to dominate in the new revolutionary Independent Force from August 1918, which was tasked with bombing industrial installations, many of them in Germany. Way ahead of its time, this force demonstrated the power of aerial bombardment and many lessons were

learned from it. While it was made up of several other bomber type aircraft, it was clear that the Handley Page had set the tone. Weather permitting, anything up to 40 O/400s were airborne almost every night over Germany during the latter months of the war. No.215 Squadron managed to fly as far east as Mannheim on 25 August 1918, attacking the city with two aircraft.

Economically, the O/400 had also set a high standard in favour of the use of the heavy night bomber. It was very cost effective; a single O/400 cost £9600 and with a crew of four it would take the equivalent of five DH.9As at a cost of £16,000 to deliver the same amount of bombs. The loss rate of the single-engined bombers was also four times higher than the O/400 and only had the capability to carry, at best, a pair of 230lb bombs.

There is no doubt that the O/400 was the greatest heavy bomber of World War One. But unfortunately for Handley Page, it was obvious that the type had reached its own technological limits and further development, although attempted, did not extend the production life of the machine beyond 1919. The RAF looked to the Vickers Vimy for its early peacetime operations, although a single O/400 remained in service with 216 Squadron until October 1921. ■

This O/400 runs up its Rolls-Royce Eagle VIII engines before embarking on a sortie over India in 1919. **Via Time Line Images**

TVAL's FE.2b '6341' being flown by Gene DeMarco, with his observer ready to open fire on the camera ship! **Alex Mitchell**

Port fuselage bearing the name *Zanzibar No.1*, as the reproduction machine represents a World War One presentation aircraft. **Jarrod Cotter**

The 'Fee' is powered by an original 160hp Beardmore engine. **Jarrod Cotter**

'Fee'

With its 'pusher' engine and 23ft long spruce outriggers, FE.2b reproduction '6341' must class as one of the world's most unusual airworthy fighters.

For a short time after arrival on the Western Front in great numbers during January 1916, the Royal Aircraft Factory FE.2b was an effective fighter. Prior to the advent of interrupter gear, formations of 'pusher' types could wreak havoc on their enemy.

German ace Max Immelmann was killed during a fight with an FE.2b on 18 June 1916, and while Manfred von Richthofen's first victory was an FE.2b, he was later shot down suffering a severe head injury during combat with a formation of FE.2ds on 6 July 1917. However, as faster and more manoeuvrable fighters came on stream the large and slower 'Fee' quickly became obsolete. It was withdrawn from frontline daylight duties during the autumn of 1917, although being a stable platform capable of carrying a large payload it was instead used as a bomber and FE.2bs carried out night bombing operations until late in the war, as well as flying with Home Defence squadrons.

The first production aircraft were fitted with a 120hp Beardmore engine and later machines with a 160hp Beardmore, while the more powerful 250hp Rolls-Royce Eagle powered the FE.2d.

One major weak spot of the type was its lack of rearward defence. As losses mounted, the step was taken to fit a second Lewis gun on a telescopic mount behind the observer. To fire it, the observer had to raise the gun above the top wing and stand on his seat, obviously being hampered all the time by the severe buffeting of the slipstream and putting himself at even greater risk from enemy gunfire.

The Vintage Aviator Ltd's reproduction FE.2b took to the skies during 2009 and is powered by an original 160hp Beardmore engine, which after a long search was located in South America. Adding to its provenance further, it features many other original parts including fuel tanks, wheels and interplane struts. The latter items were manufactured by Boulton & Paul in 1917, and the original company decals and AID stamps were clearly visible bearing the date '21 Mar 1917'.

It is painted in the colours of 6341 of 25 Squadron RFC, flown by Capt Douglas Grinnell-Milne and observer Corporal D MacMaster. This was a presentation aircraft gifted to 25 Squadron by the Government of Zanzibar, hence on its port side carries the name *Zanzibar No.1*. To starboard is a second name *The Scotch Express*, reflecting the fact that 25 Squadron was formed at Montrose, Scotland. On 16 May 1916 this aircraft was forced down by Ltn Gontermann of Jasta 5 and extensively photographed by the Germans. This photographic record allowed TVAL to faithfully replicate the paint scheme. ■

RAF FE.2B (FIGHTER) SPECIFICATION

Dimensions:	Wingspan 47ft 9in; Length 32ft 3in; Height 12ft 7½in
All-up weight:	3037lb
Powerplant:	One 120hp or 160hp Beardmore
Performance:	Maximum speed 91mph at sea level, 76mph at 10,000ft; Climb to 10,000ft 39 minutes 44 seconds; Service ceiling 11,000ft
Armament:	One bracket-mounted 0.303in Lewis gun mounted on the front of the observer's cockpit, later one additional Lewis gun on a telescopic mount in between the cockpits for firing rearwards

Top: '6341' breaks from formation. **Alex Mitchell**

Below: In flight close-up, highlighting the observer's precarious position. Note the second gun for rearward firing over the top wing, which required the observer to stand up on his seat putting himself at full exposure to both the slipstream and hostile gunfire. **Alex Mitchell**

'Father of the RAF'

Hugh Trenchard is generally known as the 'Father of the Royal Air Force'
and became the first Chief of the Air Staff, but his life encompassed
much more than even that, as François Prins relates.

There is an imposing statue of the first Marshal of the Royal Air Force outside the Ministry of Defence main building in Whitehall, London. He stands alongside other great British armed forces wartime leaders, but who was he and what did he do?

Hugh Montague Trenchard was born on 3 February 1873, and he was rather a poor scholar and only just succeeded in meeting the minimum standard for commissioned service in the British Army. At the age of 20, he was gazetted as a Second Lieutenant in the Second Battalion the Royal Scots Fusiliers and posted to India.

On the outbreak of the Boer War, Trenchard volunteered and was posted to South Africa. He was critically wounded on 9 October, lost a lung and was partially paralysed. Trenchard returned to Britain and on medical advice travelled to Switzerland to recuperate; boredom made him take up bobsleighing and on one run he crashed heavily but found that his paralysis was gone and that he could walk unaided.

Trenchard returned to active duty and was back in South Africa in July 1901. He was involved in various operations as the Boer War drew to a close and promoted Brevet Major in August 1902. Following the end of the Boer War, Trenchard applied for service in the West African Frontier Force and was granted the position of Deputy Commandant of the Southern Nigeria Regiment. He arrived in Nigeria in December 1903 and spent the next six years on various expeditions to the interior, patrolling, surveying and mapping the area which later came to be known as Biafra. He was appointed to the Distinguished Service Order in 1906.

'WINGED' LEADER

Early in 1910, Trenchard became seriously ill and after several months he returned home once again. In October 1910, he was posted to Derry to take command of the Second Battalion of the Royal Scots Fusiliers. In 1912, an old friend from Nigeria, Captain Eustace Loraine, urged him to take up flying. Trenchard acted quickly as he was just short

of 40, the maximum age for military student pilots at the Central Flying School. He was granted three months paid leave to train as a pilot. When Trenchard arrived at Thomas Sopwith's flying school at Brooklands, Surrey, he told Sopwith than he only had 10 days to gain his aviator's certificate. Copeland Perry instructed Trenchard, who succeeded in going solo on 31 July, gaining his Royal Aero Club aviator's certificate (No.270) with a total of 64 minutes airborne.

On arrival at the Central Flying School, Upavon, Hugh Trenchard spent many hours improving his flying and after he had finished the course, was officially appointed as an instructor. However, he did no instructing and was involved in administrative duties. In September 1913, Trenchard was promoted temporary Lieutenant Colonel and on the outbreak of World War One, replaced Lieutenant Colonel Sykes as Officer Commanding the Military Wing of the Royal Flying Corps. His duties included providing replacements and raising new squadrons for service in France.

In August 1915, General Henderson moved back to the War Office and handed command of the RFC in the field to Trenchard – promoted Brigadier General – who established his headquarters at Merville. He would serve as the head of the RFC in the field until the early days of 1918 and would define the RFC's role in support with ground forces, reconnaissance and artillery co-ordination and later tactical low-level bombing of enemy ground forces.

Following the Gotha raids on London in the summer of 1917, the Government considered creating an air force by merging the RFC and the Royal Naval Air Service. Major-General John Salmond succeeded Trenchard in France, who returned to London on the morning of 16 December and met the Air Minister, Lord Rothermere, who offered him the post of Chief of the Air Staff (CAS). In the 1918 Honours List, Hugh Trenchard was made Knight Commander of the Order of the Bath and began work as CAS on 18 January.

However, it was not easy, and he and Sir David Henderson clashed with Rothermere on numerous issues; neither man could work with Rothermere and they resigned from the new Royal Air Force, which came into being on 1 April.

Trenchard's resignation was accepted on 10 April, and he was asked to write a report ➤

Sir Hugh Trenchard addresses a meeting during the late 1920s when he was campaigning to expand the RAF. **All via author unless noted**

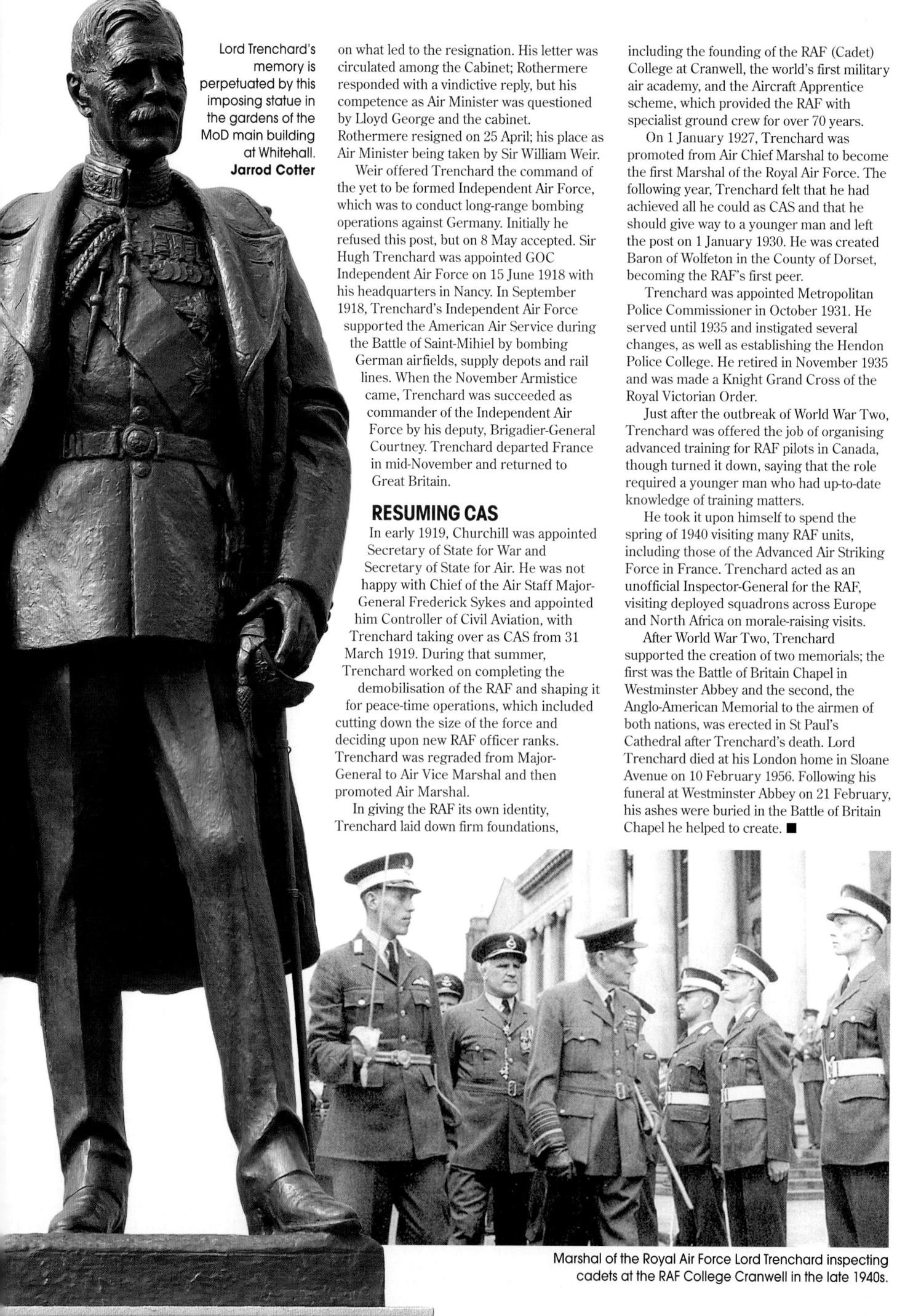

on what led to the resignation. His letter was circulated among the Cabinet; Rothermere responded with a vindictive reply, but his competence as Air Minister was questioned by Lloyd George and the cabinet. Rothermere resigned on 25 April; his place as Air Minister being taken by Sir William Weir.

Weir offered Trenchard the command of the yet to be formed Independent Air Force, which was to conduct long-range bombing operations against Germany. Initially he refused this post, but on 8 May accepted. Sir Hugh Trenchard was appointed GOC Independent Air Force on 15 June 1918 with his headquarters in Nancy. In September 1918, Trenchard's Independent Air Force supported the American Air Service during the Battle of Saint-Mihiel by bombing German airfields, supply depots and rail lines. When the November Armistice came, Trenchard was succeeded as commander of the Independent Air Force by his deputy, Brigadier-General Courtney. Trenchard departed France in mid-November and returned to Great Britain.

RESUMING CAS

In early 1919, Churchill was appointed Secretary of State for War and Secretary of State for Air. He was not happy with Chief of the Air Staff Major-General Frederick Sykes and appointed him Controller of Civil Aviation, with Trenchard taking over as CAS from 31 March 1919. During that summer, Trenchard worked on completing the demobilisation of the RAF and shaping it for peace-time operations, which included cutting down the size of the force and deciding upon new RAF officer ranks. Trenchard was regraded from Major-General to Air Vice Marshal and then promoted Air Marshal.

In giving the RAF its own identity, Trenchard laid down firm foundations,

including the founding of the RAF (Cadet) College at Cranwell, the world's first military air academy, and the Aircraft Apprentice scheme, which provided the RAF with specialist ground crew for over 70 years.

On 1 January 1927, Trenchard was promoted from Air Chief Marshal to become the first Marshal of the Royal Air Force. The following year, Trenchard felt that he had achieved all he could as CAS and that he should give way to a younger man and left the post on 1 January 1930. He was created Baron of Wolfeton in the County of Dorset, becoming the RAF's first peer.

Trenchard was appointed Metropolitan Police Commissioner in October 1931. He served until 1935 and instigated several changes, as well as establishing the Hendon Police College. He retired in November 1935 and was made a Knight Grand Cross of the Royal Victorian Order.

Just after the outbreak of World War Two, Trenchard was offered the job of organising advanced training for RAF pilots in Canada, though turned it down, saying that the role required a younger man who had up-to-date knowledge of training matters.

He took it upon himself to spend the spring of 1940 visiting many RAF units, including those of the Advanced Air Striking Force in France. Trenchard acted as an unofficial Inspector-General for the RAF, visiting deployed squadrons across Europe and North Africa on morale-raising visits.

After World War Two, Trenchard supported the creation of two memorials; the first was the Battle of Britain Chapel in Westminster Abbey and the second, the Anglo-American Memorial to the airmen of both nations, was erected in St Paul's Cathedral after Trenchard's death. Lord Trenchard died at his London home in Sloane Avenue on 10 February 1956. Following his funeral at Westminster Abbey on 21 February, his ashes were buried in the Battle of Britain Chapel he helped to create. ∎

Marshal of the Royal Air Force Lord Trenchard inspecting cadets at the RAF College Cranwell in the late 1940s.

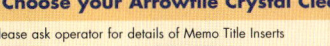
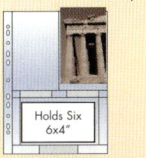

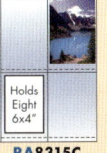
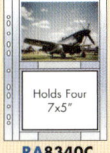

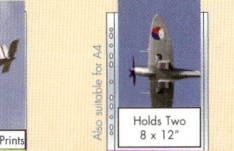
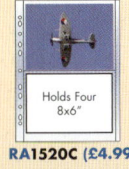

TVAL's Albatros D.Va reproduction being flown in the vicinity of Masterton by Gene DeMarco.
Alex Mitchell

Close-up of the part of pattern making up the colourful lozenge fabric.

Deadly Albatros

Profile of a perfect reproduction of one of Germany's formidable fighters.

By late 1916, the Albatros D series had developed to the D.III, which proved itself a capable match for the Allied fighters of its time. As the Allied technology continued to improve with new types such as the Sopwith Camel and RAF SE.5a arriving on the Western Front, so too did the development of the Albatros need to be addressed to keep pace.

The result, in mid-1917, was the D.V, which closely resembled the D.III and retained the Mercedes D.IIIa engine. The most notable difference was the fuselage, which was lighter than that of the D.III and had an oval cross-section instead of the D.III's flat-sides. It also had major modifications to its wings.

It entered service in May 1917, though quickly began experiencing structural wing failures as had its predecessor. It also offered little improvement in performance, leading some pilots to claim they preferred the D.III. That July, Germany's leading ace Baron Manfred von Richthofen was most critical of the D.V, stating that it was already obsolete and inferior to the Allied types.

Albatros consequently modified the design and the result was the D.Va, which among its improvements featured stronger wing spars, heavier wing ribs and a reinforced fuselage. Although an excellent fighter overall, it didn't offer superior performance to its enemy's best types which arrived towards the end of the war. ➤

Deliveries of the D.Va began in October 1917, and structural problems of the Fokker Dr.I left the D.Va as one of Germany's best fighters until the Fokker D.VII entered service in the summer of 1918. Production ceased in April 1918, but the D.Va remained in front line use until the Armistice on 11 November 1918.

PERFECT REPRODUCTION

One of The Vintage Aviator Ltd's most recent products is a perfect reproduction of a late war Albatros D.Va. Adding to its authenticity, the aircraft is powered by an original Mercedes D.IIIa engine.

It first flew in late October 2009, wearing the paint scheme of 5284/17 as flown by Vfw Josef Mai of Jasta 5, circa late 1917. This German ace scored a total of 30 victories, 11 of which came while flying Albatros scouts and seven in the machine represented.

The aircraft took around two years to build and has been constructed using appropriate materials and manufacturing techniques ensuring that it is almost identical to what would have emerged from the factory in 1917.

Just one of the many aspects of its construction that took a great deal of research is the newly printed lozenge fabric which covers the wings. TVAL craftsmen wanted to ensure that the shapes and colour hues which create the camouflage pattern were accurately reproduced – and the attractive results add greatly to the overall colourful paint scheme. ■

The Albatros is powered by an original Mercedes D.IIIa engine.

Topside view of the D.Va at Masterton in November 2009 showing its faithfully reproduced lozenge fabric to good effect. **All Jarrod Cotter unless noted**

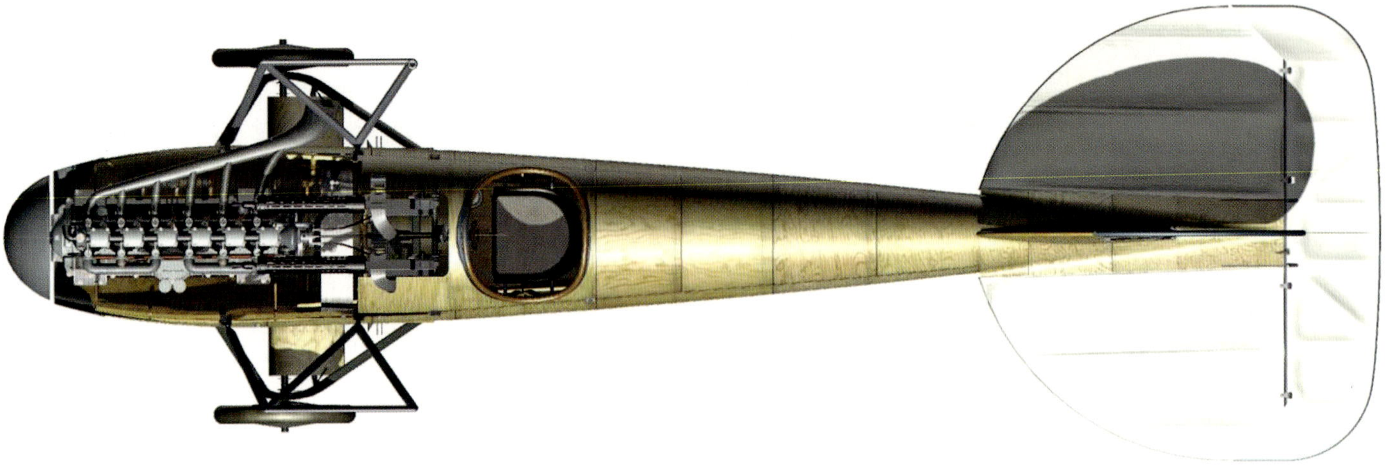

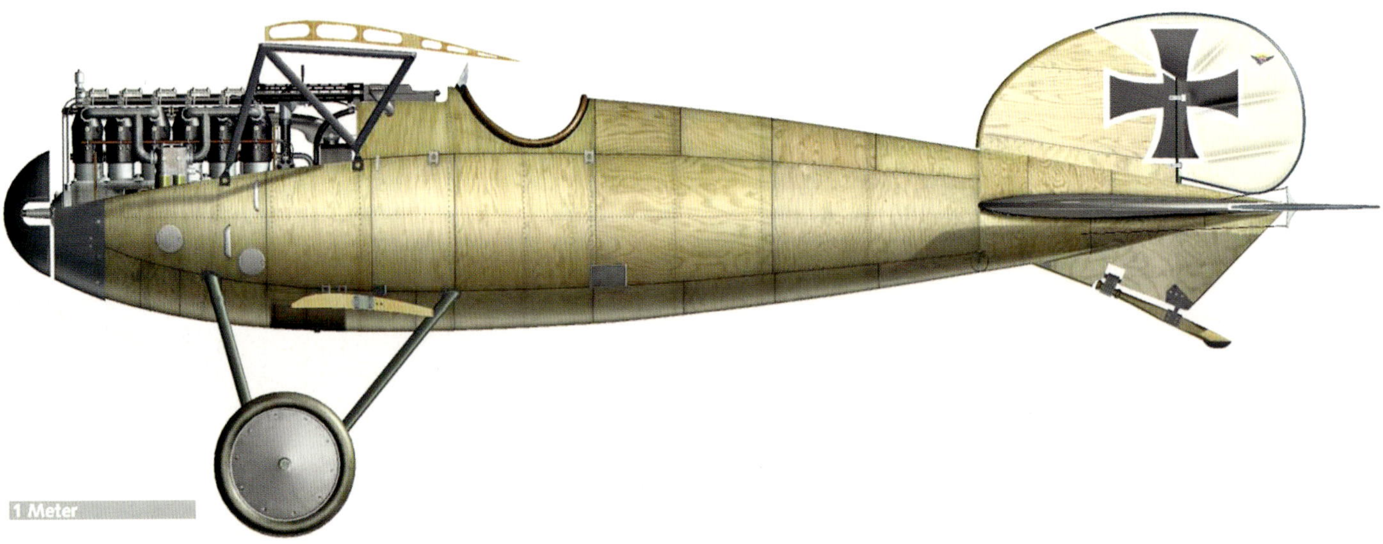

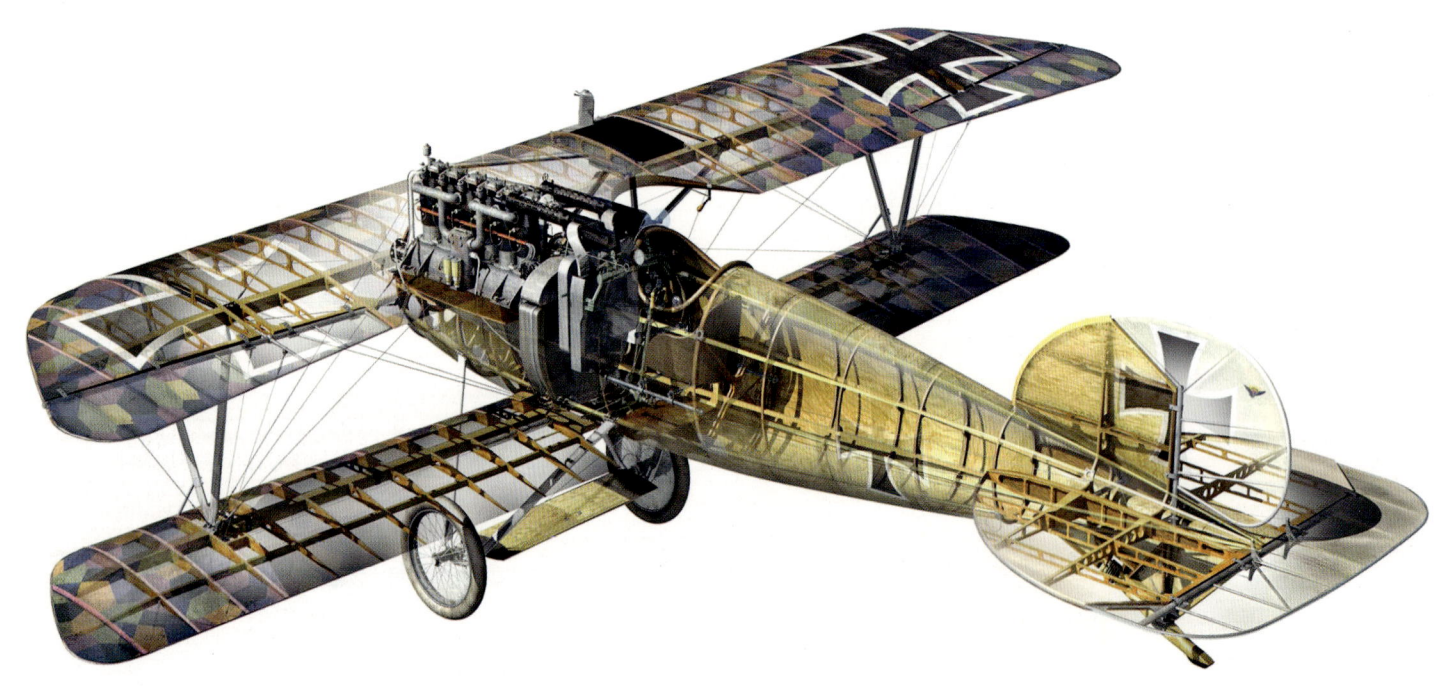

1 Meter

Albatros D.Va cutaway

Mark Miller's superb artwork shows the construction of the Albatros and some of its equipment in great detail.

All artwork Mark W Miller © 2010